ROBOTIC LAW
THE LEGAL PERSONALITY OF THE ROBOT

ROBOTIC LAW
THE LEGAL PERSONALITY OF THE ROBOT

MARCO AURÉLIO DE CASTRO JÚNIOR

Andradina
2020

Editorial assistance Leonam Liziero
Book formatting and English translation Hermilo Santana
Book cover Adriano Castro
Back cover photo Gil Ramos

Meraki Publisher

C355 Castro Junior, Marco Aurélio de
        Robotic Law: the legal personality of the robot/ Marco
Aurélio de Castro Junior. Andradina: Meraki, 2020.
        Bibliografia
        ISBN 978-16-526-4543-6
        1. Direito 2. Direito Civil.
        1. Título
        CDU – 349 CDD – 346.001

Mãos dadas.

Não serei o poeta de um mundo caduco.
Também não cantarei o mundo futuro.
Estou preso à vida e olho meus companheiros
Estão taciturnos mas nutrem grandes esperanças.
Entre eles, considero a enorme realidade.
O presente é tão grande, não nos afastemos.
Não nos afastemos muito, vamos de mãos dadas.
O tempo é a minha matéria, o tempo presente, os homens presentes,
a vida presente.

Carlos Drummond de Andrade[1]

Hands in Hands.

I shall not be the poet in a fugacious world.
Likewise, I shall not sing the future world.
I am chained to life and look upon my comrades.
They are sullen but filled with great hopes.
Among them, I consider the immense reality.
The present is so grand, let´s not be apart.
We shall not walk apart, let´s go hands in hands.
Time is my matter, the present time, the present men, the present life.
(Carlos Drummond de Andrade)
* Free translation by the Author.

[1]Andrade, C.D. (1983). *Nova reunião: 19 livros de poesia* (Vol. 1, pp. 78). Rio de Janeiro: Livraria José Olympio Editora S.A.

I dedicate this book, my first one, to my daughter Maria, who has made my life and my world better; in the hope of a better world for everyone and that each and every Man shall have the privilege of finding their own Marias.

PREFACE

This is the 2nd edition of the book, this time in Kindle format. It deals with the technological singularity of the robot that could happen in a few years. To assert that this robot must be treated as a subject of law, as an individual person, the author has done deep research on what characterizes Man, presenting his concept in philosophy from pre-Socratic to contemporary philosophers.

It then seeks to understand which features of the human being the law appropriates or uses to treat Man as a subject of rights as opposed to the objects of law.

The book goes through the analysis of the Darwinian theory of evolution to present the idea that the robot of the technological singularity, a unique phenomenon that may happen in the coming years, could be the evolution of Homo Sapiens.

It also seeks to demonstrate that the slow evolutionary process may not be characterized as intelligent and, therefore, it is possible that from an unintelligent based intelligence may emerge and from a less intelligent one a more intelligent one may arise.

The book advances in the treatment of the subject always trying to present enlightening examples.

It goes through Newton da Costa's paraconsistent logic and Göddel's incompleteness theorems, as well as Ray Kurzweil's Law of Accelerating Returns.

From Freud and Lacan's psychoanalysis, it seeks to extract the concepts of consciousness and the unconscious to treat them from the perspective of robotics, cybernetics and artificial intelligence.

It also discusses the factors that may lead to the occurrence of technological singularity, such as nanotechnology, quantum computing, and big data.

The author also deals with themes such as natural, animal, human and artificial intelligence and the concept of biological life and artificial life to emphasize that the robot of the technological singularity should be treated as a living being.

What is most striking is that Marco Aurélio de Castro Júnior has been dealing with this subject, whether in lectures, in Brazil and abroad or in publications, since 2000. He is a pioneer in this field of study in Brazil and one of the first in the world to deal with this subject that way.

The first edition of the book came to light when no other book, whether in Brazil or abroad, had been published specifically on the subject.

It is a seminal book to deal with robotic law and a must-read for all who want to be up to date with the most amazing advances of humanity.

Rodolfo Pamplona Filho

Chief Judge of the 1st Labour Court in Salvador/BA (Regional Labour Court of the Fifth Region). Senior Professor of Civil Law and Procedural Labor Law of the University of Salvador — UNIFACS. Adjunct Professor for Graduate and Post-Graduate Courses in Law (Master's and Doctoral degree) at the Federal University of Bahia (UFBA) Law School. Coordinator of the Extension Courses in Labor Law and Procedural Labor Law at JusPodivm/Ba. Master's and Doctoral Degrees in Labor Law at the Pontifical Catholic University of São Paulo (PUC/SP). Extension Degree in Civil Law at the Federal University of Bahia (UFBA) Law School Institution. Member of the National Academy of Labor Law (Vice-president) and the Academy of Letters of Bahia (Secretary-General).

ACKNOWLEDGMENTS

In the first edition, I was grateful to the people who contributed directly to the completion of that edition. Regarding this new English edition, I would like to express my thanks to:

All who have followed and follow me since then, especially my parents, Carmen and Marco, for the immense love and permanent encouragement to the good intellectual and moral formation.

My late grandparents, Oscar, Hilda, Zelina and Claudionor, who populate many of my fondest memories.

My beloved wife, Celia, for the patience, understanding, and encouragement for this and so many other works to come to an end, albeit at the expense of a greater and more desired coexistence and for, at all times, making me see the world from another perspective.

My daughters Maria and Rafaela for the greatest joy of being their father. Being the father of intelligent, beautiful and caring girls is the greatest gift I have ever received.

My brother and buddy, Adriano, for showing me that art is essential to life.

My friend and teacher Rodolfo Pamplona Filho, who always had a word of encouragement when others criticized. Although we have differing opinions from time to time, he has agreed to preface this book once again.

My teacher Augusto Aras for the frequent and interesting philosophical discussions on the subject of this work and others that have always followed in our conversations. Because of his example, I became a teacher.

My colleagues at the office, the Prosecutor's Office, and the Faculty of Law. They are always ready to help me and they are alert to show other worldviews.

My students, all of them, for being a permanent stimulus to keep alive the desire to learn and discover. From them, I learn more than I teach.

TABLE OF CONTENTS

1 INTRODUCTION

The ever-increasing speed at which technology advances have turned into reality what was, until recently ago, fictional. The dematerialization and deterritorialization of human activities caused by the increasing access to computer global networks, the popularization of portable communication platforms, the detachment of the production tools from their physical devices together with the cloud computing, creates a reality, unthinkable until a while ago, deconstructing long-established paradigms.

At first glance, one could even think that this work refers to a science fiction novel, but will soon see that this is not what I propose. I won't be surprised with this reaction, but one must recall that there was a time when space travel, wireless telecom, and cloning were all considered science-fictional, but they soon proved to be real. The mobile phone became an essential tool in the day to day life, even for the children. The GPS technology is spreading rapidly, even in developing countries such as Brazil, and is used for several purposes, whether being recreational, for personal safety or goods in transit. Cloning is approaching at a fast pace towards the implementation of its procedure in human beings. As to the replacement of human organs by manufactured parts, what was, until a while ago, science fictional, is becoming reality, and this enables Man to take a step closer to immortality, by means of "cyborgization", like what already happened to some people, including famous ones, such as Stephen Hawking, who without his technological apparatus wouldn't be able to walk nor communicate.

This very much resembles, in an inverted perspective, the novel The Bicentennial Man[2], in which the main character, a robot, yearns to humanize itself, even knowing that, to become a human, implies having a limited life span. He so strongly desires to achieve such a condition that he goes to court for that proposal.

The objective of this work revolves around the discussion of issues that haven't yet reached the general public or the courts: The advent of machines smarter than humans will result in their legal personality? Does the legal concept of the person currently established in Brazil comprise the understanding of robot as a legal person? This is not a visionary work; it's just a legal planning of a reality yet to come.

It's already noticeable, in the legal field, the existence of debates regarding themes that would have been unthinkable until recently, like the rights of clones, the evidence originated from the internet, the legality of arrests of people located through the triangulation of GPS signals and mobile phones, the international treaties on extraterrestrial exploration and the social welfare issues concerning human longevity due to scientific developments. Soon, philosophical, moral and legal questions regarding human longevity (if not human immortality) will be discussed under different framings from those existing today.

Thus, one doesn't need to go far to see that the current reality surpasses the fiction, making the work of authors of this literary genre ever more difficult, because what is imagined is soon carried out in a short space of time. By the way, Darwin's ideas have gained worldwide popularity and changed the world forever in a period of ten years; Einstein went from a total stranger to one of the greatest geniuses of mankind in a few decades; and not to forget that only seventy years separate the first plane flight and the arrival of man on the moon! All these events were witnessed, since the beginning until peak development, by the same generations. It all happens very fast and in an increasing and exponential acceleration, and the

<hr>

[2] Asimov, I. (1994). *O homem bicentenário* [The Bicentennial Man] (R.S. de Biasi, Trans.) (pp. 251). Rio de Janeiro: Record.

perception here revealed is that the current generation might come to know machines that are as intelligent as men, or even more, still in the first half-century of this millennium.

But the poetry is latent for those who know how to see it, and from the title till the last word, the great little poem "Hands in Hands", by Carlos Drummond de Andrade[3], in its entirety, seems to harmonize with what I think about the theme. Truly, one must be hand in hand to face this subject, that might be trailblazing in the near future. Aside from the need to commune efforts, forecasted in the title of the poem, I feel, "even though ill-compared"[4], quoting another's Drummond poem, like him. I am not a science fiction fan and I don't want to talk about futurology, all I want to do is to, when facing this "immense reality"[5], real or virtual, understand it.

It's extremely complex to deal with the subject matter addressed in this book. It addresses, all at the same time, humanistic, philosophical, religious, biological, existential, technical, psychological, and especially psychoanalytic and legal concepts, which are the ending point of this book and guide the perspective under which it was drawn up.

Of course that it wouldn't be possible, within the scope of a legal paper, to get into details of all related issues, without the risk of deviating from its main focus, however, they were all referred to in some level in what I thought to be relevant to the understanding of the ideas set out here.

Hence, that is why before entering into the actual legal themes, I first walk through basic concepts of Computer Science, and within it, notions related to cybernetics, artificial intelligence, and robotics, with referral to artificial life.

It was also inevitable to examine psychological and cognitive aspects linked to topics such as intelligence, mind, personality, consciousness, and unconsciousness.

---

3 ANDRADE, C. D., op. cit., loc. cit.

[4] Ibidem, pp. 460.

[5] Ibidem, pp.78.

As to philosophy, I lay out the differentiation between the definitions of Man and person, and question which characterizing elements in the concept of Man are embraced by the legal system to set the definition of legal personality.

In the fields of logic and mathematics, studies developed at a fast pace from antiquity until the paraconsistent logic, which serves, among others, as a basis to artificial intelligence systems, as well as it trails the intricate and somewhat misunderstood pathway of all systems' incompleteness.

Within biology, I collect elements from the theory of evolution and use to correlate it with the Law of Accelerating Returns, applicable to biological and technological evolution. Furthermore, it was in the work of the biologists Maturana and Varela, in conjunction with cybernetics, from which I extract the definition of a living being, and that is used throughout this book.

From psychoanalysis came the definitions of consciousness, id, ego, superego and most importantly, unconsciousness, and I relate them with information technology, due to their similarity with *software* and *operating system*.

All of the above mentioned related topics are referred just to enable the discussion of whether or not it's possible for a robot to acquire legal personality and whether or not the legal system allows such understanding.

I didn't go beyond to discuss which rights of personality could the robot attain, restricting myself to make mere references to variations resulting from the stage development of these machines, since such effort would require the need of a new book, to be written in the future, whether by myself or by others.

I also took an inroad into the Anglo-Saxon legal system, not only to show how this theme is being addressed by scholars but also to highlight, like one would expect, that the paths to answers, specifically in Portugal and Brazil, may diverge from those settled by the European legal system.

From the common law, I extracted legislation and case-law pertaining robots, given the absence, at least up until the completion of this book, of Brazilian and Portuguese – our nearest example – laws about the subject.

I intentionally pushed aside the Asian legal systems, restricting me in only bringing philosophical ideas as to the existing about Man's place and other living creatures' place in nature.

Within this context, I noticed that Brazilian books regarding this theme are almost nonexistent, having identified only one article written by myself in the year 2000 and a reference to the topic in another subsequent article. Even overseas, there is not, as far as verified, a single book about the theme addressed here, there are only a handful of articles and rare titles in which robotics is related to law.

This book contains six chapters: introduction, five chapters regarding the subject-matter and conclusion. The **first of the four chapters** concerning the subject-matter presents some **basic notions of anthropocentrism and different anthropocentric views within philosophy, from the cosmological period until today. Also, this chapter brings considerations regarding the human condition**. Thus, it can be determined if such elements are exclusive to human beings or if they can be transferred to other living and inanimate beings, through the deconstruction of the concept of Man.

The **second chapter** presents a **study on the legal concepts associated with Man and person**, as well as the **legal treatment given by Brazilian Law and other legal systems**. It was also analyzed, under a deconstructive view, the post-human condition as a counterpoint and a complement to the idea of humanity, to reinforce the arguments presented here. The closure of this chapter comes with a study of the legal personality and the concept of life.

The **third chapter goes deep into technical issues associated with robotics**, dealing with subjects such as cybernetics, artificial intelligence, robot, superconductivity, nanotechnology, quantum computation, Law of Accelerating Returns, among other factors that may contribute to the advent of technological singularity. This chapter brings elements essential to the understanding of the proposal presented in this paperwork. Without such information, the reader won't fully understand the exposed arguments.

The **fourth chapter**, the heart of this book, reaffirms systematically what was said in the previous chapters. **This chapter provides the criteria and reasoning as to why a robot shall have legal personality**. At last, it unveils the three laws of robotics, case law and the limited existing legislation regarding the subject.

I took a while to understand that this book cannot reach its total completion at the present moment. But, why publish it then? Because I must. Because it took me ten years of research and I consulted almost four hundred works to create this doctoral thesis. Before that, however, all my studies were latent and silent, with eventual glimpses in the form of two published articles and a handful of lectures.

This latency between the conception of ideas and the publication of this book also occurred to, at least, two other authors from different areas (other than the legal one), to whom I talked with. And, instead of being harmful, it proved to favor an internal dialectic within me, yielding good results.

This work is a thesis and doesn't represent absolute truth. This very thesis was postponed, left aside, discouraged by some professors and misunderstood when partially disclosed in lectures. It only became a reality by chance, after the line of research for the doctoral degree to which I applied for was abruptly extinguished from the University curriculum soon after my entrance. At that time, I already had in hands my initial thesis (almost finished) regarding the use of treaties to avoid double taxation within Brazil-China trading business (which has demanded two years of investment in research, travel, time and money).

If that was so, then why not move forward with my research on Robotic Law? This was the motivation that I needed to, within two months, write a new thesis. After my oral presentation, I took over one year to absorb new readings and to give further thought to the theme, which resulted in this work, still in constant development.

I invite you for a reading that, perhaps, demands a detachment from the anthropocentric vision of the world, without bias, and an acceptance of other views on life and the individual person. Maybe without that, one cannot fully understand my ideas. I also invite you to explore new meanings to concepts already so deeply enrooted within society, because, maybe they soon won't be useful anymore.

What really helped me was my personal and irreverent stance, sometimes almost anarchic, my respectful and still sustained agnosticism, my *a priori* and persistent systematic questionings and my openness to the new without disregarding the voice of experience, not least because what I point out in the book wasn't created out of the blue, but, rather, it was built on existing foundations, some over a century old.

This book comprises other areas of knowledge aside from the legal one, adjusting to the notion that the legal area represents only a small share of human knowledge, an important one, but not the only one; it's not an isolated island but rather, an inland territory. That's why it needs to communicate with the world.

I needed the Law to construct and deconstruct the core theme of this work, which was insufficient, thus, it was important and necessary to wander through other areas of knowledge such as biology, logic, mathematics, psychoanalysis, informatics, cybernetics and philosophy, to then, return to the legal field and create the concept of a legal individual and analyze if a robot can be considered as such.

These ideas aren't easy to understand nor even to be accepted, but I believe that there is an internal coherence within it, which enabled me to write what is put here.

I don't intend to attract followers nor address a prophecy. The work delivered here is not yet finished. Many other sources which I think are worthy of examination are already in my library waiting for me, and, in time, will be incorporated into this book.

Nonetheless, if a decade of latency of ideas set here was important, it's not anymore, because now I am aware that this book only represents a bridge to a future that might not even happen. However, if it, indeed, does happen in the way outlined here, the reader may find the following pages quite useful.

This book, even though, permanently unfinished, doesn't undermine its comprehension, because, any addition will only represent a new element, but will never be able to give closure to it, at least, not with my current concept and understanding about the theme.

Other authors might come to deconstruct it, adjust it, rebut it, complete it, ignore it, in short, to make it exist.

I hope that this reading will be as pleasant as the pleasure to write it, without the pain of having to confront it with enrooted ideas. But I must warn the reader that he/she won't be able to find easy answers nor any manifestation even close to approval.

In reality, I had to put a great amount of effort into this work, having to sacrifice a good portion of my family life. Many of these pages were written during Bahia's Carnival, in Praia do Forte, on new year's eve, on holidays and vacations, always in family moments, never again recoverable. Those days will never come back; I will never again hear my daughter, Maria, at the age of 3 or 4, asking me to be with her in the pool; the moments with my beloved Celia, also, cannot be relived. Thus, I paid a high price and the result of it I entrust to the readers with my heart and soul.

This book isn't mine anymore. It belongs to the readers. Make good use of it.

2 SOME GENERAL NOTIONS ABOUT ANTHROPOCENTRISM

Man has always been the starting point and the ending point of Law. Historically and universally, Law has always been considered under an anthropocentric point of view, in which it was created by Man, for Man and because of Man.

This legal perspective of Man may soon undergo a dramatic change if all the forecasts, backed by technical and empirical data, materialize itself and intelligent robots come to life, or better said, that seems to be intelligent because they act as if they were intelligent, indistinguishable, in its results, to what a human could do.

The fundamental paradigm of Law, like almost everything of human origin, lies in its anthropocentrism. Under this paradigm, Law wouldn't exist without Man, without people.

Vasconcelos[6], while lecturing about the anthropocentric nature of Law, adds:

> The human being is the ethical and ontological foundation of Law [...] Without people there would be no Law. Law exists due to the people and for the people. Its objective is to regulate their social interaction in the World in a fair manner. Thus, the people are the starting point and the ending point of Law (free translation by the Author).

This perspective of the world is anthropocentric and, from what we saw in the last centuries, especially with the rise of science, the

---

[6] Vasconcelos, P. P. (2006). *Direito de personalidade* [Personality rights] (pp. 6). Coimbra: Almedina. "A pessoa humana constitui o fundamento ético-ontológico do Direito. [...] Sem pessoas não existiria o Direito. O Direito existe pelas pessoas e para as pessoas. Tem como fim reger a sua interação no Mundo de um modo justo. As pessoas constituem, pois, o princípio e o fim do Direito".

enlightenment, and the positivism, it couldn't be different. However, its flaw, like any point of view, is that it is limited.

Nevertheless, with the emergence of the latest technology, based on silicon, but not limited to it, this paradigm tends to be questioned. The machines are becoming not only omnipresent and omniscient, but, above all, intelligent, perhaps, to the point of equating with human beings, or even surpassing them. One day these machines can surpass humans regarding general and cognitive ability and rationale, like what they already did in physical strength, and reach a level of consciousness that will enable them to be aware of their existence, separated from others, and to have feelings.

At this moment, or even sooner, it will be useless a civilization based on Man, considered to be the center of the Universe, because Man may become obsolete, negligible, disposable, and even subordinated.

According to Negroponte[7]:

> The change from atoms to bits is irrevocable and unstoppable. There are many merits to digitization. Some obvious ones include data compression and error correction, which is important in the delivery of information through a costly or noisy channel. Bits commingle effortlessly. They start to get mixed up and can be used and reused together or separately. A new kind of bit is born — a bit that tells you about the other bits.

These characteristics allow the gathering of information to reach an extent never imagined before, dematerializing itself. A simple CD can contain about one hundred masterpieces, enough to make a reader occupied for five years.

The reason for this theoretical effort is to present a scenario in which robots, here also called machines or computers, without distinction, acquire rights like humans, given by the latter, and not created by robots, if possible, so that the current existential para-

---

[7] Negroponte, N. (1995). *Being Digital.* (pp. 4, 15, 18) New York: Vintage Books.

digm, the legal system in its present framework and the anthropo-centric view of the world don't shred into pieces, something that no one wants.

This anthropocentric view of the world began to be deconstruct-ed when Nicholas Copernicus followed by Galileu Galilei[8] caused the first narcissistic wound in Man by destroying his perception of a geocentric world, replacing it with a heliocentric vision of the solar system.

As a result, the World ceased to be the center of the Universe and started to gravitate around the King Star, the Sun. Thus, the dwelling place of the creature, who once thought that there was no one above him but God, the Man, who should naturally occupy the center of the Universe, was suddenly moved and dislocated to an inferior position.

A second narcissistic wound was caused by Darwin's theory[9] of evolution[10] of the species. The origin of Man ceased to be di-vine. The Human being wasn't created to God's image and resem-blance, but instead, he was a result of a lengthy evolutionary pro-cess, through which, roughly speaking, the stronger ones are able to survive while the less adapted ones succumb, resulting in the birth of new species capable of fully developing themselves in ev-ery corner of the world.

The Man started to come closer to other primates rather than to God, regarding his origin. Hence, God couldn't be considered any-more as the human creator, but only a figure of worship and belief.

The prevailing perception, then, was that Man knew everything about the Universe, aware of his position in it, and was proud to have what he thought that made him distinguishable from other species: rationality. And scientific reasoning could prove him right.

[8] Banfi, A. (1986). *Galileu* [Galileo] (A. P. Ribeiro, Trans.). Lisbon: Edições 70.
[9] Darwin, C. R. (2008). *A origem das espécies por meio da seleção natural* [On the Origin of Species by Means of Natural Selection] (A. C. Mesquita, Trans.) (2nd ed., Vol. 1). São Paulo: Escala.
[10] Desmond, A.; Moore, J. (1995). *Darwin: a vida de um evolucionista atormen-tado* [Darwin: The Life of a Tormented Evolutionist] (G. Pereira, Trans.). São Paulo: Geração editorial.

The Man considered himself to be superior, because as a rational being, he could govern himself with autonomy, aware and conscious of everything that surrounds him, knowing what he is, what he can do, what he can achieve and what he desires. Thus, he was a subject of law and not an object of law since he has achieved the pinnacle of the evolutionary scale.

The positive, Cartesian and scientific reasoning, exercised only by Man, due to his total control over himself, gave him prominence concerning other living beings.

Within this line of reasoning, there would be an evolutionary hierarchy where the human being would be the most advanced species of all; more evolved because he/she subdues other species and shapes the world to his/her desire, except for the uncontrollable forces of nature. Everything is governed by reason and by conscious human conducts.

Man would be more evolved than a cockroach, for example, even though the latter has witnessed the rise and the extinction of the dinosaurs, can survive disasters, can instinctively swim and fly, remain for days without breathing or eating, move proportionately faster than human, capture aromas and flavors better than men, are more sensitive and can react faster to attacks, eat things that humans cannot digest, in short, it can perfectly adapt to life in any circumstance and environment existent on earth, with the exception of the poles and the areas covered by water.

Where humans would die of hunger, cold, heat, diseases, smothered, drowned, etc., these insects, considered inferior in the evolutionary scale, could easily proliferate, even though they could not shape the world to its way, having to adapt to it.

And so humans continue to consider themselves superior, linking intelligence and ability to resolve problems regarding evolution, in a rational and conscious way, albeit there is nothing that proves the relationship between intelligence and evolution, not least because, the definition of evolution created by Darwin[11] is

---

[11] Darwin, C. R., op. cit.

not related with intelligence, but with the ability to adapt. There is no relationship between evolution through the natural selection method and intelligence.

As taught by Maturana and Varela[12], all living beings are equal while alive, since a living being is adapted to its environment until it perishes and, regarding that, its condition of change remains. Since all creatures are alive, then they have fulfilled the requirements for an uninterrupted ontogeny. Thus, there isn't such thing as survival of the fittest; survives the one that is in balance with its environment.

Also, we must consider that the environment is an uninterrupted "selector" of the structural modifications known by the organism in its ontogeny. In a strict sense, the same thing happens to the environment, since the structural linkage is always mutual: the environment and the organism are altered. In this context, the conservation of the organisms as dynamic systems within their environment depends on an organism/environment compatibility. This is what's called adaption[13].

Ontogeny is defined as the history of structural modifications of a unit, without the loss of its organization. These modifications occur as differentiations caused by interactions originated from its environment or as a result of its internal dynamics. The ontogenic transformations of unity continue until it perishes[14].

Therefore, intelligence cannot be an attribute of evolution, because a process that lasts for billions of years cannot be considered an intelligent one. It's prudent, indeed, but not intelligent. Furthermore, the evolution has generated an inefficient genetic code — although incredibly interesting —, full of redundancies and sequences that don't compute, i.e., that don't produce proteins. Kurzweil[15]

---

[12] Maturana, H. R.; Varela, F. J. (2007). *A Árvore do Conhecimento: as bases biológicas da compreensão humana* [The Tree of Knowledge: The Biological Roots of Human Understanding]. São Paulo: Palas Athena.

[13] Ibidem, p. 115.

[14] Ibidem, p.86.

[15] KURZWEIL, R. (2009, January 05). After the singularity: a talk with Ray Kurzweil. Retrieved from: <www.kurzweilai.net/meme/frame.html?main=/ar-

gives as an example of an insignificant sequence known as ALI, made of 300 (three hundred) pairs of nucleotides, which occurs approximately (300,000) three hundred thousand) times in the human genome, equivalent to over 3% (three percent) of its totality.

Nevertheless, the genetic program works relatively well. Just look how fast a molecule of hemoglobin is created: around 500,000,000,000,000 (five hundred trillion) times per second. If each molecule is formed of more than 500 (five hundred) amino acids, then we would have over 15×10^{18} reading operations, per minute, by the ribosomes!

Besides, the errors of chemical processing of genetic data occur once every billion of base-pair replications, which would be considered in the computer system a parity error, meaning that it can be detected and corrected by other system levels. Kurzweil[16] reveals some impressive details about DNA, regarding its processing capacity:

> The DNA strings in a single cell would measure up to six feet in length if stretched out, but an elaborate packing method coils it to fit into a cell only 1/2500 of an inch across. With four letters in the alphabet, each rung is coding two bits of data in a digital code. Special enzymes can copy this information by splitting each base pair and assembling two identical DNA molecules by rematching the broken base pairs. Other enzymes actually check the validity of the copy by checking the integrity of the base-pair matching. With these copying and validation steps, this chemical data-processing system makes only about one error in a billion base-pair replications. Further redundancy and error-correction codes are built into the digital data itself, and so meaningful mutations resulting from the one-in-a-billion error rate will result in the equivalent of a "parity" error, an error that can be detected and corrected by other levels of the system, which will prevent the incorrect bit from causing any significant damage.

So, even though they weren't divine any more, in their origin,

---

ticles/art0451.html?>.

[16] Idem. (1999). *The age of intelligent machines.* (3rd reprint., pp. 150-151) Cambridge: MIT Press.

still, the reason was the one to govern Men. The reason was the cause and the force that moved them, keeping them apart from the irrational animals, which lived by instinct and not by reason. Then, Man decided to move away from nature and become artificial, by living in an artificial environment and producing artificial resources instead of using what nature had to offer.

With the arrival of the 19th century, another narcissistic wound was opened, but not in a place, as it was with Copernicus and Galileo; not at its origin, as it was with Darwin; this time the wound was in Man himself, in his head, in his Being.

Sigmund Freud[17] has already shown that there is much of a cause and unconscious force in everything that is done. The unconscious is a unique force that if it doesn't govern Man, at least, it copes decisively with him, if not rightly dealt.

Thus, next to the impulses, "correspondent" to the animal instincts that he still maintains and to the rationality which made him proud and standing out from others, since he only acted by means of a desired and autonomous will, there was also another acting force, the **unconscious** which, during the whole time, disturbs Man, making him act, often to his detriment, causing him to lose control of his actions. In spite of not being considered absolutely or predominantly rationals — if someone is driven by reason, then he must be conscious — due to these unconscious actions, Man is yet responsible for his actions, not even the unconscious can remove his autonomy.

Near the conscious that dictates reason, there is the unconscious that dictates free human behavior, like, for example, the Freudian slips.

The increasing technological advance, right now, with the use

---

[17] Freud, S. (1996). *Além do princípio do prazer* [Beyond the Pleasure Principle] In: Edição Standard das Obras Completas. (C. Monteiro, Trans.) (2nd ed., vol. 18). Rio de Janeiro: Imago.

of artificial intelligence powered by circuits based on carbon and other materials (not just silicon, whose days are numbered), neural networks, quantum computation, superconduction, nanotechnology, biological circuits, genetic algorithms[18], opens the door to the creation of machines potentially smarter than humans, aware of their individuality, ability to self-reproduce[19] generating improved versions of the previous generation, obtaining energy from the breakdown of certain molecules as the animals and the vegetables do and, it is thought, having feelings.

> *A number of robots that people have built, including Kismet and My Real Baby, is able to express emotions in humanlike ways. They use facial expressions, body posture, and prosody in their voices to express the state of their internal emotions. Their internal emotions are a complex interplay of many subsystems. Some have drives, such as Kismet's loneliness drive, that can be satiated only by particular experiences in the world, in this case detecting a human face.*[20]

This step that Man is about to take may result in the breaking of a crucial paradigm for culture and, therefore, for the Law, allowing robots to have a legal personality like humans.

The speed of change may not allow people, on a general level, to become aware of the ongoing process. The majority of people will only be aware of what has happened *after it has happened*, when the situation consolidates or be almost consolidated. However, not only scientists, but also governments of wealthy countries or even countries that are more attuned to the pace of change and, as it could not fail to be,

---

[18] Rover, A. J. (2000). *Direito, sociedade e informática: limites e perspectivas da vida digital* [Law, society and information technology: limits and perspectives of the digital life]. (pp. 207-212). Florianópolis: Boiteux.

[19] Wiener, N. (1971). *Deus, Golem e Cia: um comentário sobre certos pontos de contato entre cibernética e religião* [God and Golem, Inc.: A Comment on Certain Points where Cybernetics Impinges on Religion] (L. Hegenberg and O. S. da Mota, Trans.). (pp. 22). São Paulo: Cultrix.

[20] Brooks, R. A. (2002). *Flesh and machines: how robots will change us.* (pp. 155) New York: Pantheon Books.

the companies are aware of the facts. Bill Gates[21] presents the following view:

> *In fact, for all the excitement and promise, no one can say with any certainty when — or even if — this industry will achieve critical mass.*
>
> *Of course, the paragraph above could be a description of the computer industry during the mid-1970s, around the time that Paul Allen and I launched Microsoft. [...] At homegrown computer clubs, enthusiasts struggled to figure out exactly what this new technology was good for.*
>
> *But what I really have in mind is something much more contemporary: the emergence of the robotics industry, which is developing in much the same way that the computer business did 30 years ago. Think of the manufacturing robots currently used on automobile assembly lines as the equivalent of yesterday's mainframes.*

Gates[22] collates some figures that show the speed of the changes that have already taken place:

> *How soon will robots become part of our day-to-day lives? According to the International Federation of Robotics, about two million personal robots were in use around the world in 2004, and another seven million will be installed by 2008. In South Korea, the Ministry of Information and Communication hopes to put a robot in every home there by 2013. The Japanese Robot Association predicts that by 2025, the personal robot industry will be worth more than $50 billion a year worldwide, compared with about $5 billion today.*

When machines become as intelligent as humans, at this very moment, they may already have surpassed them, due to the differences between humans and robots. Kurzweil[23] explains why:

---

[21] Gates, B. (2008). A Robot in Every Home. *Scientific American* Sp, 18(1), 4-11. Retrieved from https://www.scientificamerican.com/article/a-robot-in-every-home-2008-02/

[22] *Ibidem*, p. 13.

[23] Kurzweil, R. (2008). The Coming Merging of Mind and Machine. *Scientific American* Sp, 18(1), 20-25. Retrieved from https://www.scientificamerican.com/article/merging-of-mind-and-machine/

Once computers achieve a level of intelligence compa-
rable to that of humans, they will necessarily soar past it.
For example, if I learn French, I can't readily download
that learning to you. The reason is that for us, learning
involves successions of stunningly complex patterns of
interconnections among brain cells (neurons) and among
the concentrations of biochemicals known as neurotrans-
mitters that enable impulses to travel from neuron to
neuron. We have no way of quickly downloading these
patterns. But quick downloading will allow our nonbio-
logical creations to share immediately what they learn
with billions of other machines.

Perhaps, at that moment, the following sentence, still in the field of fiction, extracted from the work of Asimov[24], will become reality:

And it was that statement that cued the judge. The crucial
sentence in his decision was "There is no right to deny free-
dom to any object with a mind advanced enough to grasp
the concept and desire the state".

Would it be possible to attribute legal personality to robots? Or would our law already cover this possibility or would it be necessary to produce new rules?

In order to do so, it is necessary to investigate the legal system and then, what are the assumptions for the attribution or recognition of the individual legal personality.

Going beyond the anthropocentric paradigm to admit the possibility of existence of a robotic right[25], in other words, in which it is accepted, alone or concomitantly with humans, nonhuman beings, not (wholly or partially) biological, as right holders, is a question that demands absolute detachment — not contempt — to humanity itself and to that of others, and full scientific thought, based on the proper logic.

At this point, a dialogue like this can become a reality:

---

[24] Asimov, I., op. cit, loc. cit.
[25] Castro Júnior, M. A. (2000). Direito robótico? [Robotic Law?] *Jornal Correio da Bahia*. Salvador, December 29.

"We've done two things, Andrew," said DeLong, "both of which are good. First of all, we have established the fact that no number of artificial parts in the human body causes it to cease being a human body. Secondly, we have engaged public opinion in the question in such a way as to put it fiercely on the side of a broad interpretation of humanity, since there is not a human being in existence who does not hope for prosthetics if they will keep him alive."

"And do you think the Legislature will now grant me my humanity?" Andrew asked.

"As to that, I cannot be optimistic. There remains the one organ which the World Court has used as the criterion of humanity. Human beings have an organic cellular brain and robots have a platinum iridium positronic brain if they have one at all — and you certainly have a positronic brain. No, Andrew, don't get that look in your eye. We lack the knowledge to duplicate the work of a cellular brain in artificial structures close enough to the organic type as to allow it to fall within the court's decision. Not even you could do it." [...].

*"It all comes down to the brain, then," Andrew said cautiously. "But must we leave it at the level of cells versus positrons? **Is there no way of forcing a functional definition?** Must we say that a brain is made of this or that? May we not say that a brain is something anything-capable of a certain level of thought?"*

"Won't work," said Li-hsing. "Your brain is manmade, the human brain is not. Your brain is constructed, theirs developed. To any human being who is intent on keeping up the barrier between himself and a robot, those differences are a steel wall a mile high and a mile thick"[26].

Countless centuries of history of thought amalgamated strongly the idea that Man, before the center of the Universe, today the center of the world, he reigns supreme over the Earth, without direct competitors, without threats that are not due to his own action or the imponderable cataclysmic forces of nature.

---

[26] Asimov, I., op. cit, p. 279-281.

This Man, who lives in society, unified, but diverse, (universal), deals with all the themes that matter to him under his centralizing perspective of himself, anthropocentric, looking at the Universe that surrounds him in an egocentric way. His center, as a lens deforming the light, actually, moulder of light to his specific convictions and conveniences, in group or individual.

Thus, it is not intended to rule out the legitimacy of this paradigm, since it cannot be considered wrong insofar as Man has always felt himself alone in the world of intelligence, as it is usually defined.

However, when it is time to come across creatures so or more intelligent than Men, we must be prepared for, in legal terms, dealing with the issue and this may imply the overcoming of the anthropocentric paradigm, that, right now, has already been ruled out by the various scientific discoveries and by the new way of understanding Man as a creature among others who deserve respect, since some form of intelligence is recognized in them, as with animals, currently dignitaries of increasingly legal treatment, so to speak, in line with the anthropocentric, "human" paradigm.

This conquest or evolutionary stage of human species and culture allows us to discern some animals rights, well cared for by the Animal Law Doctrine that in Brazil has Heron de Santana Gordilho[27] as one of his scholars, responsible for, as far as it is known, in this field, a pioneer *habeas corpus* in favor of a nonhuman being[28]: Swiss chimpanzee[29].

Also, one cannot lose sight of the word of Laurence Tribe[30], which in ten lessons seeks to unveil an expansion of legal person-

---

[27] Gordilho, H. J. S. (2008). *Abolicionismo animal* [Animal abolitionism]. Salvador: Evolução.

[28] Castro Júnior, M. A., *op. cit.*

[29] Retrieved from: <http://pt.wikipedia.org/wiki/Heron_Jos%C3%A9_de_Santana>. Last access date: April 09, 2011.

[30] Tribe, L. *Ten Lessons our constitutional experience can teach us about the puzzle of animal right: the work of Steven M. Rise.* Retrieved from: <http://nabrlaw.org/Portals/10/PDF%20Files/Tribe_10ConstitutionalLessons.pdf>. Last access date: March 29, 2008.

ality. The first and third lessons stand out for the purpose of this book:

> *The first lesson that our Constitution teaches is that rights are not such a scary thing to recognize or to confer, since rights are almost never absolute. Arguing for constitutional rights on behalf of non-human beings, which some people viscerally oppose, shouldn't be confused with giving certain non-human interests absolute priority over conflicting human claims. Recognizing rights is fully consistent with acknowledging circumstances in which such rights might be overwritten, just as human rights themselves sometimes come into conflict. [...]*
>
> *The third lesson is that it is a myth – a myth that is sometimes accepted even by observers as astute as Steve – that our legal and constitutional framework has never accorded rights to entities other than human beings. [...] Broadening the circle of rights-holders, or even broadening the definition of persons, I submit, is largely a matter of acculturation. [...] our legal system could surely recognize the personhood of chimpanzees, bonobos, and maybe someday of computers that are capable not just of beating Gary Kasparov but of feeling sorry for him when he loses.*

In the same spirit, robotic law is based. If there are elements that allow the Law to have the human personality as its object of concern, or rather, the human person in its essential manifestation, which is the personality, taking care of its strand or legal approach, the same requirements have certainly been met, the same characteristics were found in a robot, the traditional logic and the equity impose the edification of the same understanding, of — if not identical — similar treatment for this creature.

In the same direction of my article, Aires Rover[31] states:

> *Thus, it is not so extravagant to think of machines or systems that respond, partially or totally, to the effects of their actions and omissions. Systems with legal personality, an*

---

[31] Rover, A. J. (2009). *Para um direito invisível: superando as artificialidades da inteligência* [For an invisible Law: overcoming the artificialities of intelligence]. Retrieved from: <http://www.infojur.ufsc.br/aires/arquivos/direito%20invisivel%202005.pdf>. Last access date: February 25, 2009.

absurd to our short-sighted legal eyes.

Also, Gordilho[32] elucidates that,

> *However, there is a worldwide tendency to overcome classical anthropocentrism, and natural elements have increasingly been the subject of moral consideration, for they are often protected to the detriment of immediate human interests.*

Although the above author expressly refers to "natural elements", it may be added that the same reasoning can be carried out for synthetic beings endowed with human characteristics. This is what the present book is about.

2.1 Introductory considerations about the concept of Man

The concept of Man, in other words, man's conception of himself, varied in its historical course. Obviously, Man's image of the Human Being could not be static.

Although in cosmic or even historical terms the existence of Man, as such, as a species identified and separated from the others, is revealed only as an ephemerality, it would not be fair to say that nothing was done in this way. Truly, several new worlds were built and destroyed, both in territorial terms and in cultural, economic, social and political terms, since Man has left prehistory.

Thus, in an unstable manner or causing a change of route, the way Man sees himself has changed, though not always as dramatic or radical as when one changes the perspective concerning God or gods, to the situation in the Universe, to the position in nature and characterization as fully rational.

Ideas about Man always seek to try to understand who he is, what he does, what he is made of, what is his origin, role, and destiny. In short, it has always been a search for answers to fundamental questions, constitutive of cultural and institutional nature.

---

[32] Gordilho, H. J. S., *op. cit.*, p. 92.

The field where these ideas were sown is that of philosophy, fertile and conducive to it. Though, when Man looks at himself, he does not show much creativity. Perhaps because he has, albeit not explicitly, the exact size of his smallness or limitations, perhaps for fear of actually facing reality, perhaps because it is about answering to questions of the highest density that only allow one step at a time, on a spiral staircase.

The purpose of this chapter is to better understand what Man is culturally made of, what makes him human and therefore, it is thought, he is unlike anything else. The intention is seeking to understand what has led the Law to create for Man an exclusive, dominant, prevalent category that possesses rights and that has everything else as the object of its plexus of rights. To this end, with a special mention of the work of Odete Maria de Oliveira[33], a historical overview from ancient Greece is traced to the present day.

One must not lose sight of the fact that this work is about robots and only in a reflexive way about Man, but that it also considers it difficult, if not impossible, to deal with the robot without dealing with Man. Therefore, one of the fundamental questions of mankind, "what man is", is not its focal point, being certain that this topic will not exhaust the question on which, one can see. From the pre-Socratics, the philosophers have always bent over and until this day it proved to be insoluble. In any case, in order to talk about robots, in an apparent paradox, it is necessary to talk about Man. The pseudo paradox arises from the fact that in order to reach the robot with personality, one asks deeply about what it is to be Man: agent, creator, arrogant, humble, conscious and ignorant of what he truly is.

The search for the robot is also, in a way, the search for Man! Therefore, talking about the robot is talking about Man.

Even so, understanding Man in his ultimate dimension is not the purpose of the chapter. It is worth mentioning that it touches only

---

[33] Oliveira, O. M. (2006). *O conceito de homem: mais humanista, mais transpessoal* [The concept of man: more humanistic, more transpersonal] Ijuí: Unijuí.

the surface of this problem, of the highest inquiry and complexity, to historicize how philosophy took care of the subject.

Therefore, many philosophers and currents have deliberately been left out, and even those who have been chosen are referred to very quickly. Also, the fact that one or the other has occupied a greater or lesser number of lines does not imply that they have dissonant importance. All are important and all have brought un-deniable contributions to the understanding, however incomplete, of Man in his superior or full dimension.

Max Scheler[34] argues that if an erudite European is asked how he understands the term "man", three levels of incompatible ideas com-monly emerge. First, the Judeo-Christian tradition and its conjec-tures about Adam, Eve, creation, paradise and fall. Then, the scope of ancient Greece, from which, first, the self-consciousness of the human being reached the level of his particular situation, through the thesis that the possession of "reason", *logos, ratio, phronesis,* etc. characterize the man as such. *Logos* here means the discourse as well as the ability to achieve the "quiddity" of things. Linked to this idea there is another idea stating that there exists, parallel to the totality, a superhuman "reason" in which only human beings would be included. The third scope, a quite traditional icon, would be that of modern science of nature and genetic psychology, which claim that man is the cumbersome product of the evolution of the planet: a being differentiated from its predecessors only by the complexity of combinations of energies and capacities, which are already found in the infrahuman nature.

These three spheres of ideas do not have cohesion between them. It is a scientific-natural anthropology, a philosophical an-thropology and a theological anthropology, all of man and which do not have a common core. Moreover, the increase of the special sciences whose object is man, no matter how important he is, does not reveal but conceals its essence. Considering also that the three

---

[34] SCHELER, M. (2008). *A situação do homem no cosmos* [The Human Place in the Cosmos] (M. A. Casanova, Trans.). (1st ed., pp. 15) Lisboa: Edições Texto & Gráfica.

points of view referred to are now shaken and that the Darwinian proposal for the question of our origin has been especially refuted, it is possible to say that at no other time in history has man made himself so *problematic*.

It is necessary, Scheler continues, to investigate the perfidious ambiguity existing in the term and concept "man" to advance against the peculiar situation of the human being. *A priori*, the word alludes to the specific characteristics, in the morphological field, that man possesses as a subgroup of vertebrates and mammals. Obviously, regardless of the conceptual point adopted, the being called man is submissive to the concept of animal, but also participates in a small group of the animal kingdom. Even qualifying humans as "the peak of the series of mammalian vertebrates", according to Lineu (information quite questionable in the factual and conceptual domain), remains true, because the summit of something still integrates this something of which is the highest part.

Dissociated from this concept, man is being built by the transformation of his spine, the balance of the skull, a powerful development of his brain and the organic conformations from his erect walk, like the opposable thumb in his prehensile hand. However, the same term "man", in everyday language and all civilized peoples, means something so different from the other meaning that one will hardly find in human language a word with similar ambiguity. He should also mean a group of characteristics that depart completely from the generic concept of the animal, which encompasses mammals and vertebrates and at the same time oppose these animals. This second concept, which the author calls the *eidetic concept of man*, distances himself from the other, of a systematic-natural character. It is clear that both have different origins.

Therefore, these chapters should be understood as intentionally limited and directed to the theses defined herein.

2.2 Philosophical Evolution of the concept of Man

2.2.1 Humanism in the cosmologic period

Western humanism is born in the Greek period, a time of great **mysticism** in which a primitive philosophy prevailed with its speculations based on **mysterious forces and hidden powers**, making it difficult to determine a concept with certainty. The next moment it was a question of **impersonating the elements of nature with human characteristics**, real forces of nature that could even dominate Men.

The cosmological period was characterized by the **polarization between the principle (arché) and nature (*physis*)**, without major worries about the Man.

Although the focus was on the world, its origin and destiny, it can be assured that it began to think about Man reflexively, since the destiny of that one would fatally be the destination of the world and of everything that surrounds it.

From the Pre-Socratic Schools, it is necessary to highlight those of greater importance for the development of this question. Evidently, it should be repeated that the author sought to make an epistemological and material perspective to include in the relationship, not only the pre-Socratics, but from every period examined, to this day, thinkers who, in their sense — and all sense is arbitrary — could contribute to the understanding and construction of the work.

2.2.2 Pre-Socratean schools

2.2.2.1 Eleatic and dialectical schools

It stands out in this period the figure of Xenophanes, of Cólofon, which asserted that **no human trait could be foreseen in the gods**: they were neither born nor died. Only the human imagination gave them shape. In fact, he preached the existence of one God.

Parmenides affirmed that through **reason** one concludes that the Being is. And being cannot be. Therefore, thinking is thinking about something. Since **Being** is the **eternal** and unchanging principle of all things, it must also be the foundation of knowledge. Hence, Being is the only true object of **thought**, the beginning, and the end of philosophical research.

Melissus of Samos saw the timelessness and elimination of the Being by another Being or by a non-being since its duration had no beginning or end so that there cannot be a mutable multiplicity, but immutable unity.

Therefore, the pre-Socratic philosophers were essentially concerned with the Cosmos, and only on the secondary level with the *humanus and his humanitas.*

2.2.2.2 Sophists

Sophists reflect a change in philosophical directions, for now, **Man** and the things of nature that surround him, the world, **are the center** of attention, the result of democracy experienced after the defeat of the Persians. With this, the **practical life** of Man has gained prominence, that is, the **human Man**, who lives and faces his **political, legal, moral, aesthetic problems**, etc.

It is imperative to note that neither Plato nor Aristotle regarded them as true philosophers, perhaps deriving from this conception the meaning which the sophist word carries to this day.

However, it was the sophists who shifted the **axis of philosophy** from cosmological to **anthropological**. In other words, now Man is in the world.

The Man now is explained by Man. The **Practical Man** comes. Thus, **there cannot be a law so general** that it applies to all and is valid for all. For men, to each one, true is what it seems to be, as well as for each one is just only what it seems to be at the very moment and how it is useful to him.

2.2.3 The Socratean Man

Socrates also stood out for his humanism, to the point of being known as a philosopher of humanity and humanism. For him, **Man who is the measure of all things does not measure anything and therefore becomes the victim of his empirics and his own experiences**. Knowing the person of Man requires the appeal to **rationality, enabling Man to be a conscious subject** of cognitive order and an objective moral order. From this comes his famous statement: "Know thyself", meaning that Man must seek within himself and what makes him a man, being a person. It is only achieved by having an awareness of what he is and what he should do.

2.2.4 The Aristotelean Man

Aristotle replaced the Platonic conception of the idea as Being by a conception of the idea and Being. He created an essentially **realistic** model. **Being is the being of the real**, there being no other being outside the real. Being is replaced as the first platonic principle by substance, which is the real. The Stagirite states that the principle of contradiction, the foundation of metaphysics and the principle of knowledge, is that it guarantees this sense of Being: it is impossible that the same thing is and at the same time is not. Therefore, it is impossible to enunciate Being and Not Being of the same thing.

It must, therefore, be said that this logic cannot be applied in artificial intelligence systems. It is also insufficient to explore man, contradictory in himself.

Aristotle inquires of **causes**: the cause by which things are made, **final** cause; the causes that reproduce, **efficient** cause; the form or essence of each thing, **formal** cause.

Based on the principle of contradiction, he understands that essences are not outside things. The **concrete reality** is the indissoluble **union** of **idea** and **matter**. In this way, **Man** is, and, being, is singular, synthesis of the intelligible elements and the real, whereas its **essential characteristic is the movement**, existing in four modalities: a) **substantial** (birth and death); b) **quantitative** (growth and decrease, or small becoming large and vice versa); c) **qualitative** (change and alteration or white becoming black and vice versa); d) **spatial** (translation or change of place).

Aristotle establishes the following principles and conditions:

I) Principle of matter, undetermined substrate, in which change occurs.

II) Principle of matter type.

He understands that the **virtual, the being in power**, is meant to be concretized by the change in its form, since the form is the final cause, whereas the impulse to movement is the efficient cause. In other words, the causes of becoming are efficient, material, formal and final cause.

He **conceptualizes Man** not as the product of external causes, but as the **inner development of inner forms of matter**. This organicity demonstrates the relationship between matter and form. There is no matter without form, nor form without matter, except God.

With this he takes care of the two moments: the virtual and the real, being matter power, and form, the real. The passage from one to the other is becoming. Thus, in Aristotle's ideas dualism also remains: matter (imperfection), and pure form (perfection).

God is the first cause of the universal movement that has nothing virtual, since Pure Act: God, absolute perfection. God is thought in action.

Man and his world are located between the poles of formless matter and form without matter. The physical world, where Man is situated, is the synthesis of matter and form, in which all movement is executed in time and space.

2.2.5 The Epicurean Man

This philosophical school is named after Epicurus of Samos, who sought to endow his investigations with a pragmatic character, to achieve happiness.

The mathematical theory was less important than physics and logic since they had a **practical end**. In the same way, he did not see philosophy as endowed with its end. It is a medium, a set of rules for living happily. The truth lies in the sensations since the opinions can be true or false, as confirmed or contested by the testimonies of the senses, residing in them the possibility of error.

Epicurus sees Man as a set of atoms of air, fire, wind and yet another unnamed element, components of his body and his soul.

Since **the end of all Man is pleasure and the only evil is pain**, one must live with wisdom and virtue, and it is not proper to live alone. As can be seen, the Epicureans do not deal with death, but with life.

2.2.6 The Stoical Man

Stoicism, which has as its founder Zeno of Citius, also gives great value to the **sensation**, considering it as the origin of knowledge, subordinating scientific-philosophical research to a practical end aiming at the achievement of happiness, only attainable by wisdom, the purpose of philosophy.

It is interesting to note that for the Stoics the **human soul is a** *tabula rasa* on which the sensations print images and signs. So, it concerns a blank file that is capable of receiving data and storing it.

What sets stoicism apart from epicureanism, although both have several points of contact, is the determination of the criterion of truth, considering that, for the first, the representation is that in which the object imprints the world in the intellect.

It should also be noted that the *Stoic* **soul is corporeal** but not mortal, since its **superior portion**, which **is the reason**, remains for some time in the sublunary region, then returns to Fire (theory of eternal return) and blend with the immensity of divine Reason.

Thus, the Stoical Man must conform to the prevailing divine order, which he achieves, agreeing with himself, being himself, respecting and loving the *Logos*. Thus he achieves it by exercising his virtue, maintaining his austerity of character, moral rigidity, impassibility in the face of pain, misfortune or adversity, unlike the Epicurean man, guided by pleasure. The rules to be followed are: living according to nature, living according to reason, living with oneself.

2.2.7 The Christian Humanity

There is no doubt about the importance of Christian doctrine in Western development, nor should we forget the founding of a new religion. For this reason, it brings a **new concept of Man in opposition to the then prevailing one**.

The doctrine is based on the fact that Jesus Christ came with the mission of instituting the Kingdom of Heaven on Earth for all Men and redeeming humanity by offering himself in atonement on the cross to save men from sin.

The **virtuous Man is the one who has faith, hope, charity** and, especially **love**, for all beings indistinctly. It is a connotation of theological nature.

Man is evidenced **as a person** who is, by divine goodness, a creature similar to God, endowed with an **inner conscience** that allows him to conduct himself without sin, seeking to realize his first and ultimate end: eternal life.

This **autonomy** deriving from the condition of God's creature, conscious in his faith, elevates human dignity to that of being autonomous, Man-person, who, though he follows his course on the basis of rules dictated by God, he does so, if he will, by being **free** not to adopt them, and thus ceasing to be truly free.

Unlike the Greek cosmological view, in which man subordinates himself to the world, to Christianity, the problem of the world is subordinated to man as a person, endowed with consciousness, freedom, dignity, love, and spirit. Man is not only an element of the real but also the very meaning of reality. Therefore, the problem of Man is Man, placing him in the center of the world — **anthropocentrism** —, taking from there the cosmos — geocentrism. Man is more than a rational, social and political animal: man is a **spiritual animal**. In his intelligence is present a truth that does not come from sense and reason: the truth of revelation, which is transcendent.

2.2.7.1 The Augustinian Man

For Augustine of Hippo, the problem of man is God's problem. Through his education, he concentrated on the Man in God, since the encounter of Man with Man is the encounter of every Man with God. His Man is a **Man in the world**, which is valid for and by the man himself, conscious.

Through his peculiar condition, Man, in addition to fulfilling his natural destiny, aspires to a supernatural destiny, in God, superior to all things. It is the conquest of Man by Man and for Man.

2.2.7.2 The Thomist Man

Also of Christian religious education, Saint Thomas Aquinas proposes the sufficiency of **reason** to the **natural knowledge** of divine revelation. In his conception philosophy and religion are autonomous. The **real** as such **is Being**.

Interiority and transcendence are balanced. The Thomist Man is formed indissolubly by **matter** and **spirit**. He takes care of the **Man-person, rational, autonomous, political**, but **spiritualized**, that is completed in God, his supernatural end.

2.2.8 The Man in the 14th and 15th centuries

The concept of Man now is linked to **erudition** and **culture**, denoting a high spirit and **proper behavior**. Man becomes the center of all cultural manifestations. It makes Man appear at the center of historical events — **historical Man** — and philosophical concerns — **speculative Man**.

This **free** and **intelligent** Man understands his aesthetic dimension and his ability to act on the things of the world, modifying it according to his needs. Although he did not forget the search for heavenly happiness, he did not cease to pursue earthly happiness.

2.2.9 The Cartesian Man

According to Simha[35], it goes back to Descartes the construction of a radical philosophy of the subject: *the cogito*, the self that through thinking apprehends undoubted knowledge, the first base of accurate science.

However, it should be remembered that the term *consciousness* is not employed by Descartes, although it is about thinking, it is about the *cogito*.

The problem of Cartesianism, as Husserl states, is to understand how it is possible to arrive at certainties in the chain of motives of perception (conscience). The self, from its place of speech and perception, cannot hold the field of possibilities of this world, which is, at first, *its* world. This world spreads the vastness of individual experience, which in turn depends on the vastness from the *cogito's* intentional relations to the *cogitatum*. From what is thought to that which remains in the structure of the ego.

Descartes separates perception from sensation: from sensation comes brief information; through thinking, an intellectual act done with the ego, is that the essence of something is truly perceived.

2.2.10 The Marxist Man

Marx considers Man as **an end in himself**: an absolute humanistic value. It is necessary to remember that there is no unity in Marxism, which includes some aspects, among which dialectical Marxism and historical Marxism stand out.

In historical Marxism, commanded by the designator himself of the current of thought, the concept of Man is that of **Man-nature**, which constitutes a relation that dominates every historical

---

[35] SIMHA, A. (2009) *A consciência, do corpo ao sujeito: análise da noção: estudo de textos: Descartes, Locke, Nietzsche, Husserl* [The consciousness, from the body to the subject: analysis of the notion: study of texts: Descartes, Locke, Nietzsche, Husserl] (E. F. Alves, Trans). (pp 59). Petrópolis, Rio de Janeiro: Vozes.

becoming. Man is the journeyman of his true liberation from all alienations, whether economic, political, social, philosophical and religious.

Man is a transforming agent of reality that needs to be interpreted since fundamental reality is matter and the dialectic represents its degree of development and method necessary for its understanding. Man interprets reality to modify it to construct his own history.

A central question is the alienation of Man, the antithesis of history, taking a glimpse into the following types of alienation:

a) religious
b) ideological
c) political
d) economical

The added value imposed by the capitalist system removes the human condition, transforming man into merchandise. Man's great achievement is to come out of alienation and become master of himself, the creator of his freedom. It is, thus, a historical, situated Man. **There is, therefore, no spirit in man.** The truth is limited to what is produced by praxis at a given moment of evolution, or at a given historical moment. Therefore, **there is no Man as a person, but Man as a member of society, and there is no such thing**, in the same way, **as a personal consciousness, just a social consciousness.**

Similarly, there is nothing to say in the construction of the Marxist Man, about being, essence, and substance, given the historical and non-ontological nature of Man.

Finally, Marx censured the denial of the existence of God and of the religions, which are considered as a temporary and transitory degree of historical becoming, doomed to the sunset, when all men reach the full consciousness of themselves.

2.2.11 The Nietzschean Man

God has already died, as Nietzsche states, and there are only Supermen, the highest moral authority. Living in Nietzsche is experiencing the dream of consolidating your project. It is necessary to break with morality and established values and replace them with others, more radical.

2.2.12 The Existentialist Man

The main concern is conceptualizing Man as a **concrete and actual, real being**: the *being-in-itself*, the *being-in-the-world*. However, it is not a matter of constructing a Man subject to concrete limitations. Fundamentally, it is understood that existence is prior to the essence – both ontologically and epistemologically. That is, if man exists, he may be intelligible insofar as he contains the universal: the essence of the human.

Since **Man is a thinker**, and this is what he is, in order to give himself existence, he must begin to think for himself and about himself. In his destiny and in the last end Man seeks to be king. Thus, clearly, existentialism places the problem of thought in the realm of existence.

When Man recognizes his existence, he can undertake the journey towards the explanation of his being. The existentialist Man belongs to himself. He exists self-referenced but related to others and to things. He is a being-in-the-world. Thus, to be for himself he must be for the world. This extraneity is part of the definition of existence, which relates to itself.

There is a paradox, a contradiction in the existentialist Man. Although he is singular, different from all, he is concomitantly equal to all Men. He is a *Uni Verse*. It is only in the combination of the singular with the universal that one can speak of the true existence of Man. Reality is found in the singular because only the Man is singular and aware of his uniqueness.

Because the system is universal, it can be anything but real, and thus, the reality is not a system. From this, from the consciousness of its uniqueness and the contradiction inherent in him, is the appearance of Man, for Kierkegaard.

2.2.12.1 The Heideggerian Man

Martin Heidegger asserts that Man is the only being who questions about being. To exist is the essence of Man, and *Dasein*[36] constitutes his possibility of realization, for being — being in the world — is the fundamental determination of existence. **Man is being-in**, being-in-the-world, and being-to-death.

It is an ontological conception of Man, which surpasses reality because it is superior to a simple existence. Being is not limited to himself, but it exists in relation to others, in the world. Therefore, Man is incomplete and only completes himself being in the world, in relation to someone else.

For **Heidegger, the finite, mortal character** of Man is his highlight, to the point of considering that the milestone of Man's existence is to look, without illusion, at the dive into the nothingness that is death, deriving from it his state of anguish.

There is no axiological connotation of existence since it is a simple phenomenon. Man is only certain of his death for the realization of his being, characterized as one of the manifestations of nothingness.

Death is a simple consequence of life. It takes form with life itself, with the unfolding of it, until it emerges. However, Heidegger does not deny the existence. Being himself, being in himself and being to the other, even if the result is death, would characterize the existence of Man.

2.2.12.2 The Sartrean Man

Jean-Paul Sartre understands that existence precedes essence.

---

[36] Keller, A. J. (2009). *Dicionário escolar alemão* [German school dictionary]. Retrieved from <http://michaelis.uol.com.br/escolar/alemao/index.php?palavra=Dasein>. Last access date: February 25, 2009.

That is, only after a man is born he can define his essence.

However, if he is not immediately definable, it is because he is not. He is nothing. Only after is that he can become something since Man is what he wants to be. In the virtual phase of Man, he has a subjective life (principle of subjectivity). Consciousness for Sartre has as its content the objects in which it is reflected.

He sees in Descartes two kinds of beings: consciousness and objects of consciousness, since consciousness, when revealing the world, does not reveal itself directly, whereas knowledge presents itself only intentionally. Consciousness itself would have existence by itself. The other consciousness, the object that reflects consciousness has an existence in itself. In addition to these, he understands that there is a third consciousness, that of being-for-other, meaning that, if there is the other, there is the beyond-subject, outside the inner subject, the external, and thus a physical manifestation, nature.

2.2.12.3 The Jasperean Man

Karl Jaspers[37] argues that being is not something given or something that everyone can know.

Moreover, the whole is never given to us. Therefore, there is no object without a subject, for everything that is an object is determined by the consciousness in general. Therefore, the existing objective being – *Dasein* – is always an appearance.

For him the world, soul, and God can be represented by three variables:

> *All that man can know is knowable within the limits of a horizon because what encompasses all horizons is the unknowable variable. The first variable is the world, the second is the man himself, and finally the third total variable: transcendence*[38].

---

[37] Jaspers apud Oliveira, O. M., *op. cit.*, p. 288.
[38] *Idem.*

Thus the existence of man makes sense, not by believing in God, but by **feeling the presence of God**.

Only the limits of existence lead one to admit that there is one from the outside as sure as there is one from within. Thus, indirectly, one can affirm the existence of a being from outside, always unknowable and the Being from within, a codification of things. Therefore, every Being needs to know its limitations, otherwise, the Being cannot be understood.

2.2.13 The Modern Man

As can be seen, from the past to the present, the concept of Man is always in construction and reconstruction. This means, on one hand, that no concept is satisfactory for a long time and everybody, and, on the other hand, that it bears something beyond the human, either by the transcendent connotations or by the incorporation of the world or the other.

Nothing indicates, therefore, that this concept has crystallized, stopped evolving, nor it is perfect and finished.

Thus, its content can and must still be completed and always in line with the perception and Man›s world experience contemporary to the concept.

In post-humanity, when the increment of the cognitive and intellectual capacity of machines and men probably will happen. The biological, synthetic and cybernetic interaction, and, eventually, the overcoming of the human by the machine may occur. The concept of person will have to be extended to include nonhuman structures.

Man and person, in this sense, are only concepts, whose contents are open and therefore not linked to the Human Being, to the *Homo sapiens* species, although it has always been referred to up to now, in a single-handed way. Perhaps, under the state of things that men encountered in their historical and evolutionary journey, it was necessary to handle the concept by relating it to the human being to, once again, overcome it.

The time comes when Man confronts new realities, in which he shares a world with beings functionally equivalent to him, the concept must be filled to accommodate that new reality.

A clear example that the concept of Man is not linked to *Homo sapiens* is drawn from history, in fact on the sad side of history, when total or partial humanity was denied from certain human beings as prisoners, Jews, slaves, blacks, American Indians, barbarians, women, mentally or chromosomally altered individuals, etc.

Even in educated civilizations — at least so considered — as Ancient Rome and Greece, modern Europe and America, 20th century Germany — which saw the emergence of geniuses — Brazil and others, the phenomenon of dehumanization has already been present, elucidating that not always being human is to be Man in the sense that was sought to conceptualize above or in the juridical sense.

Therefore, when we come across the functional equivalents of men (thinking, conscious, intelligent, sentimental, similar in appearance or partially human) from the biological point of view, perhaps we cannot deny them the condition of Man. And we will see the condition of a person, as a subject and not as a thing, as a holder of rights and not as an object of them. Since it develops relationships with other people, even though virtual, its existence already causes reactions. It is a being. We only react to what is, not to what is not.

We have to be prepared for a new concept of person that encompasses robots and intelligent machines. It doesn't mean that robots and humans are the same. There will be (always) difference, even when there is partly a machine and partly human individuals[39]. Probably, as long as there are humans, they will be different from the cyborgs and the robots, although they share several similar characteristics. Nothing, from the legal point of view, prevents

---

[39] Castoriadis, C. (2007) *Sujeito e verdade no mundo social-histórico* [Subject and Truth in the Social-Historical World]. (E. Aguiar, Trans.). (pp. 31) São Paulo: Civilização Brasileira.

robots from being considered as persons and, possibly, from the philosophical point of view, as living beings and as Men.

But what are these characteristics that allow a man to see in himself conditions of securing what the Law calls legal personality, that is, the ability to have rights and assume obligations? If they exist, they must be questioned, and one way to inquire about them is to seek to know what effectively Man is, beyond the philosophical field. What gives him that specific and special dignity that makes almost everything else subject to his rights?

At the heart of everything, in the essence of what is effectively scientifically proven, there are matter and energy, formed by subatomic particles, which make up the atoms, which in turn form the molecules, which form chains, among that which defines biological life, DNA.

Atoms are present in everything, in almost an infinite possibility of arrangements, composing everything that is known in the physical world. This makes Men essentially and ontologically identical to everything else, not making them special.

In the biological world, be it a rat, a begonia or a seal, there's the DNA, with its very rich and detailed variation telling us blatantly that there are no glaring differences, that the protein chains are the same, with only different arrangements. So much so, that Maturana and Varela[40] denounce the small morphological variation that exists. Basically, the higher animals have similar organs of sense, limbs, body and the digestive, circulatory and respiratory systems. The multicellular vegetables have a gas exchange area, supporting elements and a structure that unites them. The unicellular are almost always very similar, with the membrane, nucleus, elements of the nucleus and, sometimes, devices for locomotion.

This, because its past unites them and it distances them, in the evolutionary cycle, unraveled with greater prominence as of

---

[40] Maturana, H. R.; Varela, F. J. (2004). *De máquinas y seres vivos. Autopoiesis: La organización de lo vivo* [Autopoiesis and Cognition: The Realization of the Living] (6th ed.) Buenos Aires: Coedição Editorial Universitaria e Editorial Lumen.

Charles Robert Darwin[41]. In essence man is equal to any other living being and that is why the evolutionary inheritance makes him have in himself a little of all other creatures, with the problems arising therefrom, even showing that the (im)perfection of nature is done at a very individual cost, as, for example, hernias, arising from the past as fish and other ills resulting from adaptive (im)perfection. The very concept of evolution was used allegorically by Darwin, in the words of Maturana and Varela[42]. Chilean biologists better explain the concept of adaptation to the environment, with its structural coupling.

2.3 Identifying elements of the Man possibly valued by Law

The following is intended to illustrate some concepts related to themes connected to the apprehension of the elements that, it seems, conform and allow the Law to deal with the legal personality of *Homo Sapiens*.

None of the concepts formulated below are certainly found in the doctrine of the splendid cradle. All of which are without exception controversial, questioned and criticized. However, it was necessary to make the necessary epistemological reflections to construct the present work, being represented only the concepts considered satisfactory for the understanding of the subject under analysis, without being unaware of the difficulties it encountered.

They represent, therefore, in each sector of the examined knowledge what was considered best to exist to base this work.

If, in essence, Men and other forms of life are equal, if, physically or biologically, Man does not move away from everything else, inanimate or living, what distinguishes him?

In his evolutionary journey, at an instant of sidereal time, the Brotherhood was broken with the other primates and a proper path

---

[41] Darwin, C. R., *op. cit.*
[42] Maturana, H. R.; Varela, F. J. (2007). *A Árvore do Conhecimento: as bases biológicas da compreensão humana* [The Tree of Knowledge: The Biological Roots of Human Understanding]. São Paulo: Palas Athena.

was taken along with the related human species, destroyed from the last glaciation.

Between humans and chimpanzees[43], DNA leaves no doubt that the genetic difference is almost imperceptible, though evident at any glance. If by less than 4% (four percent), by the most cautious estimates, humans move away from them, it will be concluded hurriedly that to be human one must be 100% (one hundred percent) genetically identical to what we call humans; be endowed with genetic and chromosomal **identity**, but this also cannot be a criterion, since at least, Down syndrome causes a different count of chromosomes and neither by the divergence of chromosome numbers does the juridical personality of its carriers deviate, nor, much less, it is claimed to be another species. It's only a mutation and a mutation occurs to any species.

Also, between the Human Being and any other species it can be found in DNA very similar characteristics, even identical genes as those related to the vision and organization of body structure, common to all animals, despite the huge difference of eyes and bodies that occurs between species[44]. Therefore, the diversity that exists is not so original, but variations on the same theme.

Scheler[45] says that, based on Darwin, Schwalbe, and Köhler, the evolutionists of the Darwinian and Lamarckian schools, refute that there is one last difference between man and animal, precisely because he is also endowed with intelligence. Thus, in some way they are connected to the theory of the unity of man, which Scheler

---

[43] According to Marvin Minsky, as the evolution of man was so rapid — taking care to report that there are very few fossil records, his brain has developed so markedly over the last few hundred thousand years, that the evolutionary interval has been so short that most genes and structure remained almost identical in man and in the chimpanzee. This seems to be in accordance with Ray Kurzweil's Law of Accelerating Returns, discussed below. For more details, see Minsky, M. (1989). *A sociedade da mente* [The Society of Mind] (W. R. Carvalho, Trans.). Rio de Janeiro: Francisco Alves.

[44] *What Darwin didn't know*. Armand Marie Leroi (dir). Tima Lambit (dir. and prod.). Richard Wilkinson (ed.). BBC. Londres: 2009. CD-ROM.

[45] Scheler, M., *op. cit.*, p. 47.

refers to as *Homo Faber* theory, and, in this way, they would not know any metaphysics of man, no separating relation that man, as such, would possess with the foundation of the world.

So far, anthropocentric characters were considered. However, one could expand the scope and consider the **biocentric criterion**, that is, in the face of being alive, according to the known biological pattern, Man would have the dignity that he has. However, this is not the case, given that in this way a man would be equated with other living beings, which our (positive) Law does not do, at least in its traditional hermeneutics, since Man, and only he, is endowed with legal personality, in the predominant understanding.

Being **gregarious** adds nothing, as there are numerous cases of gregarious animals, from bees to dolphins, to primates.

The decisive criterion could then be **intelligence**. Man, for some to be supreme on the evolutionary scale, would be the only one endowed with intelligence in all animal kingdom, for plants are usually not even thought of being intelligent.

However, this conception is mistaken in that it seeks to attribute to evolution[46] itself the character of intelligent, wise. Evolution would then lead to intelligence, and since Man is the most evolved on the biological scale, he would be the most intelligent, if not the only, intelligent being. However, it has been seen that evolution is not an intelligent process, although it may result in intelligence. Natural drift seems to explain this phenomenon. Also, the concept of evolution does not carry the hierarchy when we reflect on Maturana and Varela.

Scheler says that the essence of the human being, also possible to be called the "peculiar position", is far beyond from what is called intelligence and ability to choose. It would also be wrong to say that man is what he is due to the addition of a stage: affective

---

[46] The opinion of Norbert Wiener about evolution should be consulted.
Wiener, N. (1971). *Deus, Golem e Cia: um comentário sobre certos pontos de contato entre cibernética e religião* [God and Golem, Inc.: A Comment on Certain Points where Cybernetics Impinges on Religion] (L. Hegenberg and O. S. da Mota, Trans.). São Paulo: Cultrix.

impulse, instinct, associative memory, intelligence and choice, and also a new level in the functioning of the psychic and vital actions: his knowledge would be dependent on the capacity of psychology.

The new principle is external to everything that in the broadest sense is called "life".

The author chooses to use a broader term, which encompasses the concept of "reason," "*thought by ideas*," and a certain type of "intuition" (*Anschauung*) — that of "proto-phenomena or eidetic content" — as well as, a class of volitional and emotional actions: the word *spirit* (*Geist*). However, to the center of acts, in which the spirit manifests itself at the heart of the finite spheres of being, characterizing it as "person", in dramatic opposition to all the functional vital centers which, internally analyzed, and also called the "psychic" centers.

2.3.1. Intelligence

There is much discussion about the concept of intelligence, as well as whether people are becoming more intelligent or not. Even the term "Flynn effect" has been coined to denote the significant IQ gains in the twentieth century in honor of Dr. James R. Flynn.

Flynn[47] has an interesting insight into intelligence. He recalls, for example, that a chimpanzee can defeat a man in at least one cognitive task. Before revealing this curiosity, however, he sets out to define intelligence.

He argues that A. R. Jensen wrote that

> *Intelligence, by definition, is what intelligence tests measure. This is called instrumentalism or defining what you are trying to measure by referring to the readings of the measuring instrument, and it is subject to devastating critique. If intelligence is what current IQ tests measure, we could never invent a better IQ test because the new test, by definition, would be a departure from what measures intelligence.*[48]

---

[47] Flynn, J. R. (2007). *What is intelligence?: Beyond the Flynn effect.* (pp. 49) Cambridge: University Press.
[48] *Idem.*

In fact, he elucidates, Jensen has never been so naive:

> *In 1979, he wrote a brilliant paper distinguishing intelligence from both learning and memory. He imagined Robinson Crusoe alone on his island struggling to survive. Crusoe would forget things and, therefore, have the concept of memory. He would acquire new skills and, therefore, have the concept of learning. However, it would only be when his man Friday arrived and learned those skills faster and better than he had learned them that he would develop the concept of intelligence.*[49]

One sees, therefore, the relational character of intelligence.

Flynn[50] regrets, still, that Jensen in *"The g factor: the science of mental ability"*, Westport, CT, Praeder, has abandoned the attempt to define intelligence, saying that he would never deal with the subject again, since it was a subject without any precision and that did not attract any consensus. However, in at least one opportunity the author referred to by Flynn had to rely on the word intelligence when he states in the same work that "intelligence" predicts the pattern, quality, and limit of learning[51].

> *Any attempt to avoid defining intelligence is bad faith. The only reason we can dispense with a clarified concept is that we all have an unclarified concept in mind. Imagine that Jensen presented a lecture on g to a Martian and never did use some viable substitute for the word "intelligence". The Martian would ask in bewilderment, but what kind of a theory is this, is it perhaps a theory of the tides? When Jensen answered, of course not, it was a theory about measuring who learns best and fastest, the Martian would exclaim: "Oh, you mean it is a theory of intelligence."*

---

[49] *Ibidem*, p. 50.

[50] *Ibidem*, p. 274-275.

[51] Norbert Wiener considers that 'Learning is a property we often associate only with systems endowed with consciousness — almost always living things. It is one of the attributes of Man [...]"
Wiener, N. (1971). *Deus, Golem e Cia: um comentário sobre certos pontos de contato entre cibernética e religião* [God and Golem, Inc.: A Comment on Certain Points where Cybernetics Impinges on Religion] (L. Hegenberg and O. S. da Mota, Trans.). (pp. 22) São Paulo: Cultrix.

> *Endless muddling about the definition of intelligence is a distraction from getting on with the job of theory construction, so in a sense Jensen's instincts were sound, but the distraction is not going to go away until it is exorcised. The best start is to note Jensen's reason for abandoning the definitional task: all definitions of intelligence compare badly with the theoretical construct of g. I will argue that the roles of a pre-theory concept and a post-theory concept are quite different and that to confuse the two is fatal. The best example comes from the history of astronomy. It tells us how the modern pre-theory concept of celestial influence paved the way for the post-theory concepts of whirlpool, gravity, and space warping[52].*

This would demonstrate that pre-theories are not useless and serve to pave the way for complete and more sophisticated theories in that they show a path formed of mistakes and successes as long as they are sufficiently detailed. It would be appropriate for a theory to use the concept of pre-theory in a theoretical framework with specificity to produce a prediction that can be later (confirmed or) denied.

Flynn understands that to create a pre-theory of intelligence it will be necessary to answer the following question: What elements affect our ability to solve problems that consist of a cognitive function?

And he responds like this:

I) Mental acuity: the ability to provide on-the-spot solutions to problems we have never encountered before, problems not solvable by the mechanical application of a learned method, and often requiring us to create alternative solutions from which we must choose.

II) Habits of mind: the rise of science engendered new habits of mind of enormous potency. It detached logic and the hypothetical from the concrete and today we use them to attack

---

[52] Flynn, J. R., op.cit., p. 50-51.

a whole range of new problems. A more mundane example: ten years ago, I began to do crossword puzzles. I now do them much better, not because of increased mental acuity or even larger vocabulary or store of information. My usual proclivity with words is to use them to say what I want as simply and directly as possible. I had to modify that habit to imagine secondary meanings, less literal meanings, reflect whether the clue word was being "used" as a noun or a verb, and so forth.

III) Attitudes: these lay the foundation for acquiring habits of mind. We had to learn to take the taxonomy of science seriously before we could put on the scientific spectacles through which we now view the world. We have to take abstract problem solving seriously before we will do much of it in our leisure and be adept at it as we enter the test room.

IV) Knowledge and information: the more you have, the more problems you can attack. You cannot do advanced algebra without knowing elementary algebra. You cannot put knowledge to work without data.

V) Speed of information processing and memory[53].

The author considers that "intelligence is important in three levels, respectively: cerebral psychology, individual differences, and social[54] tendency, the latter, a fact with which, I think, one cannot agree.

Finally, the author clarifies that some intelligence-related brain capacities, such as the rate of data apprehension, may vary from species to species, and he cites Matsuzawa's experiments with the

---

[53] *Ibidem*, p.53-54.
[54] *Idem*.

chimpanzee Ali, who can memorize a larger sequence of objects that should be inspected than human beings.

Possibly this occurs because in the natural drift of the cousin species, this ability proved to be more important than in our own, and thus this cognitive capacity was more developed in the ape than in the Human.

It is imagined that in their *habitat* the chimpanzee needs to be faster to visually inspect the environment for food than the human being. This variation of cognitive aptitude among species also seems to explain why leopards, for example, are faster than apes in this task, because probably in hunting, they must first define the target before they are perceived and must be accurate in their attack, under the penalty of losing the chance and getting hungry.

Thus, it is verified that the intelligence is not only human attributed; that it is a concept with a varied content, difficult to understand in all its dimensions, and that perhaps it is still at a stage that does not permit the building of a general theory of intelligence, only apprehensible with the development of the various sciences involved with it, in its different approaches.

However, even at this stage, several of its component elements can be sighted to understand its phenomenon.

To Telles Júnior, "Intelligence is the skill that sometimes denies and repudiates, sometimes accepts and exalts. It's intelligence who compares and evaluates. It is, in short, intelligence that decrees the *value* of things"[55]. The author also says that "Intelligence is necessarily *determined* by what the human being *really is*," that is, by what Man is in a certain place and historical circumstances, and intelligence is endowed with a constituent function of Man.

Kurzweil[56] elucidates that one way of defining intelligence is in terms of constitutive processes through learning, rationalization

---

[55] Telles Júnior, G. (2003) *Direito quântico: ensaios sobre o fundamento da ordem jurídica* [Quantum law: essays on the foundation of the legal order]. (7th ed., pp. 230) São Paulo: Juarez de Oliveira.

[56] Kurzweil, R. (1999). *The age of intelligent machines.* (pp. 16, 3rd reprint). Cambridge, Mass.: MIT Press.

and the ability to manipulate symbols. For him, learning is not only an acquisition of facts but also knowledge. A Freudian or Lacanian psychoanalyst would talk about **awareness** and not about **knowledge**.

He also understands that reason is the ability to have deductions and interferences of knowledge to achieve a goal or solve a problem. Thus he defines intelligence in terms of purpose — and he understands that Man has a goal, common to all species, that is to survive.

Therefore, in various fields of knowledge, intelligence is indicated as a human characteristic, though not exclusively human.

2.3.1.1 Nervous system and knowledge

As Maturana and Varella[57] postulate, it is necessary to always remember that behavior is not a creation of the nervous system, but the description of the natural changes of state of a system concerning an environment, in balancing the disturbances generated by it.

The associations common to the word behavior are everyday actions, such as eating and walking, among others. The unifying element of these actions is their relation to the movement, although it is not the universal quality of living beings, which Telles Júnior does not disagree with.

The elemental organization of the human nervous system, so intricately complex, fundamentally, has the same logic as the modest hydra, which has one of the most simplified known forms of the nervous system.

2.3.1.2 The interneuronal network

In humans, one hundred billion (10^{11}) of interneurons interconnect around one million (10^6) motor neurons, which activate a few

---

[57] Maturana, H., & Varela, F. (2007). *A Árvore do Conhecimento: as bases biológicas da compreensão humana* [The Tree of Knowledge: The Biological Roots of Human Understanding]. (pp. 158-196). São Paulo: Palas Athena.

thousand muscles, with tens of millions (10^7) of sensory cells scattered as receptor surfaces at various locations of the body. Between the motor neurons and the sensory neurons interposes the brain, a colossal "entanglement" of interneurons that interconnects (at a ratio of 10 / 100,000 / 1) in a constantly changing dynamics.

It is interesting to note that the neural system of the octopus is different from the human one and much more decentralized, as some current digital systems that use distributed computing to optimize the processes.

External disturbances are not decisive. It only articulates the constant coming and going of internal balance.

2.3.1.3 Operational cloister of the nervous system

For Maturana and Varella[58], the nervous system is organized in a way that any change that has taken place will bring about other changes within itself; it functions as a closed loop of modifications in the relations of activities between its constituent parts. Thus, it can be said that, as regards its organization, it has an **operational closure**.

Thanks to its structure and its way of operating in a cloister, the functioning of the nervous system is perfectly consistent with the autonomous character of the unit. One state of activity is followed by another, which changes the whole unit. In this way, every process of knowledge is based on the organism as an operationally closed unit in its nervous system. Hence it is known that all knowledge is about doing, having sensory-effector connections in the domains of structural coupling in which there is the nervous system.

2.3.1.4 Plasticity

The degree of activity and the chemical transit between two cells articulate the efficiency and the form of interaction that occurs between them during their continuous variation. This explains

---

[58] *Ibidem*, p. 158-196.

the plasticity of the nervous system: the points of interaction be-tween the cells compose delicate dynamic balance, articulated by countless elements that provoke local structural changes. These arise from the activity of these same cells, as well as from oth-ers, whose results travel through the bloodstream and bathe the neurons. All this integrates the dynamics of the interactions of the organism through its environment.

2.3.1.5 The brain and the computer

For Maturana and Varela[59], it would be erroneous to conceptu-alize the nervous system as having inputs and outputs, in the tra-ditional sense. It would mean that such inputs and outputs are part of the system definition, like a computer. This conduct is totally permissible when we create a machine in which the most important thing is to know how we wish to interact with it. But the nervous system (or organism) was not designed by anyone: it stems from the phylogenetic drift of units centered on their state dynamics. In this way, what is appropriate is to recognize it as a unit constrained by its internal relations, in which interactions only act by articula-ting its structural dynamics, that is, as a unit endowed with opera-tional closure. Unlike what is commonly said, the nervous system does not "pick up information" from the environment. Rather the opposite, it builds a world, by pointing out which environment set-tings are disturbances and what changes are caused in the body.

2.3.2 Consciousness

Initially, it is necessary to assert, like Minsky[60], that there is a generalized belief that we have this special entity called conscious-ness.

> Many people seem absolutely certain that no computer could ever be sentient, conscious, self-willed, or in any oth-er way "aware" of itself. But what makes everyone so sure

---

[59] *Idem.*

[60] Minsky, M. (1988). *The society of mind.* (pp. 39). New York: Simon & Schus-ter.

that they themselves possess those admirable qualities?
(...) If self-awareness means to know what's happening
inside one's mind, no realist could maintain for long that
people have much insight, in the literal sense of seeing-in.
Indeed, the evidence that we are self-aware — is very weak
indeed."[61]

Finally, he says, "There is something strange about a description of consciousness: no matter what people mean, they just cannot say it clearly."[62]

Dealing with consciousness is primarily a matter of psychology, psychoanalysis, and philosophy, but this work would not be complete without at least touching the surface of this subject.

Therefore, it is convenient to warn that conscience is a polysemic word and, therefore, presents great difficulty for its study. Just observe that in the Houaiss Online Dictionary[63], its description fills in about fifteen A4-size pages when printed.

One of the characteristics that is commonly attributed to the human being and that would make him unique, unlike anything else, would be the fact of being endowed with consciousness. Therefore, without knowing what this characterizing element is, it is not possible to examine whether Man is conscious, whether he only thinks or believes that he is conscious, whether he has this characteristic in isolation, or whether it is possible to attribute this condition to other species or beings, including robots.

Henrique Schützer del Nero[64] deals with the question by saying that consciousness is a product of the brain, whereas content is a function and also a form. Its formation would be due to the momentary, synchronized and circumstantial conjunction of the

---

[61] *Ibidem*, p.63.

[62] *Ibidem*, p.29.

[63] Houaiss, A. *et al. Dicionário Houaiss de língua portuguesa* [Houaiss Dictionary of Portuguese language]. Retrieved from: <http://houaiss.uol.com.br/busca.jhtm?verbete=consciencia&stype=k. Last access date: February 09, 2009.

[64] Nero, H. S. D. (1997). *O sitio da mente: pensamento, emoção e vontade no cérebro humano* [The site of the mind: thought, emotion and will in the human brain]. (pp. 125-126). São Paulo: Collegium Cognitio.

neurons, representing different aspects of the external and internal worlds, concrete and abstract, tied to the analogical character of the processing performed by the brain.

Thus, he immediately removes the exclusivity of human consciousness, expressly accepting its occurrence in other animals — but not expressly in the vegetal kingdom — while emphasizing that its organization in the human brain is unique.

The author limits himself, as mentioned, to dethrone Man from the condition of the only conscious being – and it could not fail to be, since numerous animals demonstrate to have some degree of awareness of what they do. This way, it is a big and important step, because it breaks one of the pillars of deeply rooted anthropocentrism in the West.

Hans Moravec[65] recalls that some people see consciousness even in insects. He quotes Donald Griffin's *Animal Thinking* which collates Otto Von Frisch's research on bees in which he announces that these invertebrates communicate the direction, distance, and value of a food reserve to other bees of the same hive, by performing an intricate dance, performed with convulsions, whose directions, length and energy transmit these pieces of information.

It also brings to light the research of Martin Lindauer who went further and proved a much more elaborate and conscientious form of communication by reporting that when a hive is overpopulated the workers go out in search of new sites for the construction of the new hive. When these workers return, they perform a dance in which they communicate the characteristics of the sites visited, such as the location and conditions to house the hive.

The most promising places are then visited by other bees that will check the information transmitted, returning and communicating their impressions to the community.

It is interesting to note that when a bee is performing the dance to communicate its discovery, it is not diverted by bees that trans-

---

[65] Moravec, H. (1992). *Homens e robots: o futuro da inteligência humana e robótica* [Mind Children: the future of robot and human intelligence]. (J. L. M. F. Lima, Trans.). (pp. 69-70). Lisboa: Gradiva.

mit information about the same place it visited. However, if a bee talks about a more promising site than its own, the worker can change its mind and stop its dancing to pay attention to the bee that brought the best news.

It must be said that in an overpopulated beehive, countless bees are performing this dance at the same time and that the number of sites to be checked decreases as they compare and select the best. When almost unanimity is found, they leave the hive, and together they go to the best place chosen by the majority, after this cycle of debates, which can last for several days.

This well demonstrates that the bees start up a smart[66], conscious process, done in a team, in stages with trial and error, until a decision is made. Now, this characterizes intelligent behavior. To verify, it is enough to replace the words "bees and workers" by "men" and "swarm" by "group", as well as *hive* by *assembly*, that no difference will be noticed in the behavior one would expect of men who usually consider themselves intelligent.

For Del Nero[67] consciousness plays the role of collector and gluer of pieces of information unconsciously in the brain and that, by its nature and the effect of analog processing performed by the brain, they have the condition to become conscious, that is, to be known by Man.

He glimpses that the characteristics of consciousness (timeless, non-spatial, subjective, qualitative, capable of generating will, holistic, mnemonic, emergent and intentional) made it move away from the physical brain, through the course of all evolution of the species, conferring on it the status of a human phenomenon.

The author, after recalling some of the various mechanical explanations for the mind, such as comparisons with fountains, telephone switchboard, etc., all seeking to locate it in the brain or in

---

[66] Kurzweil, R. (1999). *The age of intelligent machines.* (pp. 145, 3rd reprint). Cambridge, Mass.: MIT Press. p. 145. "An intelligent process is an association of intelligent and non-intelligent processes communicating and influencing each other".

[67] Nero, H. S. D., *op. cit.*, loc. cit.

some other organ, giving natural object *status*, subject to laws of physics, says that the attempts aimed to maintain nature unified and trying to explain the causes of mental pathologies. All this to avoid the complication proposed by the duality of matter and spirit in the field of science.

He also reminds us that modern physics demonstrates that, from subatomic levels, there is no reason to talk about matter, but about energy. That would, after all, support the argument of the dichotomy of the treatment of the subject, highlighting the implicit duality which, in any case, is unified in the concept of energy, consolidating matter and spirit, "unity of everything."

Also, Simha[68] teaches, in the modern sense of the term, the notion of the conscious subject implies personal identity, which is also a complex notion. Identity has two meanings: individual perception of its operations and appropriation of personal experience. Consciousness would then be the possibility of a constituted subject to perceive and understand their perceptions, as well as to interact with themselves, to notice their changes, whether suffered or realized and ultimately responsible.

Consciousness depends on the ability to aggregate representations (memories) regardless of their order of events and their temporal location. Thus, consciousness and memory are implied in such a way that there is a constant re-actualization of the past.

The modern conception of consciousness investigates the origin of mental activity capable of reflecting upon itself (being aware of what it is and what it does). Memorization ("archiving", recalling what one is aware of and what one does). Autonomy (it imputes to itself its actions and perceptions, even in a remote past). From its ethical meaning, one understands the psychological unity: identity is only formed and remains when it comes from the moral and legal demands of responsibility. Thus, the problem is placed between the subject (endowed with personal, intimate consciousness) and externality.

---

[68] Simha, A., *op. cit.*, p. 19.

Memory is distinguished from consciousness: perception is a category of action, always related to objectivity and exteriority; the memory is highlighted by the essential relation between subjectivity and interiority.

The recall of a lesson, for example, is a habit acquired by the repetition of the same effort. A memory, on the contrary, is a unique representation, an individual event that evokes the past (unlike memory-habit, which merely represents it), bringing with it the spontaneity of the image that was lived and simultaneously formed for the first time, impregnated by personal experience, subjective.

Consciousness depends on its structure and functions on the action of the subject (who performs bodily functions), on the opposition of the past formed by pure memories and the present sensory-motor (a system whose center is occupied by the human body). Memories are not contained anywhere, even in the brain: what is perceived occupies a place only in the present moment.

The true autonomy of the subject as a function of the perception of self — consciousness as a power of synthesis and reflection — arises from the specification of a human unconscious, situated between automatism and reflective knowledge of the reason of its own acts, a condition without which there is not your domain.

For Maturana and Varela[69], the lineage of hominids is more than fifteen million years old, but only about three million years ago they solidified the structural features fundamentally identical to the present ones. Some of the most important: the erect and bipedal walking, increased cranial capacity, specific dental configuration — related to an omnivorous diet, but mainly based on seeds and nuts — and the exchange of fertility estrous cycles of females by menstruation.

The unique characteristics of human social life and its constant linguistic coupling originated a new phenomenon, simultaneously

---

[69] Maturana, H. R.; Varela, F. J. (2007). *A Árvore do Conhecimento: as bases biológicas da compreensão humana* [The Tree of Knowledge: The Biological Roots of Human Understanding]. (pp. 228-257). São Paulo: Palas Athena.

so close and so far from our very existence: mind and consciousness.

When exposed for the first time in front of a mirror, the gorillas are amazed, but soon they get used to the effect and ignore it. Once an experiment was carried out: a gorilla was anesthetized and between his eyes, a colored spot was painted, so that it could only be seen in the mirror. After awakening from the anesthesia and placed before the mirror, he brought his hand to the colored spot on his forehead to analyze it. It was presumed that he would extend it to touch the point on the image, where he saw it. With these experiments, one imagined being able to indicate that, at least in the gorillas (and in other superior primates) there was a certain possibility of self-image and, thus, of reflection. It is far from understanding what recursive mechanisms allow such reflection — if there are mechanisms. And, if they exist, they are probably very limited and partial. Indeed, man is different, in which language[70] makes his reflective capacity inseparable from his identity.

In the interactions made with the two cerebral hemispheres, there are behaviors usually pointed out as belonging to a conscious mind capable of reflecting something very important. Without the linguistic resource there is no language, nor does it seem to form a mind or something that resembles as such, in our domain of distinctions.

At all levels, the living system is organized to create internal regularities. In the field of social coupling and communication (linguistic "trophallaxis"), the same effect is produced. Through the mechanisms made possible by linguistic activity and its maximization in language, this time the coherence and stabilization of society as a unit will be produced. This new level of coherence is what we know as consciousness and as "our" mind. Besides, we know that words are actions and not things that "pass from here to there".

The appearance of language in the human being, as well as in the social context in which it appears, creates the unprecedented

---

[70] *KOKO: o gorila falante* [KOKO: a talking gorilla]. Barbet Shroeder (dir.) Paris: Wonder Multimidia. 1978. DVD.

phenomenon — as far as is known — of the mind and self-consciousness as the most personal experience of the human being. Without the historical development of adequate structures, there is no possibility of entering the human domain. On the other hand, as a phenomenon in the network of social and linguistic coupling, the mind is not a "thing" located in the skull, nor a brain fluid: consciousness and the mind integrate social coupling, therefore, in it happens its dynamics. The language was not created by an individual alone in capturing an outside world. Thus, it cannot be used as a tool to reveal this world.

2.3.2.1 Identity

According to Santaella[71], there are always many identities. The view that identity is consciously unified and rigid is based on the notion of subject and subjectivity inherited from Cartesianism and, at least a century ago, was problematized by philosophy and psychoanalysis.

The Cartesian cogito established an idea of human subjectivity that prevailed for centuries in Western thought. According to this idea, the existence of the subject is analogous to his thought.

The vision of the "self", established by Descartes, has gone into a crisis that is probably irreversible. The concepts of individual, subject and subjectivity based on this vision were replaced by cultural changes initiated in the second half of the 19th century.

The radically uncentered view of the self, suggested by Freud, was one of the most revolutionary ideas in this area of knowledge. Lacan has pointed out that the ego is, in fact, a disorganized compilation of identifications and that it is the projection of the imaginary, the false unity of the self. In this sense, Lacanian postulates unite psychoanalysis with the post-structuralist attempt to evaluate the self as the result of discourse and not as something real or as a stable structure of mind. Today, the deconstruction of the subject

---

[71] Santaella, L. (2007). *Linguagens líquidas na era da mobilidade* [Liquid languages in the era of mobility]. (pp. 84). São Paulo: Paulus.

occurs not only in philosophy or psychoanalysis but also in several areas.

Who can say, that sometimes, at least, one is not contradictory of oneself? Still, one has an identity.

A different view of subjectivity reveals it as multiply developed. This image seeks to detach itself from naturalistic essentialism or social naturalism and is found in Domenèch[72], in the Actor-Network theory. This theory, based on the postulates of Michel Serres[73] and originated within the study of science, restores the role of technology — instead of increasing the distance between the human and the nonhuman, between the social and the natural — in the explanations on questions which have been formulated as distinct from this class of elements. Thus, relations of power and the constitution of subjectivities, for example, appear under a new focus, when we stop considering them exclusively as processes pertinent to humans.

Guattari's[74] polyphonic subjectivity states that collective subjectivity is generated by semiotic elements that cannot be reduced to a translation in terms of structural and systemic signifiers. Considering such a point of view, it is no longer possible to refer to a subject in general and a perfectly individualized utterance, but rather to partial and heterogeneous elements of subjectivity and collective assemblies of enunciation from which human multiplicities arise, but also to become an orderly animal, vegetal, machinal, incorporeal, infrapersonal.

Thus, the conceptual dispersion of the "self" in the human sciences is evident, observable in the considerations about subjectivity that try to highlight the falsehoods hidden in the axioms behind the beliefs.

The conclusion, then, is that the greater fluidity which the *per-*

---

[72] Domenèch, M. et al. A dobra: psicologia e subjetivação [The fold: psychology and subjectivation]. *In*: Nunca fomos humanos. Nos rastros do sujeito [We were never human. In the traces of the subject], *apud* Santaella, L., *op. cit.*

[73] Serres, M. Preface. In: L'oeuf transparente; *apud* Santaella, L., *op. cit.*

[74] *Idem.*

sona is endowed that interacts in cyberspace, compared to other life situations, comes from the possibility of consciously constructing it in the simulated environment. Because we have consciousness, we can play with ourselves in new ways of interacting with other *personas* of the cyberspace. However, this is only possible through the mediation of the Other — language, culture, cyberspace as code systems — that allow interactive forms that cannot be lived in other circumstances.

The subject is not in a fixed time/space, in a fixed opinion from which he can rationally decide his options. On the contrary, it is multiplied in databases, spread among electronic messages, involved successively in some mode of electronic transmission and capture of symbols. Now, with the appearance of cyberculture, the Other (the big other of psychoanalysis, the space of language of codes and culture) becomes more complex.

The great novelty of cyberspace is to demonstrate that human identity is naturally manifold, and to allow one to play with this truth "to the ultimate limit of transmutation, of metamorphosis; finally, of the 'metamorphosis' of identity," in the words of Santaella herself.

2.3.2.1.1 Identity under a legal perspective

Capelo de Sousa[75] states that the legal good of identity lies in the recognition of man by himself, in the connection by which he identifies himself. This good is so intrinsic to the human being that the very coexistence depends on it being reciprocally safeguarded. For this reason, the law protects not only the essence of identity but also its logical or formal reflection before society, so that each individual is an independent unit of interests, he has his way of being and of asserting itself, being incumbent on others to recognize and respect his identity.

The legal protection of identity rests on the somatic-psychic

---

[75] Capelo de Sousa, R. V. A. (1995). *O direito geral de personalidade* [The general Law of personality]. (pp. 245). Coimbra: Coimbra Editora.

disposition of each human being, especially when it regards his "physical image, gestures, voice, writing and moral portrait"[76]. It also encompasses the fact that the man is placed socially and environmentally, considering his "image of life, individual history, decorum, reputation, his credit towards third parties, sexual, family, racial, linguistic, political, religious and cultural identity[77]. It may also include social factors that identify the individual, such as "name and pseudonym", or "recognized affiliation, marital status, place of birth and address" that, although protected by other areas, end up integrating the good of identity.

However, the good of identity is limited. First, the behaviors pointed out as appropriate. Then, although the good encompasses a vastness of aspects, not all are amenable to full legal protection. Thus, for example, the offenses against the accessory aspects of identity will not be civilly indemnified, provided that it does not suffer a considerable injury. In the same sense, actions that come from common life and from human errors will not be unlawful.

2.3.3 Brain, Mind, Consciousness and Unconsciousness

Recent attempts at materializing the mind are based on the fact (the idea) that the brain[78] is a machine that calculates and that the mind would be the thought and that this is a processing of sentences or sequences of symbols.

Therefore, one cannot confuse mind and brain, nor these with thought, as will be seen below, although a relation can be drawn between them.

---

[76] *Ibidem*, p. 248.

[77] *Idem*.

[78] Taube, M. (1967). *Os computadores: o mito das máquinas pensantes* [Computers and Common Sense, the Myth of Thinking Machines]. (R. S. de Biasi, Trans.). (pp. 73). Rio de Janeiro: O Cruzeiro. "From these considerations we can get a rather simple and immediate functional definition of the brain: The brain is the organ of the body that processes the information received from a relatively stable environment (including the body itself) to ensure a successful behavior of the organism in relation to the environment".

For Del Nero[79], the great capacity of the mind is to analyze the nature of truth or falsity of sentences and the validity, or otherwise, of arguments, being certain that arguments are valid or not, and sentences are true or false. Reasoning or thinking is the articulation of both concepts. Thus, for the author to think would be:

1. recognize a proposition or not (see the difference among "Paul is bald", "Paul is Martian", "Martians turned the cheerful door green." The first is a true sentence. The second is a false sentence. The third is a non-sentence or non-proposition);

2. recognize the truth or falsity of a sentence or proposition;

3.recognize the validity or not of an argument (articulation of a set of sentences such that, if the premises are true, the conclusion follows from them);

This would serve to conceptualize logic as a science of necessary inferences or a framework of intelligent thinking, which would allow us to see the mind as computation, making it possible to make abstract or real machines that perform the above functions.

It is important to question what logic should be used. Obviously, it cannot be the classical logic with its three basic primacies, since the principle of the excluded middle has to be excluded itself to project an artificial intelligence system of an anthropological model, given the contradictions inherent to Man and therefore to his form of expressing intelligence.

In this direction, the paraconsistent logic, whose exponent among us is Prof. Newton da Costa[80], who thinks about the principle of excluded middle as inaccurate, on the way of the psychoanalytic approach developed by Freud and improved by Lacan, demonstrating that Man is also his contradiction.

---

[79] Nero, H. S. D., *op. cit.*, p. 150-151.
[80] Costa, N. C. A. da. (1999). *Lógica paraconsistente aplicada* [Paraconsistent logic applied]. São Paulo: Atlas.

Moreover, one can no longer think of a single logic or method to produce a result consistent with the present time. Induction, deduction and abduction must be used.

It is important to emphasize that the work on logic developed by Alfred Tarski in the field of logic surpassed only by Gödel and by Jan Lukasiewicz[81] (Polish notation), who developed a logic containing three values of truth: the true, the false and the possible (trivalent or polyvalent logic that is similar to what is seen in the Law). However, there are still authors who do not understand this possibility, stating categorically their uselessness for the cybernetics' rights, like Lousano[82].

Pimentel refuses to accept this statement of the peninsular jurist, for he certainly knows that this is the logic adopted in intelligent systems.

This brings to light Turing's ideas about his universal, theoretical machine, the mother of all modern computers and the basis for artificial intelligence systems, impossible to be created because of the conceptual necessity of its infinite memory, but because of its ability to formalization, it could emulate the functioning of the brain. This is the seminal text of artificial intelligence, for it conjectured on the test of imitation, as Turing called it, but which passed into history as the Turing Test[83], by which, since then, one has sought to measure the intelligence of a computer.

> *I propose to consider the question, "Can machines think?" This should begin with definitions of the meaning of the terms "machine" and "think." The definitions might be framed so as to reflect so far as possible the normal use of the words, but this attitude is dangerous, If the meaning of the words "machine" and "think" are to be found by examining how they are commonly used it is difficult to escape*

---

[81] Tarski, A.; Lukasiewicz, J. (2002). *On the Concept of Following Logically.* (Tarski, Trans.). 1936, by Stroińska e D. Hitchcock. (pp. 155-196). *History and Philosophy of Logic.* Editora 23.

[82] Turing, A. M. *Computing machinery and intelligence.* Retrieved from: <http://www.loebner.net/Prizef/TuringArticle.html>. Last access date: April 20, 2004.

[83] Turing, A. M. *Computing machinery and intelligence.* Retrieved from: <http://www.loebner.net/Prizef/TuringArticle.html>. Last access date: April 20, 2004.

> *the conclusion that the meaning and the answer to the question, "Can machines think?" is to be sought in a statistical survey such as a Gallup poll. But this is absurd. Instead of attempting such a definition I shall replace the question by another, which is closely related to it and is expressed in relatively unambiguous words.*
>
> *The new form of the problem can be described in terms of a game which we call the 'imitation game." It is played with three people, a man (A), a woman (B), and an interrogator (C) who may be of either sex. The interrogator stays in a room apart front the other two. The object of the game for the interrogator is to determine which of the other two is the man and which is the woman. He knows them by labels X and Y, and at the end of the game he says either "X is A and Y is B" or "X is B and Y is A. [...] We now ask the question, "What will happen when a machine takes the part of A in this game?" Will the interrogator decide wrongly as often when the game is played like this as he does when the game is played between a man and a woman? These questions replace our original, "Can machines think?"*

Evidently, the test and its propositions are also questioned by the doctrine, among other reasons because it would be based on a lie. For these, the purpose of the computer in the game would be to lie for its interrogator to think that he is human.

The second relevant contestation is that it would measure **a type** of intelligence.

However, these confrontations are mistaken. Initially, Turing did not say that the computer should lie. Nor he said that the computer was meant to be a human. The test is not meant to measure humanity, nor truth, but intelligence; it is not proposed to know whether the occupant of a given position is a human being. The test wants to know if a human recognizes in his interlocutor something that he considers as intelligent answers, leading to the understanding that he is dialoguing with an intelligent and supposedly human being.

The assumption that the interrogator might think that he was talking to a human, being the interrogated a computer, is based on an anthropocentric paradigm that only a human could be intelligent or establish an intelligent conversation and thus only a human manifestation would be as intelligent, and thus only by falsifying human identity would a computer pass the test.

It is a mistake. The computer, as mentioned, in the Turing test does not have to pretend to be human. It only needs to be itself, answering what it **judges** — note the verb — suitable, whether true or false, because the human players also were not asked to always speak the truth, only to be themselves. Nor are they asked to be consistent. So much so that a persistent liar can be asked to perform the test that it is not invalidated in its original terms. It can occur even if the computer feels legally like a person, but this is also unimportant to the test.

The second misconception of the supposed failure of the test is that it would measure only one type of intelligence. Now, intelligence, in the usual terms — and must be in that sense examined in the test — is the ability to express acts, including words, that have an appearance, that provoke in those who know them the feeling of being witnessing something intelligent.

The Turing test must be seen this way.

However, in this step, Gödel's[84] work must be referred to, notably his theorems of incompleteness to understand the difference between the brain and the computer[85] for his mathematical proof that certain mathematical problems can neither be proved nor un-

---

[84] Goldstein, R. (2008). *Incompletude: a prova e o paradoxo de Kurt Gödel* [Incompleteness: the proof and paradox of Kurt Godel]. São Paulo: Companhia das Letras.

[85] In this particular, *see* Kolman, E.; Frolov, I. P. (1958). La cibernética y el cérebro humano. [Cybernetics and the human brain]. (pp. 157 et seq). Montevideu: Pueblos Unidos.

proved within the system of mathematics, this being not an uncertainty, but a definite certainty, it matters in that there are truths that can neither be proven nor refuted and thus cannot be formalized.

Goldstein[86] and Gödel[87] explain:

> *In particular, what our minds could not be, so goes the reasoning, are computers. That is what Gödel's first incompleteness theorem seems to tell us. But formal systems are precisely what captures the computing of computers, which is why they are able to figure things out without having any recourse to meanings. Computers run algorithms and we, it seems, do not, from which it straightforwardly follows that our minds are not computers.*

> *The first of the arguments claiming a connection between Gödel's first incompleteness theorem and the nature of the mind was published in 1961 by the Oxford philosopher John Lucas:*

> *Gödel's theorem seems to me to prove that Mechanism is false, that is, that minds cannot be explained as machines. So also has it seemed to many other people: almost every mathematical logician I have put the matter to has confessed to similar thoughts but has felt reluctant to commit himself definitely until he could see the whole argument set out, with all objections fully stated and properly met. This I attempt to do. Lucas's argument was stalwartly straightforward. No matter how complicated a "thinking" machine we engineer, he argued, this machine will run according to hard-wired rules that can be stated in a formal system, and when we ask this machine to tell us what the true propositions are it will be able to do this only by seeing which propositions follow according to the rules of the system. There will, therefore, be a proposition that eludes its grasp of truth, which is nothing but rule-determined provability — a proposition that our minds will nonetheless be able to grasp as true. No matter how we strengthen the machine, by adding in the previously elusive propositions as axioms, there will be yet another proposition that will elude it... but not us. This formula the machine will be unable to produce as being true, although a mind can see that it is true. And so the machine will still*

---

[86] Goldstein, R., *op. cit.*, p. 168-169.

[87] GÖDEL, Kurt. (1992). *On formally undecidable of principia and related systems.* (B. Meltzer, Trans.). (pp. 37-72). New York: Dover publications Inc.

*not be an adequate model of the mind. We are trying to pro-
duce a model of the mind which is mechanical—which is
essentially "dead"—but the mind, being in fact "alive,"
can always go one better than any formal, ossified, dead
system can. Thanks to Godel's theorem, the mind always
has the last word.*

*The mathematician Roger Penrose, also an Oxford don, has
published two books, The Emperor's New Mind and Shad-
ows of the Mind, arguing the case that Gödel's incompleteness theorems entail the falsity of mechanism, the dead-
endedness of the field of artificial intelligence if artificial
intelligence presumes to fully explain our thinking.*

*Among the things that Gödel indisputably established was
that no formal system of sound mathematical rules of proof
can ever suffice, even in principle, to establish all the true
propositions of ordinary arithmetic. This is certainly remarkable enough. But a powerful case can also be made
that his results showed something more than this, and established that human understanding and insight cannot be reduced to any set of rules. It will be part of my purpose here
to try to convince the reader that Godel's theorem indeed
shows this, and provides the foundation of my argument
that there must be more to human thinking than can ever be
achieved by a computer, **in the sense that we understand
the term "computer" today.***

*Penrose believes that even though the mind is not a comput-
er, it is nevertheless a physical system. The mind is identical
with the brain. Therefore, the nonmechanistic nature of the
mind following, he claims, from Godel's first incompleteness theorem, should direct our thinking toward nonmechanistic physical laws of just such a sort as are suggested by
quantum mechanics. The mathematically intuiting mind,
which demonstrably can't be captured mechanistically, is
nonetheless a physical system; we should, therefore, look
toward developing a nonmechanistic, radically new sort
of science—the mysteries of quantum mechanics should
be our guide here—so that the noncomputational aspects
of mind can be accommodated. The noncombinatorial but
nevertheless physical nature of thinking shows us the noncombinatorial nature of basic physical laws.*

*Gödel himself was far more reserved about drawing con-
clusions concerning the nature of the human mind from his
famous mathematical theorems. What is rigorously proved,
he suggested in his conversations with Hao Wang as well*

as in the Gibbs lecture that he gave in Providence, Rhode Island, 26 February 1951 (which he never published), is not a categorical proposition as regards the mind. Rather what follows is a disjunction, an "either-or" sort of a proposition. That is, he was admitting that nonmechanism doesn't follow, clean and simply, from his incompleteness theorem. There are possible outs for the mechanist.

*Gödel believed that what had been rigorously proved, presumably on the basis of the incompleteness theorem, is: "Either the human mind surpasses all machines (to be more precise it can decide more number theoretical questions than any machine) or else there exist number theoretical questions undecidable for the **human mind**.*[88]

These are noncomputable problems. Gödel thus described his discovery: "It is possible — assuming the (formal) consistency of classical mathematics — to give examples of propositions that are contextually true but not deductible in the formal system of classical mathematics."[89]

From this statement he can announce the two theorems of incompleteness. The first, briefly, is that

there are arithmetical truths that cannot be proved within the formal system, assuming the system to be consistent. The formal system is either inconsistent or incomplete. There are provably unprovable, but nevertheless true, propositions in any formal system that contains elementary arithmetic, assuming that system to be consistent[90].

The second theorem states "that the consistency of a formal system containing arithmetic cannot be formally proved within that system."[91]

This leads to the impossibility of the computer functioning as the brain that acts by intuition not by formalization, as it also leads to the limits of human knowledge, since it mathematically proves that there will always be something that cannot be known and

---

[88] Goldstein, R., op. cit., p. 168-171.
[89] *Ibidem*, p. 131
[90] *Ibidem*, p.141-142.
[91] *Ibidem*, p.155.

therefore neither understood nor explained.

In the same sense the understanding of Kurzweil[92]:

> *Taken together, the work of Turing, Church, and Gödel, all published in the 1930s, represented the first formal proofs that there are definite limits to what logic, mathematics, and computation can do. These discoveries strongly contradict Wittgenstein's statement in the Tractatus that "if a question can be framed, it can be answered".*

In fact, in their way, Wittgenstein and Gödel, in spite of the profound divergences, have in common the fact that both have dealt with incompleteness, since the philosopher had already expressed his understanding that there are certain things unspeakable, such as exoteric, religious statements. Before them, Freud had already dealt with the lack.

According to Taube[93], at the 1955 National Convention of Radio Engineers, it was concluded that "computers cannot be considered as structurally similar to human brains, and that the simulation of the structure of the brain by a mechanical structure is not a very promising enterprise."

It must be said that in that year, or even at the time of the original publication of Taube's work, the knowledge of the mechanics, physiology, structure, and functioning of the brain was far inferior to what we have today and will have in the future. Also, the perspective handled by the author takes into account the paradigm of computers of that time — and in a certain way still current — that can be overcome in the future, and it is premature to assert categorically the absolute discrepancy between the brain and the computer.

Human intelligence is finite, limited, and therefore can be surpassed by another that is not, if it exists, or will ever exist. However, it is important to say that the brain-machine junction, "person + artifact", has emergent properties, which surpassed the sum of

---

[92] Kurzweil, R. (1999). *The age of intelligent machines.* (pp. 115, 3rd reprint). Cambridge, Mass.: MIT Press.

[93] Taube, M., *op. cit.*, p. 75.

the specific properties of each element[94]. Thus, the technological Man has expanded his capacity for thought.

Moreover, Gödel has shown that any formal system is incomplete, whether it is it mathematics, law, or any other. Thus, it was clear that you cannot formalize everything, because there will always be something that doesn't fit, and thus computers being machines, as they are currently made, use formalization to compute, i.e. to produce their results. Computers will not, based on this understanding, be able to function exactly as brains do. Brains also compute and can produce similar results, but by different, though not completely diverse, processes.

In addition, it is well known that computers function digitally, in a binary way, whereas the brain, at least the human and probably all of the animals, functions analogically "and performs functions analogous to those of computers"[95] mixed with digital elements.[96] For David Gelernter,[97] the brain functions analogically under digital control, a fact also observed by John Von Neumann[98].

In the face of the settled confusion that the brains by virtue of being also analog are inferior and outdated in relation to computers, the analogical way has been disregarded as an investigative method in the construction of artificial intelligence systems, which, perhaps, slow the pace of development of general intelligence sys-

[94] Guimarães, A. S. O homem de seis milhões de dólares [The Six Million Dollar Man]. *Revista filosofia, ciência & vida*. Enigmas da consciência na filosofia da mente [Puzzles of consciousness in the philosophy of mind]. (I, n° 3, pp. 24). Editora Escala.

[95] Dawkins, R. (2008). *O gene egoísta* [The Selfish Gene]. (R. Rubino, Trans.). (pp. 111). São Paulo: Companhia das Letras.

[96] Tenório, R. M. (2003). *Cérebros e computadores: a complementaridade analógico-digital na informática e na educação* [Brains and computers: the analogical-digital complementarity in information technology and education]. (4th ed.) São Paulo: Escrituras.

[97] Debate at MIT to celebrate the 70th anniversary of the publication on computable numbers of Alan Turing. Retrieved from: <http://www.kurzweilai.net/meme/frame.html?main=memelist .html?m=4%23688>. Last access date: February 13, 2009.

[98] Tenório, R. M., *op. cit.*, p. 2.

tems, as the dual analog and digital capabilities of the human brain are not used as a model.

The understanding of mathematics as a closed system in which not all answers are to be sought does not denature mathematics as systematizing truths, but only sets it a limit, naturalizing it.

It is interesting to note that, at the same time that the computer sets apart from the brain, because of the impossibility of formalizing everything, an approximation occurs because both are limited.

Just like some things cannot be understood, nor explained, nor proven, nor unproven, there are problems that cannot be computed, at least in the way they are carried out today in computers and that in domestic systems leads to the "crash" of equipment.

Computers at their current stage are excellent for quantifying, but, as they function today, they are incapable of qualifying. Whereas human brains are good at qualifying, but already surpassed by computers to quantify and calculate. This does not mean that computers cannot one day be as good as the brain in this matter, by applying technologies already available with other technologies yet to come.

Marvin Minsky[99] disagrees with the general understanding that computers obey a perfect logic:

> What's wrong with the old arguments that lead us to believe that if machines could ever think at all, they'd have to think with perfect logic? We're told that by their nature, all machines must work according to rules. We're also told that they can only do exactly what they're told to do. Besides that, we also hear that machines can only handle quantities and therefore cannot deal with qualities or anything like analogies.
>
> Most such arguments are based upon a mistake that is like confusing an agent with an agency. When we design and build a machine, we know a good deal about how it works. When our design is based on neat, logical principles, we are likely to make the mistake of expecting the machine to behave in a similarly neat and logical fashion. Edgar Allan Poe once argued that a certain chess-playing "machine"

---

[99] MINSKY, Marvin. (1988). *The society of mind.* (pp. 186). New York: Simon & Schuster.

had to be fraudulent because it did not always win. If it were
really a machine, he argued, it would be perfectly logical –
and therefore could never make any mistakes!

Minsky also understands that the mind is not a thing because it
has none of the characters of a thing, although it has vital connections with the brain[100].

He further adds that he has no doubt that the brain is a machine,
operating according to the laws of physics, but that, given its complexity, nonexistent in any other machine, the difficulties of understanding it comes from our inexperience with such complexity.

Therefore, it can be concluded that what happens inside a computer, when it is in operation, is often an unfathomable mystery, as it
is still a mystery what happens in the brain when we think.

For Del Nero[101], the brain would be the *hardware*; and the mind,
the *software*. This didactic and imperfect identification with the
computer, or rather with a computer system understood as a logical
and physical system, would allow the author to assert that a machine equipped with the right program and processing analogous
to that of the brain could think.

It is necessary to affirm that human thought is worthless unless it
is expressed, and, certainly, what is examined in the concrete world
is not thought, but its expression. So if thought is a characteristic
of intelligent beings, thought itself, with its mechanisms inherent
in that or what it thinks, is not as important as what is thought in its
manifestation in the World. In addition, reflection, not thought in
itself, is what seems to denote intelligence. We all think, but only
those who demonstrate improved reflection are considered to be
intelligent.

Therefore, the way one thinks, the mechanism of thought is not
an indicator of intelligence, but its manifestation, act of reflection,
is an expression of intelligence. Thus, it doesn't matter how one ar-
rives at the expressed thought, it is not of interest to know whether

---

[100] *Ibidem*, p. 288.
[101] Nero, H. S. D., *op. cit.*, p. 149-153.

90

there is intelligence in the thought, but whether the result seems and expresses intelligence.

In this way, whether one claims to be cerebral or cybernetic, biological or electronic, digital or analog, the intelligent one is the one that seems intelligent, the one that behaves intelligently.

For Lacan[102] the thought is not in the brain:

> *You imagine that the thought is in the brain. I do not see why I would dissuade you from this. As for me, I am sure — I am quite sure, it is my business — that it is in the subcutaneous frontals in the talking being, just as in the hedgehog.*
>
> *Finally, if you can think with the frontal subcutaneous, you can also think with your feet. Well, that's where I'd like it to go, since, after all, the imaginary, the symbolic and the real, this is done for those of that grouping who are the ones who follow me, so that it helps them to walk the path of analysis." [...] In all this, then, there are no problems of thought. A psychoanalyst knows that thinking is aberrant by nature, which does not prevent it from being responsible for a discourse that joins the analyzer — to what?*
>
> *What I find comical is that one simply does not realize that there is no other way of thinking and that psychologists looking for a thought that would not be spoken would in some way imply that pure thought, if I dare say it, would be better. In what I have just advanced as a Cartesian, "I think, therefore that I am", in particular, there is a profound mistake, that is, what disturbs him is when he imagines that thought is an extension, if you can say so. But it is well to show that there is no other thought, if I may say, pure, a thought not subject to the contortions of language, but just the thought of extension. And then the subject that I would like to introduce to you today and that, after all, after two hours, nothing but failure, just crawling, is this: that the extension that we supposed to be space, the space that is common to us, namely, the three dimensions, why the heck has never been approached by the knot way?*

---

[102] Lacan, J. (1974). The third conference given at the 7th Congress of the Ecole Freudienne de Paris on October 31, 1974. Retrieved from: <http://www.freud-lacan.com/articles/article.php?url_article=jlacan031105_2>. Last access date: January 11, 2009.

Rover[103] seems to have a similar understanding which is supported by David Gerlernter[104] that intelligence and thought are not exclusive domains of the brain, but of this and of the body. Rover says: "The human brain and the body carry this wonderful, natural, old and new, problem-solving ability".[105] Gelernter asserts: "[...] *it's clear that you don't just think with your brain, you think with your body.*"[106]

The thought is not something easy to conceptualize. Marvin Minsky[107] — who has an interesting theory about agents acting in the brain to develop their activities in a hierarchical way — alluding to Seymour Papert's famous phrase that "You can't think about thinking without thinking about something", he states: "Just as we walk without thinking, we think without thinking!"[108].

The idea behind this would serve to demonstrate how an intelligent being can arise from something unintelligent, such as Man and Darwinian evolution since not all hierarchized agents of the mind can be qualified as intelligent, although they produce intelligent results and form what we consider to be the center of intelligence. The conception of a society of agents in the mind serves both for human intelligence and for artificial intelligence.

Within the biological limits, numerous animal species are proven to have brains of varying shapes and sizes. The mind, as Del Nero[109] claims, is a complex, memory-based and learning-based

---

[103] Rover, A. J. *Para um direito invisível: superando as artificialidades da inteligência* [For an invisible Law: overcoming the artificialities of intelligence]. Retrieved from:
<http://www.infojur.ufsc.br/aires/arquivos/direito%20invisivel%202005.pdf>.
Last access date: February 25, 2009.
[104] Gelernter, D. *et al. Gelernter, Kurzweil debate machine consciousness.*
Retrieved from: <www.kurzweilai.net/meme/frame.html?main=memelist. html?m=4%23688>. Last access date: February 13, 2009.
[105] Rover, *op. cit.*, loc. cit.
[106] Gelernter, *op. cit.*, p.2.
[107] Minsky, M. (1988). *The society of mind.* (pp. 63). New York: Simon & Schuster.
[108] *Ibidem.* p. 63.
[109] Nero, H. S. D., *op. cit.*, p. 387.

process for problem-solving. No other conclusion can be drawn, except that animals have minds, and therefore there is a possibility that they may have awareness.

Well, everyone agrees that Man thinks. He has thoughts. Everyone agrees that Man has a brain and body. Thus, everyone will agree that thinking happens in any brain, even Lacan, which does not limit it in any human body among the billions in the world.

However, all brains are physically different. Even so, all serve as physical support for thought. So thought, this *software*, works on any appropriate support, including electronic or photonic.

Therefore, it is possible to create, at least in theory, another support where the same type of event occurred and, therefore, would understand that what happens in this other physical support must be thought.[110]

In fact, it has already been proven that chimpanzees and gorillas are aware of themselves, the perception of their individuality, as beings separated from others. Perhaps even in a rough way, a consciousness similar to the human, manifested by the monitoring of action in society, an evaluation, justification of conduct, in the face of socially accepted standards. It would act in two stages: the first, in the planning of the action, and the second, confronted with tables of conduct or socially delineated rules, so that the second evaluation guided the first for action to take place or not, or for the act to be consonant with these tables of values. Consciousness would act as a judge of what should and what shouldn't be an act. It is important to understand that the representation of the action before its occurrence is not a copy of previous actions, but a "language-filtered version, by memories, and filled with strong valuation"[111].

As stated, it is not a copy of something of the past, because the high degree of complexity of all actions would prevent its reproduction in an analog processing system. Because there is always

---

[110] Kurzweil, R. (1999). *The age of intelligent machines*. (pp. 85, 3rd reprint). Cambridge, Mass.: MIT Press.

[111] Nero, *ibidem*, p. 388.

something that is lost — let us remember the filter of language, always unable to grasp the richness of life and of the world — that cannot become conscious, either because the unconscious does not allow it or because the memory is not rescued, either because one does not actually have memory, but memory of memory or the saying of the "Big Other." Or because, after all, all perception is formalized by the senses, and these select and then have their stimuli selected again by the brain and therefore are always partial, incomplete and interpretive.

Humans would thus have full consciousness, while other animals would only have a lesser or less precise or complex consciousness?

Consciousness would result, among other factors, of the existence of the neocortex, notably the frontal, developed in our evolution, allied to language, to the duty of justification of acts in conduct in society and synchronization, appropriate to the complexity of the action, between the projected action and its valued redescription.

Briefly, Del Nero[112] understands that consciousness would arise because:

a) Language gradually creates a pattern of social life full of conduct standards and justification;

b) The neocortex is able to create a valued analog of action, an interpretation formatted by language (after all it is the language that will be used to accuse and defend);

c) The valued analogs of action will be the contents of consciousness;

d) The synchronization of action and the valued redescription of action will be consciousness-sensation (or content);

---

[112] *Ibidem*, loco citato.

e) The consciousness will be able to inhibit or confirm certain future actions and reflect on past actions;

f) If consciousness is a valued form that serves socialization, then also in the supra-cerebral degrees there will be some form of consciousness, control, inhibition (coercion, repression) of inferior activities;

g) In this way, both the brain consciousness would become the most cultural of biological phenomena, as the society in some of its facets would be the most natural of cultural phenomena.

In the legal field, Telles Junior[113] says

> *The standard does not arise from the fact and does not arise from intelligence. It arises, rather, from the confrontation of the fact with a table of goods. It results from the judgment of the fact, in the light of an axiological system of reference. This confrontation and judgment is the work of intelligence. From this work, a judgment of duty emerges, which can be promoted to become a standard.*

Thus, the standard is the result or expression of consciousness that confronts the facts and thoughts with a set of values and acts to fit it. It acts aiming at normality, whose concept is brought in the present work.

There should be no doubt that from the psychoanalytic point of view, but also, at a similar level, from a legal point of view, consciousness is related to the capacity to reflect on something and, based on a given table of values, make a judgment, a judgment of value. The awareness of what is right and what is wrong, the exact and full notion of the appropriateness of the conduct resulting from thinking what is legally and socially acceptable, permitted or more precisely the non-forbidden, would characterize the consciousness

---

[113] Telles Júnior, G. (2003). *Direito quântico: ensaios sobre o fundamento da ordem jurídica* [Quantum law: essays on the foundation of the legal order]. (7th ed, pp. 239). São Paulo: Juarez de Oliveira.

of the human being, away from the consciousness of other biological beings.

Regarding the value of something one has to understand what it matters, the measure, the quantum of something else to which it corresponds, a relation to other things, a gradation, a hierarchy, implying that a judgment is made about it to know the real value. To Telles Junior, "Being is no more than the being of a judgment"[114].

Junior Telles understands that *"intelligence is the faculty that judges [...] to bring the agent to the ends he wishes to attain."*[115] (italic in the original), demonstrating that, at least for this author, there would be a relationship between intelligence and consciousness.

He adds that:

> The value of these goods (referring to the intellectual or spiritual goods, as you term them), as of the others, depends on the judgment to which they are subjected, and therefore on their relationship with some reference system.[116]

It is a reflective consciousness. The author understands that

> Consciousness is perception, no doubt because it is through consciousness that the human being comes into contact with his inner world. [...] But it is also memory, because a consciousness that does not retain the memories of the past and forgets its perceptions, would perish and be reborn at every moment. Now, this is not consciousness, but precisely, unconsciousness[117].

It must be clarified that unconsciousness, as defined above, is not mistaken with the unconscious[118] of Freudian / Lacanian psychoanalysis, whose complexity overflows with the simple lack of

---

[114] *Ibidem*, p. 229.

[115] *Ibidem*, p. 233.

[116] *Ibidem*, p. 237.

[117] *Ibidem*, p. 248.

[118] Perhaps one can draw a parallel from the unconscious in Freud to the agents of Marvin Minsky's mind-society who hide in the mind and influence what we have decided to do.

knowledge about what is done to advance its causes. Unconsciousness in Telles is forgetfulness. Unconscious in Freud[119] is an engine
of human conduct.

> *For psychoanalysis there is a motivation that causes us to
> forget unwanted events, which, however, would continue to
> exert influence on consciousness, resulting in acts. There
> are even elements that do not become conscious.*

> *If, on the one hand, we say that the brain processes are
> totally unconscious, on the other hand, we say that the
> mental processes are conscious or can become con-
> scious. If the motivation that takes a certain mental fact
> to situate itself outside the consciousness is of repressive
> origin or only an economy of the system, it is not the
> case[120].*

Thus, the concept of the unconscious in Del Nero[121] is not related to the concept of the psychoanalytic, Freudian / Lacanian unconscious, which is adopted in this work.

Now, if higher order values, such as spiritual ones, can be evaluated, measured against a reference system, they can be formalized
and thus transformed into *software* that can be treated by a computer. In other words, by taking the concept of Telles Júnior[122],
one reaches the conclusion that the values that characterize human
intelligence, at its highest level or expression, can be formalized,
programmed, meaning that a robot can execute them, expressing
even feelings.

In addition, Telles Júnior adds that "The ethical order results
from the meeting of the creative force of intelligence with the
real facts of life."[123]

Although it is understood that the author did not go so far in his

---

[119] Freud, S. (1996). Além do princípio do prazer [Beyond the Pleasure Princi-
ple] In: *Edição Standard das Obras Completas.* (C. Monteiro, Trans.) (2nd ed.,
vol. 18, pp. 72). Rio de Janeiro: Imago.
[120] Nero, H. S. D. *op. cit.*, p. 131.
[121] *Ibidem*, p. 126-130.
[122] Telles Júnior, G. *op. cit.*, p. 237.
[123] *Ibidem*, p. 238.

statement, there is nothing to prevent him from concluding, based on his lessons, that an ethic can be created for, or by robots, for its guidance. Since it is possible to develop intelligent machines, being the creativity the character of the intelligence, at least of the only one consensually accepted, that is the human intelligence. Because human intelligence will, in theory, be present in any intelligence that can thus be defined, and its confrontation with the facts of real life will result in an ethical order.

It should be emphasized that creativity is present not only in man but also in other animals — whether in the search for and discovery of new ways to hunt, to harvest, to cooperate, but also in the use of tools — found not only between the primates, but also, between animals considered less evolved, like birds or even arachnids.

Some understand that Man is not creative, since "neither man nor machine is capable of creating information".[124] Since any creative idea would simply be a matter of juxtaposition or combination of information previously existing in different configurations, consequently, there is in principle no barrier to the development of artificial intelligence or artificial creativity.

In fact, he goes on to say, "Computers do only what they are programmed to do in the same sense that humans only do what their accumulated genes and experiences determine that they do"[125].

It should also be said that the general concept of more or less evolved is also anthropocentric and misleading, since, in theory, all biological living beings present on the surface of the earth today have the same level of evolution, considered as the capacity to adapt to the environment and perpetuate the species, to keep the homeostatic balance.

---

[124] ROSE, J. *Apud* Lehman-Wilzig, Sam N. *Frankenstein Unbound: towards a legal definition of artificial intelligence.* Retrieved from: <profslw.com/wp-content/uploads/academic/40._Frankenstein_Unbound.Towards_a_legal_definition...
pdf>. (pp. 444). Last accesso date: February 22, 2009.
[125] *Idem.*

Thus, they are all well adapted to their niches, their habitat, the ecosystem — note that the medium or environment is a system and can also be considered as a computer, from the cybernetic perspective — otherwise they would not exist. There is no way, therefore, to assert that this or that species is more evolved than the other, to arrive at the point of saying that *Homo sapiens* is the most evolved of all, although, in a way, it is dominant. However, dominance and evolution are distinct concepts. The purpose of evolution is not the designation of the environment and/or other species, but the maintenance of the species itself, survival, and balance with the environment.

Dominance has multiple meanings. For example, bacteria and other microorganisms dominate the environment, if one considers the number of individuals.

In other animals, although it can be seen that they often seek, especially in primates, to act following social rules, with the collective expectations of the groups, it seems that there is no precise notion of the values involved. Although, for example, a chimpanzee knows exactly how to behave in his social group, it seems that he does not conduct himself by understanding that this way of acting is the best, but because if he does not do so, he may be subjected to violence or punishment, or because, in so doing, he allows himself to be molested and may even be the recipient of beneficial conduct by other members of the group, similar to human favors.

That is why, oftentimes, absent the group, he acts to transgress the social rules. It is not denied that the Human Being, sometimes, when he is freed of the looks, of the possibility of censorship of the others, he acts in a social or legally reprehensible way. But, as a rule, the honest man will continue to act honestly, even though there is no one present to scrutinize, for he will be guided by instilled values.

When seeing an open door from a third-party home, the average Man will not enter uninvited, even though there is no one observing. When seeing a valuable object unprotected, but unequivocally with signs of alien property, this Man, this typical Human Being will not get hold of the thing, in the normality of life.

The animal has no such notion of property. He is not able to judge, to evaluate, to discern whether that good is valuable — there is no reference here to economic or moral values culturally fixed by Human Beings as money, jewels, and so on — as, for example, a piece of food that belongs to another, even because he is not aware of the property. If he is hungry and has an opportunity, he will eat.

Let it not be said that there are cultures in which men do not know the private property and, therefore, the example would not fit. Certainly, in these cultures, there will be values common to all its members, such as, for example, some kind of worship, possibly directed at something that is not human. Well, an individual of this culture, as a rule, will respect the totem or icon. Probably no individual of this culture will destroy, micturate, or defecate in the clothing, bodies, drink, or food of other individuals, as may happen among animals (of course not the clothes).

He seems to have instilled, perhaps in the unconscious, the record of what is right and wrong, enabling Man to make value judgments about the facts, about the conduct of others and his conduct.

Hence, it is concluded that law is a cultural manifestation of reflexive consciousness, sedimented and reaffirmed permanently, by the axiological sieve of society, which establishes deontological criteria, through formulations endowed with this logic, denying the importance or punishing the manifestations that trespass it.

Thus, it seems that the ability to act according to judgment, an evaluation of one's conduct, would characterize human consciousness, reproducible by the robot.

Originally, Freud[126] recognized three regions in the structure of the psyche: the conscious, the preconscious and the unconscious, which did not correspond to properly delimited areas. The uncon-

---

[126] Freud, S. (1996). Além do princípio do prazer [Beyond the Pleasure Principle] In: Edição Standard das Obras Completas. (C. Monteiro, Trans.) (2nd ed., vol. 18). Rio de Janeiro: Imago.

scious comprises processes and representations that are voluntarily inaccessible, although accessible through analysis. The preconscious encompasses the accessible part when **allowed** by the subject.

These instances are commanded by censorship, by castration. They are grouped into three systems: the conscious and the preconscious, or ego and the unconscious, a pure language without punctuation, of inherent contradiction. The distinction between them is at the functional level. In the conscious and preconscious, logical thinking prevails, and the unconscious is indifferent to classical logic and Cartesian coherence, ignoring the principle of contradiction and without thinking of the law of excluded middle, and applying the principle of pleasure. Freud[127] evolved this understanding to embody the drives of life and death and proposed new concepts: Ego, Superego, and Id. The Superego is the inculcation of the saying of the Big Other (Lacan, later), resulting in castration. The Id is the libido zone.

Freud[128] teaches, as seen before, that three distinct instances can be located in the mind, the Id, the Ego, and the Superego. The Id, by the way, would be absolutely unconscious, although it is not entirely mistaken with it. It is where the drives are found, governed by the pleasure principle whose demands must be met immediately. The Ego, or I, would characterize consciousness, the part of the brain of the most superficial individual, who can act in a relatively rational way. Finally, the superego or super-I, partially conscious, partially unconscious that manifests the castration, the saying of the Big Other[129], the prohibitions, the fences and "always brings the excess, something that is not regulated."[130]. It results

---

[127] *Idem.*
[128] Freud, S., *op. cit.*, p. 72.
[129] Lacan, J. (2008). *Seminário XVI. De um Outro ao outro* [Seminar XVI. From One to Another] (V. Ribeiro, Trans.). São Paulo: Zahar, 2008.
[130] Fiamenghi, C. M. (2008). *Imperativo superegóico e culpa na clínica* [Superegoic imperative and guilt at the clinic]. In: Gerbase, J. (Ed.). Avatares do Supereu [Avatars of the Superego]. (pp. 60). Salvador: Associação Científica Campo Psicanalítico.

precisely from the confrontation of thought or act in thought, to come, virtual, with the table of values to which the individual has been exposed and which restrains the drives.

Freud still conceived the Dream Theory[131], in which he introduced the method of free association. It regards the dream as the realization of desires, easily forgotten when returning to wakefulness. The dream needs to be interpreted by the dreamer because it presents itself in the form of metaphors.

2.3.4 Unconscious

Interestingly, if consciousness is virtual, it seems, the unconscious is always real, because it is language[132], and language is constitutive of Man. If Man is understood as endowed with reality, one cannot deny the reality of language and, consequently, one cannot depart reality from the unconscious which nevertheless functions under its own logic, written in an unpunctuated language with its own grammar, read only by analysis.

The unconscious is *software*. In fact, it seems to have been this — not with these terms — the original idea of Freud, as something that has already been inscribed and therefore marked, programmed and that the neurotic follows exactly, even if this causes him prejudice.

It is more like an operating system, written in symbolic language — to be redundant — processed without the express knowledge of Man, in the background, language similar to machine binary language. (Intelligent by the brain that follows it faithfully, it needs high-level language). It needs another layer of *software*, to be interpreted by consciousness and thus be punctuated, understood. So that this primary language does not bring the whole system to a breakdown — or a crash — to problems not computable

131 Freud, S. *op. cit.*, *passim*.
132 Lacan, J. (1974). La troisième conférence. 7ème Congrès de l'École Freudienne de Paris à Rome. 31 octobre, 1974. Retrieved from: <http://www.freud-lacan.com/articles/article.php?url_article=jlacan031105_2>. Last access date: January 11, 2009.

by the brain, to systematic, unnecessary and harmful repetitions to the economy of being.

In fact, the term binary for the machine language, low-level language, to the unconscious is not the most appropriate to the case. Because it does not proceed in the fashion of zero or one, of the yes or no, submitted to classical logic and physics, locator, deterministic, in which one cannot be in the intervals, in the ambiguity. As a matter of fact, this is done in the quantum form, which is more appropriate to the unconscious, contradictory of itself when it is the case, bivalent or polyvalent, not content with markings, grammar, punctuation rules. It functions at full power, in every possible way, present in all forms, or no form, occurring simultaneously in all potentiality, and not only virtually in the places that have been reserved or predicted to them as is the case with consciousness.

It is language, written and inscribed in the formation of being by the Big Other of Lacan, who dictates a rule, a model, an image and is not mistaken with being, unless the unconscious without the filter of consciousness would act without obstacles. With this filter, it can learn to handle and reprocess to give you a safe and friendly interface. The conjugation of the supposed being with the being is the result of this processing, which, like all processing, takes place through a language of interpretation to be intelligible externally.

That is why one can distinguish the brain process from the mental process. The brain is unconscious, and the mind is conscious. The brain is the real, it is what the brain of physical existence processes and the mind is its interpretation to the external world, its interface, the mind, the conscious, a formalization.

However, this process of interpretation or translation or reading of the primary language, machine, by the high-level language, is only clearly accessible by the analytical process, by the analytical method.

All that is said shows the multiplicity of aspects without which Man cannot be understood and how much is still to be learned about him.

In biological terms, there is no doubt about the definition of *Homo sapiens*. No matter how related any other species is, one can tell apart the *Homo Sapiens*. There is an evident physical distinction of the other primates, notably by the fact of the exclusive bipedalism, aspect of the skull and language.

However, even the knowledge about the origin of man is recent, dating from the nineteenth and twentieth centuries, still unclear are the mechanisms by which the species differed from other hominids and why they were extinct. And it is not known, due to the lack of a study specimen, when the process of hominization was consolidated, moving away, it is estimated, about ten million years ago, of the other closest primates in our evolution.

The fact is that, in cosmic terms, the appearance of Man took place an instant ago compared to the presumed several billion years of the Universe and a little less billion years of life on Earth, of which only in the last five hundred million years, manifested in more complex ways.

This only reinforces the Law of Accelerating Returns, discussed below.

In the legal sphere, one could not expect something different in terms of sedimentation of knowledge about Man.

Law is a manifestation of the social instance of the humanization of life on Earth in its growing social complexity. In this field, as well, the prevailing notions of law are very recent, even in human historical terms. If the species, as it stands today, was established some ten or eleven thousand years ago, the legal structure in the West has been launched just over three thousand years ago in Rome, although previous contributions from other peoples, such as the Greeks, Phoenicians, Chinese, Arabs, etc.

2.3.4.1 Language

Maturana and Varella[133] affirm that Man is not the only possess-

---

[133] Maturana, H. R.; Varela, F. J. (2007). *A Árvore do Conhecimento: as bases biológicas da compreensão humana* [The Tree of Knowledge: The Biological

or of a linguistic domain. However, a characteristic of language is identified. It is the power to modify the behavioral domains of Man, allowing new phenomena, like reflection and consciousness. This characteristic is the possibility that language creates for the individual who utilizes it to **describe himself** and his circumstance.

The linguistic domain itself becomes part of the possible means of interactions: the observer notes that descriptions can be made by considering other descriptions as objects or elements of the domain of interactions. Only at the moment when this linguistic reflection is made, the language exists, the observer appears and the organisms begin to function in a linguistic domain. Thus, it is only when this happens that the semantic domain becomes part of the medium in which those who operate in it maintain their adaptation. All of us, humans, are affected by this: we exist in our functioning in language and we maintain our adaptation in the domain of meanings that this brings up. We describe the descriptions we make. We are observers and we exist in a semantic domain created by our linguistic mode of acting. Once language exists, there are no barriers to what it is possible to describe, imagine, relate. Although it adds the permanent risk of not communicating what was effectively desired.

A priori, the language was considered a human privilege. Although such a conception has been mitigated in recent times, what has contributed most to its softening was to discover that higher primates can learn to interact linguistically with us in an ever more extensive way.[134]

2.4 Some considerations on human condition

The paradoxical insufficiency and profusion of approaches on Man, before functioning as a disincentive, acts as an impulse to seek to understand the species and the human phenomenon, the

---

Roots of Human Understanding]. São Paulo: Palas Athena.
[134] *KOKO: o gorila falante* [KOKO: a talking gorilla]. Barbet Shroeder (dir.) Paris: Wonder Multimidia. 1978. DVD.

creation and the legal conception of a human person, to deconstruct it opportunely and open space for discussion of the legal treatment of post-humanity.

Hannah Arendt[135] considers that there are three fundamental human activities: labor, work, and action because each of them corresponds to one of the basic conditions of man's life on Earth. Also, she understands that plurality is the condition of human action, because, although all human beings thus qualify, none is exactly like another.

However, only Man can show this difference by communicating himself and not just by communicating something. Only he is endowed with otherness. Following the footsteps of St. Augustine, it is stated that only man is capable of initiating. It is with birth that the action arises and the human condition becomes effective by birth. The alterity and ability to act, very often, unexpectedly are inherent.

However, the human essence is not limited to those conditions in which life was given to man, since the Human Being is conditioned, since everything with which it comes into contact immediately becomes a condition of its existence, whether they are things of the world or arising exclusively from human activity, from their *active life*.

In the same way, for Foucault,[136] **in principle, there is no** human essence, nor a transcendent truth, since hermeneutics assumes a truth to be revealed by a supposed knowledge, as well as the supposed knowledge of the Freudian and Lacanian analysts.

The objectiveness of the world and the human condition complement each other, because it is not necessary to talk about human existence without things, and these would be stripped of meaning without Man, if they were not conditions of Man, being certain that the human condition cannot be mistaken with the human nature.

---

[135] Arendt, H. (2008). *A condição humana* [The Human Condition]. (R. Raposo, Trans.). (10th ed., 7th reprint, pp. 15-16). São Paulo: Forense Universitária.
[136] Foucault, M. *A ordem do discurso* [The Order of Discourse]. Retrieved from: <http://vsites.unb.br/fe/tef/filoesco/foucault/ordem.pdf>. Last access date: March 31, 2009.

The active life takes place in a world populated by things done by men and of men, from which they do not move away nor transcend totally, since they would lose meaning, being displaced, outside of this environment.

Although for Arendt, all human activities are conditioned by social coexistence, human action is the only activity that cannot even be imagined outside the society of men, because it is an exclusive prerogative. Thus, intrinsically human, no animal, nor God is capable of action. The work can be practiced in isolation, but, in isolation, it would deprive *Homo Faber*. Anyone who did so could be a god, but not the creator, only a demiurge in the form described by Plato.

Man is a political animal. Thus, the human condition is only realized through its action in a society.

The author recalls that:

> the Latin translation of this expression as rationale animal results from a failure of interpretation no less fundamental than that of the expression "social animal". Aristotle did not intend to define man in general nor to indicate the highest capacity of man — which for him was not the logos, that is, the word or reason, but nous, the capacity for contemplation, whose main characteristic is that his content cannot be reduced to words.[137]

Arendt recalls Marx's lessons about the definition of Man, echoed by Benjamin Franklin, as an instrument maker, when she criticizes it as an Americanism, as a loss of universal standards and standards that were necessary for Man to build the world. Vilified by the exchange market, by showing production as a way to distinguish men from animals according to Adam Smith.

In Arendt's sense, this brings about a dehumanization, very much in the fashion of Plato's admonition about the "proactive proposition of establishing man, maker of things and the use which

---

[137] Arendt, H., *op. cit.*, p. 36.

he makes of them, as the supreme measure of the latter."[138]

This shows how much the relativity of the exchange market has to do with the concept of instrument that results from the craftsman's world and the manufacturing experience. In fact, the first comes systematically and without breaking the continuity, of the second. But Plato's answer — that not Man, but a "god is the measure of all things" — would be a hollow attempt at moralization if it was true that, as the modern age presumed, the "instrumentality", disguised in utility, governs the world, once constructed, with the same exclusiveness with which it governs the activity through which the world and all things contained therein come into existence.[139]

The loss of standards to which the author refers relates to the changes occurring around the concept of the value of a product or thing, which can be understood as the value of use or value of exchange, knowing that modern society values the latter in spite of the former.

Now, alterity, birth, behavioral improbability, all this can be programmed in a robot, not being seen as a note of prominence of the human character.

But the author advances through swampy lands to say expressly that "the ultimate secrets of Being which, according to our concept of the physical world, is so stealthy that it never presents itself, and yet so tremendously powerful that it produces all appearances."[140]

Although under the cloak of a somewhat transcendental view, the author makes it possible to foresee that **it is human what appears to be human**, which presents itself as human, although in its feeling, always escapes from full understanding. This seems to fit Gödel's thinking about the limits of human thought and understanding and the lack of the Real of psychoanalysis.

In the same way, it allows to affirm that, although there is a core of what is essentially human, indescribable in its totality, the mani-

---

[138] *Ibidem*, p. 180.
[139] *Idem*.
[140] *Ibidem*, p. 299.

festation of human appearance can serve to characterize something as human, especially if it fulfills the requirements of **dualistic**, private and collective **plurality**, with its **alterity**, and the **capacity to act** in the world in order to initiate something.

Thus, if formalized in a cybernetic system, what cannot be discarded, would emulate what is eminently human and, thus, open the possibility, in another cultural sphere — the legal sphere — of treatment similar to that attributed to the Human Being.

3 REFLECTIONS ON THE LEGAL CONCEPTS OF MAN, PERSON, AND PERSONALITY

In this step, it is appropriate to bring to light legal elements that allow us to understand how law appropriates concepts from other areas of knowledge to assign them legality.

It seems evident that for man, person and personality are not treated exclusively from the legal point of view. On the contrary, they seem to have deserved the more frequent care of several other sciences and philosophy before they were of legal interest. Similarly, they are not concepts that necessarily should or have been treated viscerally linked and therefore can be split without prejudice.

Thus, for example, Man has been, as seen before, the object of numerous philosophical debates since antiquity. It is a concept that does not find a safe landing, because, with each evolutionary social step, there is a removal, aggregation, and modification of its structure to adapt it to social, political, economic, and other circumstances.

This same Man is scrutinized by sociology, anthropology, economics, medicine, and various other sciences, each with its own peculiar vision.

The fact is that Man does not cease to be scrutinized for or by the concepts.

The very same thing happens with the concepts of person and personality. The first, subject of the same concerns mentioned above, and the second, especially relevant for psychology, medicine (psychiatry) and psychoanalysis, also here, in this work, each in its own way.

However, the myriad of approaches promoted by other disciplines does not overcome the need for its legal treatment, especially in the present work. That is why we will seek here, having had contact with the approach brought from other areas, all important for the construction of these concepts in the legal scope, the specific treatment of this area of concentration.

3.1 Reflection on the legal concept of Man

It is incredible how the juridical doctrine, to a great extent, is silent on man, given the absolute prevalence of the anthropocentric paradigm. It is not common to find in the works on legal personality, in turn also proportionally in small number, express references on the concept of Man. Perhaps because jurists feel that this is the object of study of other social disciplines. The truth is that if law is taken as a cultural object, so far created exclusively by man, it would be reasonable to imagine that legal works would inquire about the center, the addressee, and creator of the Law, seeking to elucidate its concept, from the legal point of view, so as to start the discussion of the other legal issues.

> *Such apparently evident rights as those of personality, only in the 19th century achieved, with difficulties, a certain juridical consecration. In addition, the quality of "human being" has also not been transposed, right away, into Law.*[141]

It is interesting to note, as Cordeiro[142] says, that there is no simple expression in Latin for "human being" like *Mensch* in German. And he concludes, "*Man* has a less universalist scope, as a person corresponds to an abstraction that already has a juridical aspect [...]"

Hartmann[143], in his theory of the strata of reality, discusses various levels of the human being, from animal to psychic to spiritual, this exclusively human, proposing the possibility of a progressive approach to the subject.

Law is concerned reflexively with *Homo sapiens* and directly

---

[141] Cordeiro, A. M. (2004). *Tratado de Direito Civil Português: parte geral. Pessoas* [Treaty of Portuguese Civil Law: general part. People]. (Vol. 1, Part 3, pp. 14). Coimbra: Almedina.

[142] *Idem.*

[143] Hartmann, N. *apud* Cordeiro, *op. cit.*, loc. cit.

with the person, whom it elevates to the status of a legal category.

In fact, it is historically stated that the Law exists because of Man. This anthropocentric view of law still prevails today. However, the concept of person came to light only long after the legal treatment of **contract** and **property**.

These phenomena were soon apprehended by Law in social co-existence, given its evident manifestation in the life of Man. However, Man has only turned to himself, to legally regulate Being, Man, ontologically considered, as a result of the evolution of Law, gradual and continuous.

Therefore, contrary to the pragmatic evidence of contracts and property, Man himself considered, at his core and not as an agent, he was the object of the study of philosophy, not law, because it required a high degree of abstraction. He took care of Man after dealing with property and contracts.

3.2 The legal concept of person

The traditional doctrine credits to the Romans the creation of the legal theory of the personality, although this category of rights was already known in ancient Greece.[144]

José Serpa de Santa Maria[145] affirms that *persona*, in Rome, was the term to designate a mask of metallic blades that facilitated the passage of the voice, used by the Roman actors. It echoed the voice of the artist, *vox personabat*. Over time, the term carries within itself the idea of representation, not only in the scene but also in social life. The personality, in principle, was a representation in the legal scene.

According to Beltrão[146], from the etymological perspective, the

---

[144] Giordani, M.C. (2005) *História de Roma* [History of Rome]; p. 9 *apud* Szaniawski, E. *Direitos de personalidade e sua tutela* [Personality rights and their guardianship]. (2nd ed., pp. 25) São Paulo: Editora revista dos Tribunais.

[145] Santa Maria, J. S. de. (1987). *Direitos da personalidade e a sistemática civil geral* [Personality rights and the general civil system]. Campinas, SP: Julex Livros.

[146] Chaves, A. Tratado de Direito Civil *[Treatise of Civil Law] apud* Beltrão, S.

word person comes from the Latin persona and means mask, the role assigned to this mask.

> *"The primitive meaning corresponded to that of the verb personare, that is, to make resound, to make blare, to hurt with a sound, to wince. Originally, the name of people was given to the masks used by the Roman actors in the representations. It had, in an opening that fit the lips, metal blades, which increased the sound, and the volume of the voice."*

This meaning, according to Chaves, glimpsed the person as a character, translating the word in the sense that political society resembles a drama in which each man has his representation.

As one can see, since then, Law, a reflection of society, categorizes, classifies people. Only after many centuries, with the advent of Christianity has it come to conceive the idea of the subject of rights in its approach close to the present.

According to Szaniawski, from the examination of the Roman texts Gaius (1,9); (1,120); (1,121) and (4,135); Digest (30.86, 2-IUL); (50,16,125 - Paul) and (50,17, 22 - ULP), concerning the Roman Law in the classical period, the term *persona* indicated the human being, free or slave. Beyond it, the term *caput* (head) existed, which granted more or less gradation of subjective right. Any individual regardless of his personality was *caput*: the free were called *caput liberum*, and the slaves, *caput servile*[147]. It can be concluded, then, that for the Romans at that time, every human being was *persona* and *caput*, although with different rights and capacities.

But Cordeiro[148] teaches that,

> *Historically, it is not possible to define or fully explain the person through the human being: besides, "person" only recently became a manageable concept. Human beings had*

R. (2005). *Direitos da personalidade: de acordo com o Novo Código Civil* [Personality rights: according to the New Civil Code]. São Paulo: Atlas.

[147] Correia, A.; Sciascia, G. *Manual de direito romano* [Manual of Roman Law]; p.39 *apud* Szaniawski, *op. cit.*, p. 29.

[148] Cordeiro, A. M., *op. cit.*, p. 16.

> *not been recognized as "people". Dogmatically, there is also no correspondence: we have people today — known as collective people — who are not human beings. And the unborn human being himself — legally called "unborn child" — has not been, civilly, regarded as a person identical to the others.*

According to Szaniawski[149], even the dead, who are therefore no longer persons, have some personality rights under the Civil Code. Even after the death of the individual, the Law takes care of protecting his human personality, in order to preserve his dignity. This guardianship takes place in discussions about the separate parts of the body itself, in which case the special category called the *corpse right* arises.

One can see, therefore, that the person, as a subject of rights, is a mutable, evolving concept. That is why there is no correspondence between the species *Homo sapiens* and the legal concept of person, dogmatically constructed and objectively consecrated.

So much so that women, blacks, Jews, American Indians, Gypsies, foreigners, the mentally ill, children, etc., have been deprived of rights, even in very recent historical periods. Some are minimum rights, of the full condition of Person, even though they are of the same type as the groups exercising political power.

Therefore, it comes as no surprise that, with the evolution of society, or even with the importation of Eastern philosophical sources into the West — for the Japanese, for example, when something acquires a human aspect, it potentially possesses a spirit, called *tamashi*[150] —the concept of person, capable of securing rights and obligations, encompasses animals, or even inanimate, non-biological beings.

Nevertheless, even among those who are shocked at the possibility of a disparate treatment for human beings, or even for those advocating the thesis of animal law, an anthropocentric or biocen-

---

[149] Szaniawski, E., *op. cit.*, p. 183.
[150] Carta, G. (2009, nov.). Sem carne, sem osso [No flesh, no bone]. *Carta Capital*. (Vol. 15, n. 570, pp. 74-79). Editora Confiança.

tric reason exists to differentiate creatures of organic composition from cybernetic ones.

It seems evident that this human or biological premise is not based on objective criteria but is based largely on ignorance, inattention to the question, lack of careful analysis, dogmatic and religious elements, fear, prejudice and acceptance with the crystallized paradigm, even in the contemporary stage of technology.

It is worth repeating that etymologically, as Houaiss[151] teaches, a person is:

> *Latin. persóna, 'theater mask; by extension, the role assigned to this mask, character; which can be a person, individual; a grammatical person'; f. divg. pop. de persona; see person(i)-; historically, 13th century: pessoas, persoas, pessõa. 14th century: pesoa, pesoans. 15th century: peçoas, persona.*

Now, there is no direct necessary relationship in the Law between a person and a Human Being. So much so that, if one observes, there are legal entities and nobody else is shocked by this fact, nor by that denomination, just as it does not cause any oddness to accept some rights for someone other than the estate, condominium, legislative houses, the bankrupt estate, the unborn, the deceased, and so on.

It is well seen that in the purity of the origin, *persona* was an object, a mask, that served as adornment for the actors to develop their roles, passing, then, to designate the very creatures acting on the scene, the characters. It was a representation.

Thus, a person is nothing more than an object and a person who plays a role, which is attributed to him in a performance, which may well be transferred to the role that is developed or exercised in the theater of life, where everyone has certain roles.

The man enters and leaves the scene several times, often characterized in more than one way, with more of a social role: son, fa-

---

[151] Houaiss, A. *et al. Dicionário Houaiss de língua portuguesa* [Houaiss Dictionary of Portuguese language]. Retrieved from: <http://houaiss.uol.com.br/busca.jhtm?verbete=consciencia&stype=k. Last access date: February 09, 2009.

ther, relative, professional, student, teacher, patient, deceased etc.

For each act and role a character, a face and a different outfit, with different functions, different obligations, different attributions, varied rights.

It is interesting to note how law grants or withdraws personality, sometimes in a singular way, as is still the case in North Korea, where the president is still the late grandfather of the now dictator Kim Jong-un. Thus, even political and/or administrative functions can be attributed to those who are not, by common sense, a person.

This implies that it is not surprising that, linked to the real, true, original meaning of the word "person" — detached from the anthropocentrism that isolates the human being and has strength in the West and less emphasis on the East — can be attributed the noun "person" to a robot.

Here it is not intended to conceptualize as a person all robots, indistinctly, but only those who fulfill certain requirements, that is, those who are attributed the condition of transforming Man into the central character of Law, endowed with the susceptibility of securing rights and obligations or even of others that make you claim or demand something similar or equal to rights.

What is certain is that the concept of person should serve individual and collective persons. Among them, one can, in theory, include the robots. The concept of person is an independent reality, a normative communication, which, as Cordeiro[152] teaches, mentions the existence of

> *[...] an entity that is the recipient of legal norms and therefore: capable of owning subjective rights or of being bound by obligations. The affirmation of the personality will, therefore, be the consideration that the target entity can self-determine, within the space of legitimacy conferred by the rights of which it is entitled, and must act, in the field of its effects. [...] How rights are to be exercised and obligations fulfilled is no longer clarified by the summary affirmation of personality: this will depend on multiple other legal norms, the applicability of which, however, postulates the personality and derives from it.*

---

[152] Cordeiro, A. M., *op. cit.*, p. 514.

Therefore, it seems that there are no conceptual obstacles to the characterization of the robot as a person for law purposes, provided that it fulfills the necessary characteristics. It is necessary to know whether these characteristics exist, although for us in this context, it is not the most important.

3.3 The legislative treatment of the person

As stated above, the law also takes care of the concept of person, not only doctrinally, but also, legally. Commonly the laws — and in countries with continental European legal orientation, there are basic laws, such as the Civil Codes — that aim to define in each national state the concept of person.

Among Brazilian and Portuguese law, to use the closest examples, there is no difference. Both there and here, there is a basic norm of general law, called the Civil Code, that brings in its content the definition of person.

This definition, it will be seen, is not static, and follows the social, economic, political and consequently legal evolution of these nations.

3.3.1 In Portugal

The Code of Seabra required that in order for a *Homo sapiens* be a person of law, he had to be born (Article 6: Legal capacity is acquired by birth, but the individual, as soon as he is procreated, is under the protection of the law and is born for the purposes stated in this code), that the birth should be with life (art 1479) and with a human figure (articles 110 and 1776). Thus, if a being were born from a woman's womb and did not have the human figure, that is, it was, for example, a hybrid, it would not be a person under the aegis of the revoked Portuguese Civil Code.

In Spain, until July 21, 2011, it was necessary, in order to be considered as a person, that the being born present a human form and survive outside the womb for 24 hours (Spanish Civil Code, articles 29 and 30). That is, the condition of a person requires a test, a physical test of survival. Thus a human being is not born a person, he becomes a person over time. Only with the advent of Law no. 20/2011 has this situation changed and legal personality now coincides with birth.

Portuguese Law evolved and the Civil Code of 1966 no longer came to demand the human figure, and it seems licit to suppose that it no longer required human specificity, although, at the time, it was not considered the possibility of births of hybrids or even the appearance of robots.

It should be noted that if an anthropocentric interpretation does not prevail, art. 66 of the Portuguese Civil Code establishes the legal personality of any living being that is born alive since it does not make any reference to the Human Being.

3.3.2 In Brazil

In the same path that is followed by the Portuguese Civil Code, the Brazilian Civil Code, which abandoned in its legal definition of person the word Man, allows the non-anthropocentric and extended interpretation of the legal concept of a person.

Pablo Stolze and Rodolfo Pamplona[153] see in this new form of the Civil Code a politically correct expression compatible with the constitutional order to make the equality between men and women, reverberated by art. 5th, I, of the Brazilian Federal Constitution, an understanding shared by Grinberg.[154]

It seems, however, that considering the possibility of technological uniqueness, one can see beyond the generic discriminatory fence, already expressly configured in the Brazilian Federal Constitution, to understand, faced with the new and future reality, that, without legislative change of the Civil Code, it is possible to admit a robot as a person for legal effect, given, in addition to ev-

---

[153] Gagliano, P. S.; Pamplona Filho, R. (2009). *Novo curso de direito civil: parte geral* [New civil law course: general part]. (11th ed., pp. 80). São Paulo: Saraiva.
[154] Grinberg, K. (2008). *Código Civil e cidadania* [Civil Code and citizenship]. (3rd ed., pp. 71) São Paulo: Jorge Zahar.

erything already mentioned, that in its etymological origin, robot is a forced[155] laborer, a slave, a Man submitted to others, as they once were. It cannot be emphasized enough that these regrettable facts do not happen again, the Jews, the blacks, the Christians, the American Indians, the prisoners, the condemned, etc.

Although it is possible to affirm that the Civil Code allows the understanding of the possibility of conceptualizing the robot as a person, the Federal Constitution, while not impeding such understanding, impregnated by anthropocentrism, only gives dignity to the human person, although it can assert that the legal entities may suffer moral damages.

In any case, the constitutional treatment is ambiguous, since in its art. 5, *caput* and subsections X and XV, mainly, does not distinguish a human person from any other person:

> **Article 5**. *All people are equal before the law, without any distinction whatsoever, Brazilians and foreigners residing in the country being ensured of inviolability of the right to life, to liberty, to equality, to security, and property, on the following terms:*
>
> *X - the privacy, private life, honor, and image of **persons** are inviolable, and the right to compensation for property or moral damages resulting from their violation is ensured;*
>
> *[...]*
>
> *XV - locomotion within the national territory is free in the time of peace, and any **person** may, under the terms of the law, enter it, remain therein or leave it with his assets.*

The constitutional prohibition is clear when addressing any form or nature of distinction, whether it is based on biological factors or directed to synthetic beings or by being synthetic.

It is stated that, although, as expected, the Brazilian Federal Constitution does not allow a direct and broad interpretation that

---

[155] Capek, K. (2004). *R.U.R. (Rossum's Universal Robots): A play in introductory scene and three act.* London: Penguin Classics.

contemplates the robot as a person, nor does it prohibit such conception, being open to interpretations consistent with the future state of technology and social reality. That is why it can be said that the robot of the technological singularity, considered as an individual person, cannot suffer discrimination in the treatment by virtue of the constitutional prohibition.

On the other hand, this is not a subject that should be addressed by the Constitution, but by civil codes on continental European legal systems.

It is useful to make a very brief history of legal treatment in the Brazilian Civil Code. Grinberg[156] states that the concept of the person marked the discussions on the draft of the Civil Code of 1916. The abolition of slavery was recent, and former slaves and descendants of these slaves were present.

The Teixeira de Freitas Civil Code draft bill, like all other Code projects, brought differentiations among people, especially regarding the acquisition of rights.[157] Beviláqua[158] had been strongly criticized for not following the same path, the author teaches.

It should be noted that Teixeira censured the Civil Code Project of Portugal because in his inaugural article he defined that "only man is a person". The solution adopted was to establish that people are "all entities susceptible to acquiring rights." The conception of "entity" for Teixeira, according to Grinberg, was that of Man.

Although this understanding cannot be criticized, it is certain that the "Outline" had an advanced device of such amplitude that it would allow its preservation in the legislative and technological updates that came later.

Teixeira de Freitas could only understand entity as being Man, but, nowadays or in the future, nothing prevents one from being able to look at a robot, as is defended here.

---

[156] Grinberg, *op. cit.*, p.67.

[157] *Idem.*

[158] Author's Note. The Draft Bill of Clovis Beviláqua prevailed and became, after the legislative process, the 1916 Brazil's Civil Code, in force until 2002.

It is interesting that the law then in force would already have such an understanding if, of course, there were any technical possibility of considering the existence of the robots treated here. In this sense Grinberg[159], referring to Beviláqua, says: "[...] As a person, according to all current definitions in law, every being capable of having rights, there was no need for definition since it was a notion defined by all."

And Beviláqua, according to the author, understood that it was not necessary to define a person because he had understood that it was coupled with the concept of the human being.

It seems fair to say that in current and future times the same legal reasoning can be applied to defend the idea that the legal concept of person can be linked to the robot and not only the human being, because the concept of person, in fact, is linked to the entity that holds rights and obligations under the Law — as contemplated by Teixeira de Freitas — and not to a particular species or structure, because the law cannot crystallize a position on something that can be modified by natural or technological evolution.

It will not be the first time that a concept appropriate or created by law and deontologized based on real-life (ontological) situations, evolves with the winds of change, as indeed the legal concept of the person itself.

It should be recalled with Grinberg[160] that, when Beviláqua used the expression "human being", in art. 2 of his draft, the review committee had him modify the text to use the word "man" in an attitude that could be interpreted as sexist — and, I believe, possibly, this happened back then. This sexist interpretation was refuted by the author of the 1916 Code.

However, one cannot refute the idea that, under the Civil Code of 1916, there were women who were more citizen-minded, closer to men in their rights than others, not only because society understood it, but because in the Civil Code the treatment was different for the various "women": honest, single, married, widowed, dis-

---

[159] *Ibidem*, p. 68.
[160] *Ibidem*, p. 70.

honest, etc. Each had a different plexus of rights, varying levels of legal capacity.

Therefore, the only valid justification for filling in the characteristics required by robots if they insist on attributing the condition of the human being to an exclusive characteristic is the prevalence of the anthropocentrism paradigm.

3.4 Personality

Personality is understood as a "set of characteristics of the individual himself; consisting of the intrinsic part of the human being. It is a legal good, being the first good belonging to its person, its first utility."[161]

Regarding personality, as Elimar Szaniawski[162] teaches, the expression for the Roman law was limited to individuals who had the following three *statuses: status libertatis, status civitatis,* and *status familiae.* He who was not a possessor of liberty, had no other *status*, like the slaves, though they were human beings and, for part of the doctrine, a person.[163] The slave, according to Justinian law, was a human being who lost his freedom and became the property of any citizen, who could free him, trade him or even kill him. The birth — the son of a slave was born a slave — the maximum *captio diminutio* — a punitive form for the insolvent debtor, the one caught red-handed, those who did not register in the *census* and the deserted soldier — the prisoners of war of the publicly declared campaigns by Rome to any people and the free woman who sexually relates to an alien slave, becoming the property of the master of his slave lover, are some situations that caused the loss of liberty. In addition to these, the ungrateful freedman to his former owner could once again become a slave, and anyone who pretended to be a slave, without being, to gain an undue advan-

---

[161] Szaniawski, E., *op. cit.*, p. 70.

[162] *Ibidem*, p. 183.

[163] Chamoun, E. *Instituições de direito romano* [Institutions under Roman law], p. 48 *et seq. apud* Szaniawski, E., *op. cit.*, p. 26.

tage could also lose *status libertatis*. Regarding freedom, in Rome, people were divided into naive, who had never been a slave, and freedmen, those who were slaves and obtained manumission.

According to Orlando Gomes[164], the purpose of personality rights would be to protect the human personality, being fundamental to the development of the human being, preventing it from being attacked by other individuals. In this way, the personality rights are, by legal determination, the conversion of the physical and psychic planes, which individualizes the person, and they are then protected.

In the course of history, the dignity of the human person was consolidated as a conquest made by the human being, arising from ethical-juridical reasons against the barbarism practiced by the humans themselves, against each other.[165]

Over time there have been robots that take on the most diverse tasks, for some time, such as controlling airplanes, nuclear weapons, ships, submarines, drug dosage, air quality, water, food, safety, suggest medical diagnostics etc. There are already robots to take care of the elderly and children, to have sex[166] or keep company. In short, several activities previously only entrusted to humans.[167]

It is a machine that now stores what I type and keeps my ideas in a more or less secure and perennial environment.

Surely the time will come when our respect for them approaches or surpasses what we have for humans.

It seems reasonable to suppose that we can see in them a dignity similar to ours, for they are acting in a similar way to us, even in tasks in which moral or morally founded decisions are demanded, and it seems reasonable to suppose that our dignity is in some way tied to the moral form and ethics with which we conduct ourselves

---

[164] Gomes, O. Direito da personalidade. Introdução ao dir. Civil [Personality rights. Introduction to Civil Law]. *Revista Forense*, n° 216, p. 132.

[165] Szaniawski, E., *op. cit.*, p. 141.

[166] Levy, D. (2008). *Love and sex with robots: the evolution of human-robot relationships*. Harper Perennial.

[167] Wallach, W. e Allen, C. (2009). *Moral Machines: Teaching robots right from wrong*. Oxford: University Press.

or let ourselves be led.

The time can come when it will not be possible to distinguish whether the act was human or robotic, and no longer can one deny a dignity proper to machines.

Nowadays the need to construct machines endowed with ethics and morals is already discussed, precisely because they act in the likeness of humans[168].

3.5 Post-Humanity

Once and if mankind has been overcome by the advent of technological singularity, with a possible end to the purely biological evolution of man, a new phase of human evolution would arise by overcoming the human, either by its cyborgization, by its superhumanization resulting from cyborgization, or by the enthronement of machines, with fulfillment of human function and its consequent perishing.

The fact is that, as we will try to confront later, the moment will come when the purely human will be outdated. This would be the post-humanity era.

It is a process that began with the appearance of Man himself, his primitive cyborgism by the use and incorporation of technology, some transparent; his permanent departure from nature and the search for artificialization and which has not yet been fully realized by the lack of technological means to do so and which may be delayed by moral or fear.

However, the means of overcoming Man are becoming more real each day. The devirtualization of the necessary means is proportional to the virtualization of life, the deterritorialization, and dematerialization of relations and tools and the displacement of the local situation to the informational cloud.

Furthermore, two central dialects involve the formation of the post-human: presence/absence and pattern/randomness. As information becomes increasingly important, it tends to prevail over

---

[168] *Idem.*

presence/absence. Just remember the form of archiving and retrieval of digital data and the dematerialization and deterritorialization that we witness to understand the phenomenon.

Lemos[169] understands this new reality by stating that "Micro-electronic technology is at the same time magical (abolition of space and time, telepresence) and aggregating (corporate, community)".

It is also necessary to consider that the concept of the individual will changes, since, being the conscience expressed as processes that can be created by *software*, it can be displaced from the mind and from the subject itself, wandering in several places. Therefore, it can no longer be ensured that consciousness guarantees the existence of the subject. One must be prepared for a post-conscious subject.

3.5.1 Introduction

Here it is a matter of seeking to understand what Supiot[170] called *homo juridicus*.

For Alain Supiot, "Nothing is more difficult than to apprehend our foundation. We all believe in the first article of the Universal Declaration of Human Rights [...]"[171]

Referring to St Augustine's stupefaction, he understands that the human mind, like his own, cannot fully comprehend itself and seeks out the reasons for its being. Like animals, Man is in the world by his senses, but, through language, he has access to a universe that transcends the circumstance of sensory experience. It is the limitation already demonstrated by Göddel, as seen before.

The necessity of reason is to allow Man to combine his existen-

---

[169] Lemos, A. (2008). *Cibercultura: tecnologia e via social na cultura contempo-rânea.* [Cyberculture: technology and society in contemporary culture] (4th ed., pp. 181). Porto Alegre: Sulina.
[170] Supiot, A. (2007). *Homo juridicus: ensaio sobre a função antropológica do Direito* [Homo juridicus: essay on the anthropological function of Law]. (M. E. de A. P. Galvão, Trans.). São Paulo: Martins Fontes.
[171] *Ibidem*, p. 4.

tial and material finitude with his infinite mental universe[172], but reason itself has limits which reason does not know.

He considers **birth, sex** and **death** to be the three limits of the human condition, which are now in perspective of supplantation by human cloning, by which the limitation of generation, the dependence on sex, and the time limit of life can be eliminated. This can also occur as a result of cybernetics, the application and symbiosis of technologies with the human body and mental equipment, whose occurrence is fixed in post-humanity.

Supiot asserts that, as in any society, the present Western society rests on a conception of Man that gives meaning to human life. Although from a legal point of view, Man is subject to law, endowed with reason, for other sciences he is an object, whether it is medicine, biology, economics, sociology, etc.

This scientific dichotomy, the concepts of subject and object, of person and thing, of spirit and matter, are defined by mutual opposition.[173] It is not possible to conceive of one without recognizing the existence of others.

With its appearance in Rome and its development to the present day, the human conception as *Imago Dei* allows it to surpass nature and to emerge the ambivalence of three attributes of humanity: **individuality, subjectivity**, and **personality**. Image and likeness of God, Man gains extraordinary but limited dignity, because he is not God. As an individual he is unique, but also similar to all others; as a subject, he is sovereign, but the word does not allow him to forget that he is submitted to the Law of Men; as a person he is a spirit, but incarnate in matter.

It is interesting that this same man who puts himself on a pedestal, who is unique and identical, consecrated of a sovereign dignity, by creating, within the scope of the Law, the legal person, made possible that any gathering of people, thoughts or things can be elevated to the status of a person. "The *homo juridicus* thus manages to treat the plural as a singular, the 'we' as an 'I' susceptible to

---

[172] *Ibidem*, p. 9.
[173] *Ibidem*, p. 13.

negotiate on an equal footing with all other individuals."[174]

For Supiot, the divine prescription of reign over the Universe reached its logical end with the dismissal of God and Man monopolized the quality of the subject, in a world ruled by him and filled with objects modeled in his image.[175]

Maybe that's what Man expects after the creation of machines that surpass him. Human characteristics are already assigned to machines, their data processing outcomes are already accepted as truth (just remember how often it is heard that 'This is not in the system, sir" when searching for information in a call center or airline counter, for example.

On such occasions, by hypothesis, even if the Man is carrying his flight ticket, the first reaction, if not the definitive one of the clerk, will be to verify if the system confirms that the physical evidence translates the truth.

If the physical evidence (the flight ticket) doesn't comply with the system records, the tendency is that the employee of the company will believe in the system, in the pure information, dematerialized and not in the person of flesh and blood and the document.

Also, Man has already adapted to the machines, having to learn to use their interfaces and not making them adapt to him, regardless of whoever uses them. It should be added that those who design and develop these interfaces are, as a rule, men and not machines, but men whose thoughts resemble those who have become accustomed to thinking as machines think, or at least as they are or should be.

More and more systems control the lives of people and talk to each other, gaining importance and power and having on them the widespread trust of people and even of institutions. Systems are taking more and more decisions for Men, either in choosing the best route for the space shuttle, in dosing the venom to execute a prisoner, on the right day for the birth of a child, whether the indi-

---

[174] *Ibidem*, p. 20.
[175] *Ibidem*, p.24-25.

vidual can buy their own home, if one can be elected in a poll, to vote, to contract with the public administration, to marry, etc.

Since machines are being made, especially robots, in the image and likeness of Man, trying to make machines surpass Man, there is nothing to prevent them from firing Man, reigning as absolute subjects, as a natural consequence of human evolution, now no longer in a purely biological stage, or even in any biological degree.

Recalling the juridical concept of person, it is necessary to remember that in Rome the *summa divisio* represented by the antagonistic division between people and things was relative, having evolved to reach normative value. No longer was it allowed to treat people as things and vice versa. This separation thus acquired dogmatic value in the West.

It was Christianity, as seen before, by its historical origin at a time when Jews were persecuted and enslaved, treated as objects, that personality became an attribute that should be recognized to all men, including, of course, Jews, Christians, slaves, etc., a concept that allows the body and the spirit to reconcile and remain together.

For Supiot,[176] legal personality is no more than a means by which the law guarantees to each one the aptitude so that one can realize in the Earth his own personality, in the eyes of all. That is, it is no longer necessary to wait for the ascent to heaven so that one's soul, which gives him autonomy, freedom, communion, and obedience to God, manifests itself.

It becomes evident that, when dealing with the human person, reference is constantly made to freedom, a broad concept, with variable content as well. According to Fernandez and Fernandez[177], "The problem of freedom can be analyzed in two ways: as a meta-

---

[176] *Ibidem*, p. 20.
[177] Fernandez, A.; Fernandez, M. (2008). *Neuroética, direito e neurociência: conduta humana, liberdade e racionalidade jurídica* [Neuroethics, law and neuroscience: human conduct, freedom and legal rationality]. (pp. 77). Curitiba: Juruá.

physical problem (contemplating freedom as something internal to the human person) and as a social problem (accentuating the outer freedom of the person)."

In this way, one can see negative freedom, by the absence of coercion and positive freedom resulting from individual autonomy. It is understood that by "speaking of human freedom, we can distinguish three basic types:"

I) Sociological freedom: autonomy enjoyed by the individual concerning society;

II) Psychological freedom: "self-ownership";

III) Moral freedom: Man's ability to decide to act according to reason.

Claiming that man is free means first of all to say that there is in him a principle or fundamental ability to take his own action in his hands so that he can be completely responsible for what he does.

Another way to understand freedom is to conceive it as self-possession. In this case, it refers to that state of man which, to a large extent, has freed himself from alienations and determinisms in his own action, so that his action can be called truly free. The development of freedom is discontinuous and is never a definitive possession, as the authors understand.[178]

3.5.2 The Post-Human Condition

When dealing with the new reality to come, Habermas[179] understands that the differences between man and machine, a

---

[178] *Idem et. seq.*

[179] Habermas, J. (2006). *O futuro da natureza humana: a caminho de uma eugenia liberal?* [The future of human nature: on the way to a liberal eugenics?]. (M. B. Bettencourt, Trans.). (p. 89). Coimbra: Almedina.

consequence of the development of post-human systems, will disappear:

> As the random evolution of species enters the field of in-tervention of genetic engineering and, in this way, in the field of actions for which we are responsible, there is a de-differentiation of categories that, in the world of life, still remain clearly the category of what is manufactured and the category of what is naturally generated. For us, this an-tithesis draws its evidence from the familiar forms of action of material-technical transformation, on the one hand, and from the relation of cultivation or therapy to organic nature, on the other hand.

This doesn't mean that he complies with the course of events, for what is done today will affect (the Law) of future generations who did not want to — even because they did not participate — in such development. He sees a definitive change in the human species:

> It is, of course, a power of the now on the coming defense-less objects of the previous decisions of these today's plan-ners. The reverse of the power of today will be the future subjection of the living to the dead [...] the domain of nature becomes degeneration of the nature of the species itself.[180]

In principle, it seems, this does not differ in anything from what has always occurred. This subjection of the living to the dead has always existed. Everything that has been done until today was re-alized by the then living ones and left marks, often deep, in those that were to come. These came and left their marks, died and their effects were felt by those who succeeded them.

It is evident that the generations to come often suffer the con-sequences, whatever they may be, from previous generations, for acts for which they have not at all contributed. Contrary to this, only if the march of the time were different from the one experi-enced.

Thus, to suffer the effects of a cause promoted by the dead is the nature of life itself, the effect of the dead or of those who will die,

---

[180] *Ibidem*, p. 91.

although it is now known, death is not the inexorable consequence of all life[181].

In a certain way, the philosopher would be correct if what he intended to characterize is the severity of the effects of what is done today, with the persecution or inevitability of a post-humanity, since the biological and anthropocentric paradigms could be broken. However, such or more important paradigms have already been broken before, though not by Man.

The crystalline, non-biological organization has given way to biological systems at the origin of life as we know it today. The monocellular paradigm was then broken. Then the aquatic paradigm was abandoned. The saurian model gave place to the mammal predominance and over time to the primate and last, but not probably least, to the human.

The African world was left behind, Greece was overcome, Rome was surpassed, the Mongols were overcome, the Christians were overcome and then defeated the Moors. The European world expanded with navigations, Portugal lost its power, Spain too, France too, England and the USSR in the same way, the United States now reign, seeing the accelerated development of China, followed by Brazil, India, and Russia.

Each historical step of these nations, every related change, all made by the then living and the deceased, represented, in its own way and once, subjection of the living to the dead. Therefore, in this particular nothing new under the sun. In addition, many of these changes have broken important paradigms.

Rover[182] expresses himself on this subject in the following terms:

> *From this unprecedented advance, we can affirm the appearance of a new nature, neither human nor mechanical.*

---

[181] Cinquepalmi, J. V. (2010, February). Você pode ser imortal [You can be immortal]. *Superinteressante*. (Vol. 275, pp. 42-51). Editora Abril.

[182] Rover, A. J. *Para um direito invisível: superando as artificialidades da inteligência*. [For an invisible Law: overcoming the artificialities of intelligence]. Retrieved from: <http://www.infojur.ufsc.br/aires/arquivos/direito%20invisivel%202005.pdf>. Last access date: February 25, 2009.

The invisibility of technology would have its peak at that time, in which man would have machine attributes in his flesh and machines would have biological attributes typical of mankind. There will be no clear distinction between humans and robots. Machines would be capable of feelings like fear and love, of dreaming.

Like any paradigm, the anthropocentric takes some time to develop or to undo, which may occur in one or a few generations.

Just to give an example, hypothetical and extreme, of the many possibilities. Imagine that in a given society children are told from a very early age that a dog is, for example, a person, and, thus, should be treated this way — as, for example, in Japan, it is called mister dog or mister cat, or lady Moon or mister Sun.

These children may grow up treating them by referring to and considering dogs as people, like themselves, with just another form and way of communicating and with different habits, but not to the extent of treating them like animals. They will be adults who will treat these animals as people and perpetuate the idea that they are holders of rights like humans.

This would change the anthropocentric paradigm. There are real examples like cows in India, endowed with even higher *status* than some Men.

Moreover, in Japan, when something takes on human features, it gains new status, acquiring a spirit.[183]

It is merely a matter of perspective and conception of the world, which comes from the experience of being in the world. Thus, in a world populated by intelligent, conscious robots, with unconscious thought, eventually feelings, occupying jobs in various sectors, caring for children, deciding about various human factors, cooperating with humans, fighting with them, killing and being put out of operation or dead, competing with men, etc., a new conception of the world will surely arise, and at that moment it will not be the purely anthropocentric paradigm that will prevail anymore.

---

[183] For more details see: Sem carne, sem osso [No meat, no bone]. *Carta Capital.* (Vol. 15, n. 570, pp. 74-79). Editora Confiança.

It is necessary to discuss the issue of childbirth survival, a concept that will be discussed later, in order to see the appearance of the legal personality.

At this point, it is important to remember that Habermas[184] does not accept to talk about a person before birth. In addition, the German author does not sacralize the biological nature.[185]

The philosopher, however, is not only attentive to the questions of post-humanity but he is also not satisfied with the explanations given until now.

Habermas expresses that in the work examined, he also doubts to succeed in the explanation, just making an effort to clarify the situation further: "The disturbing phenomenon is the fading of the border between the nature we are and the organic equipment we give ourselves."[186]

It should be said that the unborn is a potential[187], virtual[188] person, endowed with rights. As a potential virtual person, it resembles ontologically a workable and feasible design of a robot, which is a virtual, potential robot. Both can become real, in theory, one, biological, the other, cybernetic, provided they come to the outside world, real, with necessary and sufficient characteristics, thus acquiring a legal personality.

As Szaniawski teaches, it is not a question of any novelty in Brazilian law to propose to be the unborn possessor of personality, that is, a person. As Teixeira de Freitas taught, a person of visible existence is any entity that bears typical signs of humanity, regardless of the distinction of qualities or accidents. The people not yet born, but who were in the maternal womb,

---

[184] Habermas, J., *op. cit.*, p. 18.

[185] *Ibidem*, p. 22.

[186] *Ibidem*, p.64.

[187] Telles Júnior, G., *op. cit.*, p. 303. "In every *being that acts*, there are certain beings with power. [...] The *beings with power*, existing in a certain being that acts, are competences proper to that same being that acts, competences that exist in him because he *is* precisely what he is".

[188] LEVY, Pierre. (1996). *O que é o virtual?* [What is virtual?]. (P. Neves, Trans.). São Paulo: Editora 34.

Teixeira de Freitas called them "unborn people."[189] However, because they are people, they carry personality and legal capacity, the law is conferring upon them the indispensable representation.

He goes on saying that the 2002 Brazilian Civil Code rules in the same way as the 1916 Brazilian Civil Code: in the single paragraph of article 1.609, allows the recognition of the child even before his birth; in article 1.779, disciplines the guardianship of the unborn; in article 1798, authorizes, at the opening of the probate proceedings, persons already conceived as legal successors. In this last article, the new Code recognizes and assigns the name "person" to the unborn.

In this way, the old genetic-developmental understanding must be disregarded. It claimed that the unborn child was protected by the law, without being granted any subjective right. The Law ruled the unborn child the same way that it ruled an inanimate object. Therefore, those who maintain that the Civil Code reject the natural personality of the unborn person, but already conceived, are against the author's opinion. The virtual is the real in power.

In post-humanism, we have two possibilities: one, the occurrence of singularity will produce effects so overwhelming and rapid that almost immediately man will perish, and in the other, there may be a gradual replacement of *Homo sapiens* by hybrid beings before his disappearance.

Hayes[190] says that for the mentors of post-humanism, Man can be content to be placed next to the dinosaurs or to try to survive by becoming a cybernetic machine, through some form of symbiosis or to be supplanted by the machines he creates. However, there will be a limit to this merge of Man and machine, before there are only them.

---

[189] Esboço: arts. 35; 53; 221 and 226 *apud* Szaniawski, *op. cit.*, p. 64.

[190] Hayles, N. K. (1999). *How we became posthuman: virtual bodies in cybernetics, literature and informatics.* (pp. 283). Chicago: The University of Chicago Press.

In addition, other partially or wholly non-biological life forms are discussed by the doctrine of post-humanism, such as *cyborgs*[191], and others:

An initial taxonomy of Forms of Life (FOL)

In the first three decades of the new millennium, all of the following 10 or so life forms will emerge. Today we tend to think in terms of two life forms: animal and vegetable. The vegetable is open to 'open slather' genetic manipulation and, since 'Dolly and co(w)', animals also — not yet us though. Not yet that is. By 2030, while our children will still be alive, most of these forms of life will exist and be integrating with Artificial Intelligence (AI) and nanotechnology (NT). Life forms include: • *Cyborgs — human/machine composite FOL — $6 million man/woman, Frankenstein.* • *GEborgs - genetically engineered FOL eg through modifying orgoborgs and cyborgs by cloning, food modification etc. [see Humborgs]. An interim life form only. [See Technoborg.* • *Orgoborgs — organic FOL — animal, vegetable, microscopic etc. on planet earth Inc.* • *Humborgs (organic conscious FOLs commonly called humans). These FOLs can be cloned [see GEborgs]. Ultimately humborgs will be implanted with bioborgs. As these chips are used to operate mechanical arms, or negate brain or nerve damage. The issue of man-robots, cyborgs, will arise — the advent of nanotechnology, which is forcing a re-definition of our conception of life.* • *Bioborgs — The development of living biochips will further blur the definition of a living machine. By synthesizing living bacteria, scientists have found a way to program the bacteria's genetic development to mimic the on and off switching of electronic circuitry. Many scientists presently feel silicon miniaturization has reached its limit because of the internal heat that they generate. The biochip is then expected to greatly expand the capabilities of computerization by*

---

[191] Clynes, M.; Kline, N. apud Lima, H. L. A. de. (2004). *Do corpo-máquina ao corpo-informação: o pós-humano como horizonte biotecnológico.* [From the body-machine to the body-information: the post-human as a biotechnological horizon]. Ph.D. Dissertation (Doctor's Degree in Sociology) – Faculdade de Direito, Universidade Federal de Pernambuco, Recife. Retrieved from: <http://boletimef.org/biblioteca/757/Do-corpo-maquina-ao-corpo-informacao-o-pos-humano-como-horizonte-biotecnologico>. Last access date: April 28, 2011. The term *cyborg* was created in 1960 by Manfred Clynes and Nathan Clynes, doctors of the Rockland Hospital, New York, in order to adjust the human body to the space conquest.

reaching the ultimate in miniaturization. Biochips, when combined with nanotechnology will also have the unique ability to correct design flaws. Moreover, James McAlear of Gentronix Labs notes because proteins have the ability to assemble themselves the (organic) computer would more or less put itself together. • Siliborgs — silicon based FOL i.e. AI, self-repairing computer programs, Rights of Robots, HAL in 2001. Possibly silicon is nearing its design limitation as to its ability to dissipate heat and is about to be replaced by organic computers using biotech nano-engineering. • Symborgs — symbological FOL — three types: • 1 Conscious/external — culture, computer virus, World Wide Web • 2 Unconscious/internal –Mythic/unconscious i.e. archetypes i.e. FOL that are mythical, real yet not empirically real • 3 Bridges — between consciousness and unconsciousness eg the Cape York Rainbow Serpent Dreamtime stories/myths. Here the three prerequisite conditions of life are symbolically rather than literally met. In the case of the Rainbow Serpent story, however, the control over the physical aspects of the three aspects of tribes life is very 'real'. • Technoborgs technological FOL as shown in movies such as Batteries Not Included. By 2050 Technoborgs will become fused with GEborgs and Bioborgs. Humborgs as we know us will become indistinguishable. It is this life form that is likely to populate the life ecology of the near future. FOL relatively discrete from our humanoid terrestrial world: • ETborgs —FOL from other planets eg. ET, Predator, Alien (usually hostile to humans, maybe they represent our own fear of future). • Macroborgs (macrocosmic FOL) eg. the Gaia hypothesis, which sees the world, indeed the universe as a living organism/entity demonstrating the requisite aspects of life, outlined below. • MVborgs — Micro Vita — microscopic FOL that blend mind and matter also called orgones, diatoms etc. cp. Macroborgs. • Psyborgs — psychic FOL, entities originating in the non-material realm eg angels, Dracula.[192]

The cyborg is the most well-known creature of this new cybernetic fauna and is defined as a system that is part human and part machine.[193] It cannot be mistaken with the android, which is a

---

[192] Wildman, P. (1999, autumn). Blood sweat and gears: some present implications of cloning and other life futures. *Australian Rationalist*. (N. 49 pp. 33-37).
[193] Rosenberg, J. M. (1986). *Dictionary of artificial intelligence and robotics*. (pp. 42) Toronto: John Wiley & Sons.

human-looking being — usually referring to a synthetic being — whose female is gynoid.[194]

Indeed, again, the path of post-humanity has been paved for a long time. There is the confluence of natural selection and artificial selection, possibly the replacement of one by the other. This began with the development of medicines. "People with genetic defects, who used to be fatal, now survive and have children. Natural predators no longer affect the rules of (human) survival."[195]

Some, like Professor Steve Jones[196], of University College London, consider that the end of human evolution has been reached since it will now be more memetic than genetic.

Richard Dawkins[197] clarifies the etymology of the memetic word: that "Mimeme" comes from a proper Greek root, but I look for a shorter word that sounds more or less like "gene." I hope my classicist friends will forgive me if I abbreviate mimeme for meme. He further stated that meme remembers the word memory.

Some understand, like Hans Moravec[198], that DNA will become useless when machines, pursuing our cultural evolution, correspond to all our essential human functions, resulting in intelligent robots capable of thinking and acting like a human being, that will develop faster and faster without human need.

Moravec[199] further mentions that AG Cairns-Smith, in his book, *Seven Clues to Origin of Life*, concludes that genetic seizures of power like this have already existed, when microscopic ceramic

---

[194] Vaz, R. de O. Sentimentos fabricados [Manufactured Feelings]. *Revista filosofia, ciência & vida. Enigmas da consciência na filosofia da mente.* (Year 1, n°3, pp. 43). Editora Escala.

[195] Ward, P. (2009, February) Que futuro espera pelo homo sapiens? [What future awaits for homo sapiens?] *Scientific American Brasil. Evolução dirigida.* (Year 7, n. 81, pp. 59). Editora Duetto.

[196] *Idem.*

[197] Dawkins, R., *op. cit.*, p. 330.

[198] Moravec, H. (1992). *Homens e robots: o futuro da inteligência humana e robótica* [Mind Children: the future of robot and human intelligence]. (J. L. M. F. Lima, Trans.). (pp. 11-12). Lisboa: Gradiva.

[199] *Idem.*

crystals reproduced by the simple process of mineral growth were surpassed by biological reproduction, as previously mentioned.

Yes, this was a model of reproduction existing before biological reproduction, because the mutations that suffered and suffer in everything and for everything are adapted to the Darwinian evolutionary model, which requires reproduction, heredity, mutation and different degrees of reproductive success.

Thus, with the species of ceramic crystals competing Darwinianly, some of them began to encode genetic information in the exterior, in the form of long chains of carbon, which successively reproduced and changed, becoming less and less dependent on the crystals, eventually abandoned, resulting in the appearance of life.

Today, according to Moravec[200], there is a similar process, a change in the way information is transmitted from generation to generation. In addition to the genetic information that is carried in the genes, a growing volume of cultural data is stored outside of these, in the nervous system, in the libraries and in the computers, that have grown in cultural importance, in the form of guardians and diffusers of information. In the future, these cultural elements will be dispersed without any human intervention — as is already happening on the internet and in cloud computing.

When this cycle is fulfilled, a new genetic takeover of power will be completed, because culture can develop completely independent of human biology.[201]

Scientific American[202] magazine even goes so far as to say that some scientists consider that we face an involution due to certain characteristics of modern life that can lead to changes that even prevent our survival: the need for greater study time has delayed reproduction. This would result in less intelligent population growth and population decline of the more intelligent.

---

[200] Moravec, H. *op. cit.*, p. 12.

[201] *Ibidem*, p. 11 et. seq.

[202] Ward, P., *op. cit.*, p. 57 et seq.

There is, in fact, a misunderstanding in the interpretation of this modern phenomenon, since it relates intelligence to formal education, which is not correct.

In addition, it seems that there is no relation between evolution and intelligence, since, as seen before, Darwinian evolution is not intrinsically intelligent, although it may result in intelligence. It seems evident that there is the possibility of something different from what the antecedent generates, otherwise the various species would not have appeared.

Moreover, the magazine itself concludes that human intelligence has a low degree of heredity and that researchers have found no sign that average intelligence is actually decreasing.

Another aspect of human and post-human evolution, as seen before, leads to the appearance of cyborgs. Man is more and more dependent on machines and cannot, even under certain circumstances, do without them.

In fact, in all cultures, Man has always used them, and he would not get where he is now without them. If all were simultaneously paralyzed and Man no longer could create machines, he would remain forever in prehistory, or could not even constitute himself as a species. We would, therefore, be from the first chipped stone, cyborgs. In addition, new tools, many times, are a mere evolution of previous equipment.[203]

Therefore, it seems strange the aversion sometimes found when it comes to more and more perfected machines because that has always been what Man has done until now. The machines are so viscerally linked to Man that tasks like calculations, which have always been related to intelligence, as one of their manifestations, when they were made by computers, much better than if done by humans, not only did not stop doing part of the list of intelligent things, but they have also become, for

---

[203] See HILLIS, Daniel. (2000). *O padrão gravado na pedra: as ideias simples que fazem os computadores funcionarem.* [The pattern engraved on stone: the simple ideas that make computers work.] (L. Neves, Trans.). Rio de Janeiro: Ciência Atual Rocco.

the general understanding, boring and therefore destined to be the field of computers, the machines that perform them. In this sense, besides examples of machines that play roles, previously strictly human and considered intelligent, check out, Enric Trillas.[204]

Thus, modern urban man must be equipped with modern technological tools, similar to his ancestors, equipped with war clubs and other tools considered high-tech[205] at the time. Thus, "...the human and the technological construct each other".[206]

To overcome the adversities of modern life, there are all sorts of machines and equipment: cell phones, glasses, and sunglasses, watches, vehicles, computers in various forms, extra batteries, chargers, cars, airplanes, clothes, etc. "The process of contemporary cyborgization is nothing more than the ineluctable continuation of this order that was formed by man, his departure from nature in the construction of a second artificial order".[207]

Concomitantly with the creation of technology by Man, technology has changed Man. "When he creates an artifact and uses it, man inserts it, in a way, into his own thinking".[208] As it happens, in the viewpoint of Guimarães, a parabiosis between Man and machines.

Man is constantly adapting to his tools, adapting himself to his interfaces, in the end, by changing his behaviors to submit to the demands of machines. As they become more complex and interconnected, man will be forced to serve them, as George Dyson states in his 1998 book: "Darwin among the machines":

> *all that humans are doing to make it easier to operate computer networks is at the same time, but for different reasons, make it easier for computer networks to operate*

---

[204] Ruiz, E. T. (1998). *La inteligencia artificial: máquinas y personas.* [Artificial intelligence: machines and people.] (pp. 13-14). Madrid: Editorial Debate.

[205] Aires Rover understands that technology is an artificial instrument of nature control (in the strict sense).

[206] Lemos, A., *op. cit.*, p. 165.

[207] *Idem.*

[208] Guimarães, A. S., *op. cit.*, p. 26.

> *human beings [...] Darwinian evolution, in one of those*
> *paradoxes that life has in abundance, can be the victim of*
> *its own success, unable to deal with the non-Darwinian*
> *process that it has created.*[209]

It seems that in this case the man/dog relationship is repeated, in which they no longer have the tasks that the wolves had with shelter, food, physical activity, hygiene and even reproduction and genetic improvement, since there is always a human being conforming to their needs and providing them. There are a number of other species that have evolved by specialization, which vitally depend on other species or other individuals of their own species to survive, either symbiotically or by other adaptations, such as koalas, pandas, and at least one species of abyssal fish. It should be added that sparrows only live in human settlements.

This happens because, according to Lemos[210], "the history of the artificial and humanity coincides fully since for man, to produce the artificial is an absolutely natural activity."

Lemos[211] understands that

> *The artificial, far from what we imagine in common sense,*
> *is deeply human. Thus, the dichotomy between the artificial*
> *and the natural loses its meaning and the question of the*
> *cyborg can be placed as a structure of humanity itself and*
> *as an undeniable characteristic of cyberculture. [...] The*
> *becoming of humanity is a cyborg becoming. The first man,*
> *who makes a weapon and an instrument from a stone, is the*
> *oldest ancestor of the cyborgs.*

In addition, medical science has developed a lot, making Man tend to eternity[212]. Yes, people live longer and better, with more quality of life — the appearance of so many diseases of modernity

---

[209] Ward, P., *op. cit.*, p. 61.

[210] Lemos, *op. cit.*, p.165. In this passage the author collates the lesson of MAZINE, E. (1991). *Artefacts. Vers une Ecologie de l'environnement Artificiel.* [Artifacts. Towards an Ecology of the Artificial Environment]. Paris: CGP. [211] Lemos, A., *op. cit.*, p. 165.

[211] Lemos, A., *op. cit.*, p. 165.

[212] Cinquepalmi, J. V., *op. cit.*, p. 42-51.

is not denied — and medicine has provided the appearance of increasingly advanced and complex prostheses.

This phenomenon was foreseen by Wiener[213], still in the fifties of the 20th century:

> There are a large number of problems concerning automatons that have nothing to do with our manufacturing system, but which serve to illustrate and shed light on the possibilities of communicative mechanisms in general, or for semi-medical purposes, for the prosthesis and replacement of human functions lost or weakened in certain unfortunate individuals. [...] There is a second class of machines that have much more direct medical value and more immediate relevance. These machines can be used to supply the limitations of the mutilated and the sensorially disabled, as well as to give new, potentially dangerous capabilities to the strong ones.

The author still mentions hearing aids and artificial lungs, anticipating a future in which human beings could replace mutilated, debilitated or even not functioning organs by functional cybernetic correspondents, such as those nowadays, just over fifty years later.

According to Loureiro[214], "under the cover of the post-human they shelter": "a) Projects of intervention in the genome that, in the limit, lead to a process of "creation" (*Züchtung*, in the same way as happens with animals). b) Robotics and *cyborg*, the "scenario of a fusion between man and machine".

It is interesting to note that the process of human cyborgization is characterized by the breaking of the border between two kingdoms: animal and mineral, for the rise of an animal-mineral creature. Truly it is to a certain extent the opposite path to that which has already been traced by evolution. As Moravec[215] recalls, citing

---

[213] Wiener, N. (1993) *Cibernética e sociedade: o uso humano de seres humanos*. [The Human Use Of Human Beings: Cybernetics And Society]. (J. P. Paes, Trans.). (9th ed., pp. 161) São Paulo: Cultrix.

[214] Loureiro, J. C. Nota de apresentação [Presentation note], *in*: Hebermas, J., *op. cit.*, p. 15.

[215] Moravec, H. (1992). *Homens e robots: o futuro da inteligência humana e robótica* [Mind Children: the future of robot and human intelligence]. (J. L. M. F. Lima, Trans.). (pp. 11-12). Lisboa: Gradiva.

Cairns-Smith, at first some crystals began to support organic material in their structures, resulting in the appearance of life. There was the mineral-animal junction. Now one sees the animal-mineral fusion with the cyborgs, descendants of the crystals, the first cyborgs, so to speak.

Perhaps the real question is whether the human being, like other animals, is a machine. It will be seen that one can conceptualize a machine as a living system and vice versa. Consequently, one can define a Man as being a machine.

If this conception is apprehended, the advent of the cyborg, human-machine part, cybernetic machine part, will not be so astonishing. There would only be the replacement of one type of machine, partly, by another type of machine.

Minsky[216] recalls that many people are offended when compared to a machine, having their brains compared to a computer (and their mind to a computer program, he adds). However, he asks:

> But if you're not a machine, what makes you an authority on what it feels like to be a machine? A person might reply, "I think, therefore I know how the mind works." But that would be suspiciously like saying, "I drive my car, therefore I know how its engine works." Knowing how to use something is not the same as knowing how it works.

This brings to light the ancient Taoist story of the sages by the river fishing. One of them turns to the other and says "I wish I was like the fish. They are so happy." To which the other questioned: "But how can you know if the fish are happy if you are not a fish?" The first sage retorts: "How do you know I do not know what the fish feel if you're not me to know what I know about what the fish feel?"

However, Minsky[217] says that one cannot keep in mind the traditional concept of machine, mechanics, pulleys, levers, locomo-

[216] Minsky, M. (1988). *The society of mind.* (pp. 30). New York: Simon & Schuster.
[217] *Idem.*

tives, typewriters. He concludes that the term machine does not lead anywhere.

This question did not go unnoticed by Kurzweil[218]:

> *It seems to me that we have a problem with the word "machine," because we grew up believing that machines can only behave in a mechanical way. This view is obsolete, because the ways we use the word "machine" are outdated. For centuries, words such as "machine" and "mechanical" were used to describe simple devices such as pulleys, lever, locomotives, and typewriters. The word "computer" has also inherited from the past the sense of insignificance that comes from doing boring arithmetic through many small, boring steps. Because of this, our prior experience can sometimes be a disability. Our preconceptions of what machines can do date back to what happened when we put together systems of only a few hundred or thousands of parts. And that did not prepare us to think about assemblies of billions of type-pieces like the brain. Although we are already building machines with many millions of pieces, we continue to think as if nothing has changed. We must learn to change how we think about phenomena that work on larger scales.*

It is clear, therefore, that the application of the Law of Accelerating Returns, which will be dealt with later, to human evolution, will only bring out the virtual cyborg that exists in man, endowed with an artificial nature.

Thus, post-humanity — not only by the denomination which has as reference the humanity itself, the Man — will be only the continuity of the human evolutionary process, no longer in totally biological bases, or even, at a certain moment, partially biological but in a cybernetic basis. This is due to the very human nature that has been moving away from the biological and mineral nature since prehistoric times, creating its own surrounding nature and, in creating it, constituting itself as a Man, as a being who has opted, to the maximum extent possible, to go away from the biological nature, to live the way

---

[218] Kurzweil, R. (1999). *The age of intelligent machines.* (3rd reprint, pp. 215). Cambridge: MIT Press.

that is peculiar to him, among the artificial world created by himself.

With a special mention in J.M. Balkin[219], who went beyond Derrida, what is intended is not to destroy man or humanity, but to deconstruct it so that one can apprehend new ways of conceiving Man or, more specifically, life and Person for purposes of protection and legal regulation.

Here the end of Man is not advocated for its destruction, but rather as a consequence of the singularity and, before it, the cyborgization of Man, which began in prehistory, concomitantly with the use of tools.

Man as a species, purely biological, may even survive this remarkable event, but, theoretically, he will probably lose its dominance of preponderance in the world, being replaced by smarter beings, whether synthetic or cyborgs, in the usual conception of the term.

This deconstructive philosophical orientation allows the absorption by the concept of a cybernetic living being, autopoietic, of the traditional concept, since it presents only a reinterpretation and a re-signification of the polysemic concept of life.

Similarly, the legal concept of person and the legal definition of person, at least in Brazil, Portugal, and Spain, can perfectly accommodate the robot as a legal person, once again, what is intended is only a re-signification of its terms, constructed from the characterizing elements of the person who were used by the Law to achieve the legal concept of person.

Once the concept is constituted, the next step is its deconstruction to amplify its meaning, without, however, removing or erasing the original meaning. Thus, the legal concept of the person includes not only human beings, but also any being or

---

[219] Balkin, J.M. *Deconstructive Practice and Legal Theory*. Retrieved from: <http://www.yale.edu/lawweb/jbalkin/articles/decprac1.htm>. Last access date: March 30, 2008.

entity that holds the characteristics that served as a basis to the construction of the legal concept of the person for the human being.

Hence, the post-human condition, although it may mean the disappearance of the human species in its present configuration, will have as its protagonist the species created by the Man himself. By renouncing his condition of being biological, Man will have made the choice — although the practical result cannot be assured — of being succeeded by his creature, cybernetics, totally away from the natural and completely artificial, perhaps eternal, aiming to realize an idea of building a reality that is his own and inherent, created by himself and not found in the raw state.

Maybe Man will reach the ultimate end — long pursued, perhaps in an unthinking or inconsequential way, of being the creator and no longer the creature, even if he has to, in the transformation of creature into creator, renounce his biological nature.

Finally, in post-humanity, Man will still persist in his creature. By his extinction, it will become eternal.

3.6 Legal Personality

The law regulates legal personality as being, in general, the ability to exercise rights and assume obligations, distinguishing the holders, legal subjects, from the legal objects.

These two categories are not mistaken because they are in such a situation that one depends on the other to exist, since it is not possible to talk about the subject of rights without the corresponding objects of these rights.

Likewise, there can be no objects of rights without the existence of the holder of these rights.

The fact is that positive law regulates legal personality taking care of its emergence and extinction, conditions for its exercise and requirements for the aptitude to have it, while in doctrine, it is considered the nature of the norms that care of it: constitutive or declarative, as well as its subjective and objective aspects, among other important issues.

3.6.1 Declaratory or Constitutive Nature?

Traditionally, one can reason that it takes two primary aspects: the right of the individual personality is beyond legal, that is to say, the Man is endowed with personality independent of the Law that can only recognize it. When it does not, it violates the anthropocentric character of the Law.

Thus, the norm that violates any rule contrary to the individual legal personality departs from its legal character and becomes unlawful or contrary to the declaratory nature of Law regarding the human personality.

The other current considers that the Law would be constitutive of the personality, that is, instead of being a logical legal concept, the personality — legal when treated by the Law — would be an objective or positive legal concept.

For Vasconcelos[220],

> *The Law has no power or legitimacy to attribute the individual personality. It is limited to determine, to verify the hominity, quality of human being. It has neither legitimacy nor power to exclude. If any legislator, judge or official decrees or decides to exclude or fail to recognize the personality of a human person, his personality does not cease to exist. It continues, just like before. It will only have been disrespected or disturbed. If through the exercise of power, the personality is disrespected, if the person is treated as non-person, as an animal or as a thing, he does not cease to be what he is: a person, with all the dignity inherent to him.*

This debate may be unnecessary in practice because, by any traditional way, the Human Being can be considered as a person and, thus, as a subject of law, as endowed with legal personality. However, it is doctrinally important for the development of the theme.

In any case, those who understand the declaratory nature seem to mix extra-juridical elements with legal ones, causing

---

[220] Vasconcelos, P. P. de, *op. cit.* p. 6.

an unnecessary confusion and without connection with the historical context, since the right of the personality was not always recognized for all Men.

Thus, if there are extralegal or metalegal elements that inform what constitutes the Man as subject of rights, its fulfillment, by any entity, takes, by virtue of the logical reasoning, notably the deontic logic and its system of major premise, minor premise and conclusion, to the understanding that whatever meets these requirements will deserve the same treatment, unless it remains tied to the anthropocentric paradigm. The anthropocentric paradigm that, emphasizing, with all reason presently prevails — to allocate the condition of human being as a presupposition of legal personality. However, as can be seen, this does not hold true as in previous times, when some men had no personality (partial or full), nor at present with the legal person and in the future, under the premise of technological singularity, with the robots.

What matters in this work is knowing what allows man to be endowed with personality, what makes him human and thus, in the eyes of the anthropocentric paradigm of the Law, **person**, and then, from that perspective, to search and try to answer if a robot with the same characteristics would deserve the same legal treatment.

If, on the other hand, it is a positive law that defines the legal personality, it is sufficient to verify whether the law allows other entities to be considered as subjects of law, expressly or implicitly.

It should be emphasized, revealing the elements that, together or individually, result in the personality of the individual in legal form, it is legitimate to say that if another entity is found endowed with these same elements, the logical conclusion is that the same legal *status* of person, of individual and not of person is attributed to him by equivalence or fiction, as it happens with legal persons.

Therefore, whatever the current adopted — apart from the anthropocentric paradigm — one can conclude, attained the technological singularity, by the occurrence of the singular legal personality of the robot.

The human person certainly has its legal personality tied to a legal fact, while the legal person has it bound or resulting from a legal act. This is a very important detail that allows asserting that the legal entity is a fiction, under which, usually, some physical persons desired its creation. And the physical person, although this person results, with the conception, from a desire, from a human will, this person does not have at its base another physical person, since his personality derives from the fact of its birth, live birth, or even of its conception.

As the cybernetic/autopoietic concept of life is defended, the robot can be alive and therefore arises from a legal fact, birth.

3.6.2 Objective and Subjective Personality Right

Along with the doctrinal discussion about the nature of the right of personality, a lesson can be learned from Vasconcelos[221]:

> *The Law deals with personality in an objective and sub-jective way. The guardianship of the human personality has an objective and a subjective aspect. The first can be called the objective right of personality and the second, the subjective right of personality. This distinction corresponds to what exists, in general, between objective law and subjective right, now referred specifically to person-ality.*

When discussing the subjective right of personality Vasconce-los[222] manifests this way:

> *The subjective right of personality is a legal position: the legal position of that individual, in his capacity as a person in law, in the circumstances surrounding him and the other people who surround him and who are in personal, family and professional contact, neighborhood or of another order, with him. It is a concrete personal position, it is not an objective, abstract position, like that of a citizen.*
>
> *It is a legal position because it is a position in the Law, with*

---

[221] Vasconcelos, P. P. de, *op. cit.*, p. 47.
[222] *Ibidem*, p.56.

legal content, which is not confused with its moral position, although it has a close contact with it.

It is an advantageous position. Being an individual legal person is good, not bad. It is better to be so than not to be.

The subjective right of personality is surrounded by skillful legal means for the successful defense of the dignity of its holder. These legal means are powers.

Regarding the objective law, the author clarifies his universalist, supranational position, founded on reasons of public order, good customs and the common good, unrelated to private autonomy. It relates to the very defense of humanity, of globality and the whole human species. Thus, as in the lessons of Arendt[223], a dual character arises: the defense of the universality of Men and each of us individually. Finally, it aims to respect the dignity of the human person.

It would be better to say the dignity of the **person**, to be able to embrace all people, although not human. Even because

> *It should not be forgotten that the very idea of equal moral dignity among men was the result of a long process of struggle, which was only consolidated when the written law became a general and uniform rule applicable indiscriminately to all members of an organized society.*[224]

Later, commenting on the treatment of the issue in history, Vasconcelos[225] reveals:

> *The guardianship of personality has to do with the community and with the person, with the State and with the Citizen, with oneself and with others. In it, the objective guardianship and the subjective right coexist harmoniously.*

This dialogue, Vasconcelos[226] understands, must be deepened. In its origin is the great difference in the way of thinking the in-

---

[223] Arendt, H. *op. cit.*, p.
[224] Gordilho, H. J. de S. *op. cit.*, p. 92.
[225] Vasconcelos, P. P. de. *op. cit.*, p. 49.
[226] *Idem.*

sertion of the person in the world, between Platonic-Aristotelian objectivism and Stoic subjectivism. These two modes of thinking have divided and continue to divide European-minded thinking.

In discussing the protection of the dignity of the human person as an object of the general right of personality, Garcia[227] states that "There is, therefore, an intimate relationship between the rights of the personality and the principle of the dignity of the human person." And he adds:

> *Thus, the 'dignity of the human person' stems from the recognition of the person as a being integrated with nature, endowed with an **evolved rationality**, with the **capacity to recognize oneself** in the other, to relate to him, exercising his aptitude for dialogue and love (our emphasis).*[228]

However, the same author[229] acknowledges that,

> *However, this notion of 'dignity of the human person' underlies a particular conception of the person ('insular conception'), which is being challenged. [...] The "insular conception" — according to ANTONIO JUNQUEIRA DE AZEVEDO — proposes that only Man is endowed with reason and will, he notes that he would distinguish it from other living beings, placing Man on a higher level.*

> *[...] ANTONIO JUNQUEIRA DE AZEVEDO: "From an ontological point of view, or a view of reality, the insular conception of the human person is dualistic: man and nature do not encounter, they are at different levels: they are respectively subject and object. The man 'king of creation' sees and thinks about nature. Only man is rational and capable of wanting. Man is radically different from other beings: only he is self-conscious. Nature is a raw fact, that is, without value in itself.*

> *INGO WOLFGANG SARLET: "[...] both Kant's thinking and all the conceptions which hold that dignity are the exclusive attribute of the human person — are at least in*

---

[227] Garcia, E. C. (2007). *Direito geral da personalidade no sistema jurídico brasileiro*. [General personality rights in the Brazilian legal system.] (pp. 118). São Paulo: Juarez de Oliveira.

[228] *Idem.*

[229] *Ibidem*, p.125.

> *theory subject to criticism of excessive anthropocentrism, notably in that they maintain that the human person, in function of its rationality, occupies the privileged place in relation to the other living beings."*

> *ANTONIO JUNQUEIRA DE AZEVEDO states "[...] the proper conception of a new ethic, founded on man as being integrated with nature, a special participant in the vital flow that has been going through it for billions of years, and whose specific note is not in reason and will, which also the higher animals possess, or self-consciousness, which at least chimpanzees also have, but in the opposite direction, in the capacity of man to leave himself, to recognize in the other an equal, to use language, to dialogue and even more especially in his vocation to love as a spiritual gift to others".*

3.6.3 Legal Personality and Subjective Rights

It is also necessary to clarify the distinction between legal personality and subjective rights, these being the permission given by the legal norm to do or not do something. Whoever has this permission has a subjective right. Whoever does not possess it may not have the right, but still have the ability to have it.

Vasconcelos[230] defines that legal personality is the quality of being a person of law.

For Garcia[231],

> *The word "personality" has in its meaning the notion of a set, a collection of different aspects. Thus dictionaries define: "Personality: a set of qualities that define the individuality of a moral person; set of characteristics that distinguish a person, a group of people, a nation; set of psychic aspects which, taken as a unit, distinguish a person, especially those directly related to social values".*

The faculty is the power of subjective right, latent, in theory, virtual, which may or may not come to be carried out, if the Law

---

[230] Vasconcelos, P. P. de, *op. cit.*, p.5.
[231] Garcia, E. C., *op. cit.*, p. 109.

thus allows or deny, resulting or not, in subjective rights, that is, these rights belong to the individual.

The faculty is not an act, for this is what has already been done, that is, it's perfect, done. The faculty is not yet being done, although it is a being. For the simple fact that the faculty is something, it is, it is a being. Only what is nothing is not being. Nothing virtual cannot be or become anything real.

The virtual is apt to become a being. The robot in question, although not for the legal doctrine in general, a being, a person, by the mere fact of being, is potentially a person, just being, as said, becoming, becoming in the real world, in the same way as the unborn child, with the characteristics that allow him to be treated in this way.

Thus denying the possibility of the robot becoming a person is denying itself the existence of the robot, denying that it is, since admitting its existence, in the real world, logically one must admit that it can be and will be within its own order of realities, which, at the moment, has not yet reached the real capacity to be a person, but that it is virtually. It is enough, therefore, that circumstances allow the virtual person of the robot to fulfill itself, that it will become a real person and it is up to the Law to allow, under its field of activity, its scope of material validity, so that the robot becomes a person, in a legal sense; and that the robot be endowed with legal personality.

It is always noted, in the more than ten years of the term robotic law in Brazil, manifestations of astonishment or amazement in the juridical interlocutors, crystallized in their anthropocentric conceptions when the legal personality of the robot is affirmed.

Regarding the laic and even abiding disbelief, the words of Moravec[232] are included: "Shock was also the first reaction when we suggested the number of atoms contained in a fragment of mat-

---

[232] Moravec, H. (1992). *Homens e robots: o futuro da inteligência humana e robótica* [Mind Children: the future of robot and human intelligence]. (J. L. M. F. Lima, Trans.). (pp. 269). Lisboa: Gradiva.

ter, or the distance to the nearest stars, or the size and age of the universe. "

Australian futurologist Paul Wildman[233], in discussing different artificial life forms, argues that tomorrow's robotic lifestyle must be legally considered a 'person' or a 'unit of life'. He predicts the possibility of tomorrow's economic entity to be set up in a *'compcornation'*, that is, a computer-directed corporation, e.g., *technoborgs*, *orgoborgs* etc. In fact, he notes that, in a way, this is already happening with the companies that deal with the Stock Exchange — in the fall of the 1987 stock exchange, computers continued to sell while share prices fell. The issue of the rights and responsibilities of robots would include the rights and responsibilities of robots themselves, other life forms and their right to existence, democracy, etc., and the rights and responsibilities of computer-driven corporations.

Also, it is convenient to keep in mind that the faculty is not mistaken with the subjective right. Classic is the example given by Telles Júnior[234] of the mother who married again and lost the parental right (article 393 of the former Brazilian Civil Code of 1916), as for the children of the previous marriage. She lost the right to exercise power, not faculty. The law did not allow her to exercise this right, so much so that, widowed, she was able to exercise the right denied, demonstrating that the subjective right can be granted, withdrawn and granted again.

Restrictions also exist concerning the public servant, in relation to the business administration and the bankrupt. The person who stops being a public servant can once again enjoy the right to run a business and the bankrupt, once rehabilitated, can resume business activity. These are legal limitations to full capacity that can be restored in supervening legal facts.

Thus, the reality, the concretization of the virtual person of the robot, occurring as predicted, will force the objective right to deal with it, for those who understand that the Civil Code no longer

---

[233] Wildman, P., *op. cit.*, p. 36.
[234] Telles Júnior, G., op. cit, p. 305.

allows it. Because the real human being is a being in time, a historical phenomenon, there is nothing that prevents the robot from being considered in the same way except an anthropocentric preconception.

3.6.4 Legal Person

It is adopted the understanding that the legal person is a fiction of the law, a creation of it, as a result of the economic and social evolution of the society that started to demand a form of specialization of material assets focused on the development of its own activities with previously calculated risks.

The present work does not delve into the issues related to the legal entity because it advocates the thesis that the legal personality to be eventually attributed to the robots will be individual, such as that of natural persons and not collective as that of legal entities.

3.6.5 The Appearance of Legal Personality

It is important to emphasize that art. 45 of the Brazilian Civil Code does not expressly state that the legal person is *born, arises* with the appropriate registration. The phrase used is "The legal existence of legal persons of private law begins...".[235] It should be noted, therefore, that although the registration of the company is a constitutive act, it is, according to the Civil Code, for **legal** and non-legal purposes.

By this we mean that the Brazilian National Law recognizes the existence of the company, of the legal person, *before* registration, which serves to be assigned the legal capacity, autonomously, under the terms of the Law and for *legal* purposes, for purposes set forth in *Law* — and not, more broadly, legal — to be able to establish rights and assume obligations.

---

[235] *Código Civil, Código de Processo Civil e Constituição Federal* [Civil Code, Code of Civil Procedure and Federal Constitution]. (2004). (6th ed., pp. 281). RT, São Paulo.

So much so that the Brazilian Civil Code itself recognizes the existence of a special asset (article 994) and the retroactivity of the effects of the registration, if done within the legal term after the constitution of the company, so that it has a personality since the date of its creation, before registration.

Thus, the Law recognizes that the **real** existence of the legal person, in the form of a company, begins before registration, so that, if the registration occurs within thirty days of the creation of the corporate legal entity, its effects retroact to reach the inaugural date, of the real-world appearance of that person.

Also, the doctrine takes care of a *de facto* corporation, which, although it is a company, is not registered and, therefore, does not have legal personality, in the form of the law, to securitize, *per se*, rights.

The verb to be in the present tense has imponderable force. After all, the reality *is*, and the Law says how it *should be*. In other words, the Law is based on reality and cannot depart from it, unless exceptionally, for, in its restricted, shallow and limited field of incidence, to say how the Law will treat reality, as it should be, in the legal sphere, what it is, or even what it is not.

It is clear, therefore, that the legal entity exists independently of the record, but this assures personality, legal capacity and legal existence in succession to real existence. This way, one clearly sees the separation between real existence, legal existence, legal personality and person, concepts that are not mistaken, as well as that of a human being with a person, which is endowed with legal personality, under the terms of the Civil Law.

It should be noted that when a legal entity does not yet have a legal existence, although it has a real existence, those who respond by its acts are its partners, one, some, or all, as is the case with the incapable, by its representative.

The fiction legal person, the creation of positive law is the consecration in the law that there are other people besides human beings whose existence are independent of the Law, which may have legal personality, provided that the Positive Law so desires.

3.7 What is life?

Although it may seem obvious what life is, much of the scientific doctrine is grounded in an organic conception of life, in the way it presents itself on Earth.

This can be and is only a way of understanding this phenomenon that arose on planet Earth, but whose probability of occurrence in other systems of the Universe is quite high, not only in forms similar to those found here but in completely different ways, obeying to the own circumstances of these other systems.

However, the discussion of the existence of extraterrestrial life is not the object of this work. Even so, one cannot fail to argue that the traditional biological conception of life can be deconstructed and reinterpreted, as did Maturana and Varela[236], with their autopoietic theory of life and with the cybernetic conceptions of life, both used here to construct the thesis that robots can be considered as living beings.

Even traditional biological approaches to life are still subject to much controversy.

3.7.1 Characteristical Elements of Life in Traditional Doctrine

A recurring idea is that being alive[237] is being dynamic, detaining the capacity to reproduce, to evolve as a species, resulting from a process that ends with death.

In fact, one tries to define what it is to be alive by enumerating its properties and not by the search of its essence.

---

[236] Maturana, H. R.; Varela, F. J. (2004). *De máquinas y seres vivos. Autopoiesis: La organización de lo vivo* [Autopoiesis and Cognition: The Realization of the Living] (6th ed.) Buenos Aires: Coedição Editorial Universitaria e Editorial Lumen.

[237] Wiener, N. (1971). *Deus, Golem e Cia: um comentário sobre certos pontos de contato entre cibernética e religião* [God and Golem, Inc.: A Comment on Certain Points where Cybernetics Impinges on Religion] (L. Hegenberg and O. S. da Mota, Trans.). São Paulo: Cultrix. p. 152. The author understands that "In addition, living things are not alive (according to all indications) beyond the level of molecules."

Relating life to reproduction is absolutely incongruous. Not all life can reproduce. Take, for example, beings that, for whatever reason, endogenous or exogenous cannot produce a lineage, as it does even with humans. Would sterile people — or any living being — lose their living condition?

It would be argued that it is something accidental, episodic and that in general, human beings reproduce themselves, as the rest, in general the other living beings reproduce themselves as well.

In this way, the *reproducible* adjective only comes to be considered as one of the definers of the living condition if applied generically to all genetically identical individuals, even if one or the other is sterile.

But what to say when all individuals with the same genetic traits are unable to reproduce as the mules or lingers or male tigon (resulting from the crossing of lions and tigers)? Are they not beings? Is it possible to assign them the adjective "alive"?

Of course, reproduction cannot define the living being.

Another characteristic that presents itself as inherent to living beings is autonomy, so much so that, according to Maturana and Varela,[238] whenever one observes something that seems autonomous, the spontaneous reaction is to consider it alive. This idea arose with the vitalism of Aristotle, who influenced the whole history of biology, always seeking to explain the phenomenology of living systems under some peculiar organizing force. By the way, check out Freud's approach to the subject[239].

However, some species are not autonomous but are completely dependent on other species or other individuals of their own species. Not even mortality, which would be the opposite of the eternity of life, can be a valid criterion, since it is known of beings that, it seems, do not die, at least from natural causes. Thus death cannot be in a broad and general way, the opposite of life, to sustain a concept of life.

---

[238] Maturana, H.; Varela, F., *op. cit.*, p. 63.
[239] Freud, S. (1996). *O estranho*. (The stranger) *In*: Edição Standard das Obras Completas. (J. Salomão, Trans.). (Vol. 17, pp. 273). Rio de Janeiro: Imago.

Given the complexity of the topic and not being at the heart of the present work, those elements adopted here are considered sufficient.

3.7.2 The Autopoietic Concept of Life

It seems evident today that only physical factors operate on living beings and not an inexplicable immaterial force. Therefore, for Maturana and Varela, any biological phenomenon can be described as arising from the interaction of physical-chemical processes whose relations are specified by the context of its definition.[240] In this attempt, these Chilean authors focus on the individuals instead of the species, presenting a mechanistic view and not being influenced by factors that are outside the physical environment.

But again, it is questioned, is it possible to consider a machine as a living system as if it were alive? For Maturana and Varela only prejudice and an, *a priori,* resistance would justify a negative response.

First of all, one must take into account that "machine" is just a word!

These authors understand that living beings are machines, autopoietic systems since they transform matter in themselves in such a way that their product is their own organization: *"In other words, we hold that the notion of autopoiesis is necessary and sufficient for characterizing the organization of living systems."*[241]

The authors enumerate some reasons that critics point out not to accept that living beings are machines and, of course, it is argued that machines can be living beings if they are autopoietic machines:

> In general, machines are considered to be man-made artifacts with deterministic properties that are perfectly predefined, at least conceptually. Living systems are considered autonomous and therefore unpredictable. If living systems are machines they could be man-made and it seems incredible that man can make a living system.[242]

---

[240] Maturana, H.; Varela, F., *op. cit.*, loc. cit.
[241] *Ibidem*, p. 73.
[242] *Ibidem*, p.63.

The aforementioned authors find it easy to disqualify this thought because it leads to the understanding that living systems are too complex for human intelligence, or that they derive from unknown principles, or that the principles that generate them are decidedly impossible to be known, judging it to be of aprioristic judgments without proper proof.

I would add that, therefore, the defenders of that idea fought by Maturana cannot use the theorems of Göddel's incompleteness.

Kurzweil[243] states that "human intelligence, though quite complex, is not infinitely complex." Hence it is not difficult to conclude that the complexity of living systems is not infinite as well, resulting in that it must be understandable by the human brain.

Although Gödel's[244] incompleteness[245] is well known, which allows saying that we can neither prove nor deny, in the scope of mathematics, that certain mathematical problems are true or not, this does not mean that the answer cannot be known, which is just that. It is not that the solution should point to the possibility or the impossibility of proving itself, but that there are truly issues that cannot be proven or refuted, a fact that can be meta-mathematically proven.

Thus, the Chilean authors' reservation that the premises were not proven does not imply that they cannot be proven or that they cannot be refuted as the authors do. Therefore, it does not seem to be a matter of incompleteness. What should be sought is to demonstrate that they cannot effectively be neither proven nor refuted.

What these biologists assert is that anyone who manifests a view contrary to the possibility of considering living beings as autopoietic machines does so either with mistaken assumptions or without substantiating what they assert, which cannot be scientifically tolerated.

However, with a special mention in Gödel, the authors can be contradicted in their information that the principles that generate

---

[243] Kurzweil, R. (1999). *The age of intelligent machines.* (pp. 16, 3rd reprint, pp. 146). Cambridge, Mass.: MIT Press.

[244] Goldstein, R., *op. cit.*, p. 139.

[245] Gödel, K., *op. cit.*

life would be unintelligible by man, that is, beyond the human capacity for understanding, since it is possible that they cannot be effectively known by Man if, inexorably, they cannot be proved, in the ways advocated by logic and mathematics, not being a human limitation, but a characteristic of these principles, which has yet to be demonstrated.

Therefore, there are certain questions for which it is possible to demonstrate that there are answers, but that these can never be discovered. So much so that no man has ever solved an insoluble problem, nor has a computer treated an incomputable problem. "Many post-Gödel, scientifically minded thinkers have stated that they have heard, within the strange music of Gödel's mathematical theorems, news of essential human nature".[246] From the theorems of Gödel's incompleteness, they came to conclusions about what Man is; or, to be more precise, about what he *is not*. It should be emphasized that Gödel's theorems inform, according to this line of reasoning, "what our minds simply cannot be".[247]

In the same sense, Church-Turing's[248] thesis indicates that if a problem can be solved by the human brain, it can be solved by a computer, or rather by a Turing machine. Therefore, using this reasoning, if a problem cannot be solved by the human brain, it may not be for a Turing machine.

This is the heart of artificial intelligence: it is possible to construct machines to perform intelligent functions whose solutions are attributed possibly to human brains. However, this assertion takes into account the current paradigm under which computers are made, nothing preventing that under the paradigm of technological uniqueness, computers cannot solve problems beyond the capabilities of the human solution.

Thus, even though adhering to the critique of the aprioristic resistance to accepting that living beings are autopoietic machines,

---

[246] *Ibidem*, p. 167-168.

[247] *Idem*.

[248] Check out an explanation of the thesis in: <http://plato.stanford.edu/entries/church-turing/>. Last access date: February 23, 2009.

one cannot, concerning Gödel's lessons, also aprioristically deny that the principles from which life is derived are unintelligible, although they may be or are still misunderstood, as well as certain that those who think so do not prove what they say.

To the extent that the nature of the living organization is ignored, it is not possible to recognize when one is faced with a system that possesses it. Generally, it is accepted that plants and animals are alive, but this is done based on the enumeration of their properties, which the Chilean authors refute. Even so, they claim that when these same characteristics appear in a concrete or conceptual system made by Man, critics begin to emphasize other properties and no synthetic system is accepted as alive.

Thus, it seems that those who do not accept synthetic and cybernetic systems as living, they do so because they are linked to a biocentric or organic paradigm, glimpsed only by experience, without a theoretical basis, by the observation of its components and not by its relations as a game of interactions and transformations.

For Maturana and Varela[249], it cannot be demonstrated that a system is alive with an appeal to its components, but to its mechanistic organization, so that it is evident how all its properties arise from it:

> *"The fact that living systems are machines cannot prove to be tied to its components, but one must show its mechanistic organization in such a way that it is obvious how all its properties arise from it. To do this, we will first describe the class of machines that are living systems, and then we will indicate how the peculiar properties that characterize them can arise as a consequence of the organization of this class of machines.*
>
> *Among machines, there are those that keep some of their variables constant or within a limited range of values. In the organization of these machines, this must be expressed in such a way that the process is defined as fully verified within the limits that the same organization of the machine specifies.*

---

[249] Maturana, H. R.; Varela, F. J. (2004). *De máquinas y seres vivos. Autopoiesis: La organización de lo vivo* [Autopoiesis and Cognition: The Realization of the Living] (6th ed., pp. 66) Buenos Aires: Coedição Editorial Universitaria e Editorial Lumen.

Such machines are homeostatic, and all feedback is internal to them. If one says that there is a machine M with feedback around it, in such a way that the effects of its output affect its input, in fact, it is speaking of a larger machine, M, which in its defining organization includes the medium to its return and the feedback loop.

Autopoietic machines are homeostatic machines. However, its peculiarity lies not in this, but in the fundamental variable that keeps it constant. An autopoietic machine is a machine organized as a system of concatenated components production processes in such a way that they produce components that 1) generate the processes (relations) of production that are realized through their continuous interactions and transformations, and 2) constitute the machine as a unit in physical space. Consequently, an autopoietic machine continually specifies and produces its own organization through the production of its own components, under conditions of continuous disruption and compensation of these perturbations (component production). "[250]

The Chilean authors are not isolated among those who consider non-biological systems as living beings. Although using different criteria Lehman-Wilzig[251] says:

But the essential question remains — can these machines be considered to be alive? Kement presents six criteria which distinguish living from inanimate matter: metabolism, locomotion, reproducibility, individuality, intelligence, a 'natural'(non-artificial) composition. In all six, he concludes, AI servomechanisms clearly pass the test. Even an AI critic such as Weizenbaum admits that computers are sufficiently 'complex and autonomous' to be called an 'organism' with 'self-consciousness' and an ability to be 'socialized'. He sees "no way to put a bound on the degree of intelligence such an organism could, at least in principle, attain", although from his critical vantage point, not in the visible future. [252]

---

[250] *Idem* et seq.

[251] Lehman-Wilzig, S. N. *Frankenstein Unbound: towards a legal definition of artificial intelligence*. Retrieved from:
<profslw.com/wp-content/uploads/academic/40._Frankenstein_Unbound.
Towards_a_legal_definition...pdf>. Last access date: February 22, 2009.

[252] *Ibidem*, p. 2.

3.7.3 The Cybernetic Concept of Life

The cybernetic concept of life resembles that defended by Maturana and Varela[253]. Among others, someone who sought to build it was Korzeniewski[254]:

> *A definition of life (a living individual) in cybernetic terms is proposed. In this formulation, life (a living individual) is defined as a network of inferior negative feedbacks (regulatory mechanisms) subordinated to (being at service of) a superior positive feedback (potential of expansion). It is suggested that this definition is the minimal definition, necessary and sufficient, for life to be distinguished from inanimate phenomena and, as such, it describes the essence of life.*

This set of negative *feedback* should serve the purpose of the individual, that is, maintain their identity. This negative *feedback* is present, according to Dawkins,[255] on several machines that behave as if they are motivated.

This concept, Korzeniewski understands, will serve both the biological life currently found on Earth as well as the extinct, beyond the existing life, extraterrestrial.

It is interesting to note that the author sees in the robots the existence of the following characteristics related to life:

I) High complexity because computers and robots can be more complex than simple organisms like bacteria;

II) Hierarchical structure, because they are characterized by complex internal processes ("functions") and have negative *feedback* and,

---

[253] Maturana, H.; Varela, F., *op. cit.* p. 66.

[254] Korzenieswski, Bernard. *Cybernetic formulation of the definition of life.* Institute of Molecular Biology, Jagiellonian University, al. Mickiewicza 3, 31-120 Kraków, Poland. Retrieved from: <holtz.org/Library/Natural%20Science/Biology/DefiningLife.doc>. Last access date: January 27, 2009.

[255] Dawkins, R., *op. cit.*, p. 113.

III) They are structurally and functionally integrated entities.

However, he does not envisage robots being living beings because they do not have the purpose of maintaining their identity. There seems to be a limited and contextualized perception in the state of contemporary technology on the author's concept, since, when singularity occurs, robots may indeed be self-conscious and thus possibly wish to maintain their individual identity.

It should be noted that the author does not consider as a living being, in the cybernetic sense, sterile varieties such as worker bees or even queens, because they do not have a purpose of their own, but that of third parties, of the group to which they belong, "They are not cybernetic individuals (evoluons) because they serve the purpose of a larger entity (the colony)."[256]

Interestingly, the author considers cancer cells as cybernetic individuals, citing that they, despite being in an individual, have their own goals, including an example of cancer that has become parasitic and transmissible.[257]

The importance of Maturana and Varela's studies for cybernetics is recognized by many, even being a milestone for the perspectives of post-humanity. Hayles[258] thus states, in dealing with the second phase of cybernetics, marked by the reflexivity that has become the self-organization:

> It all started with a frog.
>
> But a young neurophysiologist from Chile, Humberto Maturana, was also on the research team [...]. Pushing the envelope of traditional scientific objectivity, he developed a new way of talking about life and about the observer's role in describing living systems. Entwined with the epistemological revolution he started the three stories we have been following: the reification of information, the cultural and technological construction of the cyborg, and the transformation of the human into the posthuman. As a result of

---

[256] *Ibidem*, p.280.

[257] *Ibidem*, p.283.

[258] HAYLES, N. Katherine, *op. cit.*, p. 131.

*work by Maturana and his collaborator, Francisco Varela,
all three stories took decisive turns during the second wave
of cybernetics, from 1960 to 1985.*

She recalls that Maturana described the nervous system and the subsystem of the frog's vision, saying that between them a high processing capacity and specific communication is established (regarding this species). He got these data by implanting a circuit in the brain of the batrachian that happened to be an amphibian cyborg, that is, the brain was reprogrammed not to meet the will of the animal, but, from third parties. He no longer belonged to the animal.

He could see that what the eye sent to the brain was a set of data already properly subjected to sophisticated processing, resulting in the conclusion that is one of the foundations of his theory: "All that is said is said by an observer."[259]

One can see, therefore, that, contrary to the original cybernetic manifest that informed that the important thing was the behavior of the system, Maturana understands that the autopoietic process, generator of the behavior is what counts.

As we have seen, first-wave researchers concentrated on building artifacts that would behave as cybernetic mechanisms: John von Neumann's self-reproducing machines; Claude Shannon's electronic rat; Ross Ashby's homeostat. By contrast, Maturana and others in the second wave look to systems instantiating processes that count as autopoietic. The homeostat might behave cybernetically, for example, but it does not count as an autopoietic machine because it does not produce the components that produce its organization. Perhaps because of this emphasis on process, autopoietic theory has proven readily adaptable to the analysis of social systems. In autopoietic theory, the machine of interest is much more likely to be the state than Robocop or Terminator.[260]

---

[259] *Idem.* Hayles is mentioning the work *What the Frog's Eye Tells the Frog's Brains* by J. Y. Lettivin, H. R. Maturana, W. S. McCulloch and W.H. Pitts, published in 1968, in the book *The Mind: Biological Approaches to its Functions*, p. 233-258.
[260] Hayles, N. K., *op. cit.*, p. 141.

Nowadays, the possibility of artificial life is considered, like the one created in computer systems, through specific programs.

This is the third phase of cybernetics. Here, unlike the circularity of Maturana's autopoiesis, the image of a spiral better describes this phase, since the emphasis is on making the system evolve by accumulating all previous gains. The one who paves the way to the third phase of cybernetics is Varela, co-editor of the annals of the first European conference on the subject. In his introduction, "For a Practice of Standalone Systems," he and co-author Paul Borgine expose their view of what artificial life should be.

They trace their origin to cybernetics, referring to William Gray Walter's electronic turtle and Ross Ashby's homeostat. Autopoiesis is succeeded by artificial life, by the evident connotation of closed systems it presents. However, as it could not fail to be, they bring new elements, such as a new conception of autonomy:

Autonomy, in this context, refers to the basic and fundamental capacity of being, of affirming its existence and carrying forward a world that is significant and pertinent without being pre-elaborated. Therefore, the autonomy of the living is understood here, both concerning its actions and to the way it models the world in a meaning.[261]

That is to say that the living being itself modifies itself, presenting an emergent behavior.

3.7.4 Artificial Life

Although it seems that artificial life systems are incorporeal organisms, this is not generally accepted, for there would always be the figure of the observer, now in a peripheral position, as a narrator who tells the stories of artificial life.[262]

But ideas about artificial life have proliferated in the world. At the fourth conference on artificial life in 1994, evolutionary biologist Thomas S. Ray presented two proposals: the first was a plan to

---

[261] *Ibidem*, p.222.
[262] *Idem et seq.*

preserve biodiversity in the tropical rainforest of Costa Rica, and the second, the suggestion to free the Tierra *software* on the internet, which creates artificial forms of life on the computer, so that it could generate several species on computers around the world. For him, the two proposals were complementary. The first objective was to extend biodiversity to protein-based life forms, and the second to do the same with silicon-based life forms. The idea was to introduce the natural form and the life process into an artificial medium. For him, the lines of codes that make up these creatures become natural life forms. Only the medium is different.

Thus, for him, not only the lines of programming combined and concatenated are alive, but also, the natural ones. And this is not the only perspective under which (artificial) life has been seen.

Briefly, studies on artificial life are subdivided into three lines of research:

I) *wetware*, which is the attempt to create biological life by techniques such as the construction of components of single-celled organisms in test tubes;

II) *hardware* which is the construction of robots and other forms of life embodied and

III) *software* which relates to the creation of *software* that establishes emerging and evolutionary processes.

All these aspects seek to create life from the bottom up. For example, programs that create simple rules and then, through highly recursive structures, allow the appearance of complexity spontaneously.

Hayles,[263] frustrated with the slow speed with which the natural evolution of organisms occurred, questioned whether there was no possibility of accelerating this process by creating artificial organ-

---

[263] *Ibidem*, p. 225-227.

isms that could be evolved within the computer. To do this, she first had to face the challenge of creating programs that were resistant enough to withstand mutation without, however, crash. She envisioned a "virtual computer" made of *software*, which would use the *address by template*, a technique in which a segment of the code would find its reverse binary, fitting into each other, similar to what happens to the DNA bases. The *address by template* only works on the virtual computer, having the advantage of keeping the organisms inside that computer, without the possibility of external reproduction.

Following in her investigative process, Hayles observed the work done by Ray in this field. She noted that Ray, to enable mutation, created the equivalent of cosmic rays by changing one-bit polarity to every 10,000 instructions performed. Also, reproduction occurs once every 1,000 to 2,000 instructions copied, introducing a new mutation source. Still, to control the number of organisms, Ray introduced a program he calls *reaper*. The *reaper* monitors the population and eliminates the oldest and most defective creatures, that is, those who have made the most mistakes in the execution of their programs. If a creature finds a way to replicate more efficiently, the *reaper* moves it down its list, and thus it becomes more "young".

The virtual computer begins its evolutionary process by sharing a block of memory called by Ray of *soup*, analogous to the beginning of life on Earth. Within the soup are released auto-breeding programs, usually starting with an 80-*byte* creature, called "ancestor". The ancestor is made up of three segments. The first counts the instructions to analyze the length of the ancestor; the second segment reserves a space in the closest memory, inserting a protective membrane around that space; and the third segment copies the ancestor's code to a placeholder, thus completing the reproduction process, creating a cellular offspring from the original cell.

Ray left his program running at night, imagining that he would find, at most, 1 or 2-*byte* variation of the 80-*byte* ancestor. By checking the program, the next day, he discovered that an entire ecology evolved, including a 22-*byte* organism. Among the mutants were parasites that lost their copy instructions but developed the ability to invade a host to remove the copy procedure. A 45-*byte* parasite evolved in a benign relationship with the ancestor; others were destructive, expelling the ancestor with his offspring. Subsequently, the development of hyperparasites, which evolved to compete for time and memory, was also observed. Hyperparasites await the invasion of parasites. When these attempt to reproduce using the hyperparasite copying procedure, it directs the program to its third segment instead of reverting the program to the parasite segment. Thus, the hyperparasite code is copied in the processing time of the parasite. In this way, the hyperparasite multiplies the time it has for its reproduction because it appropriates the time of the parasite.

Hayles[264] teaches that, according to Christopher Langton, the main assumption of artificial life is that the logical form of an organism can be separated from its physical support and that its life can be found in its logic and not in the support. Langton removes tautology by defining life in a way that programs qualify and, then by virtue of they qualify, he claims that they are alive. The form can be logically separated from matter. Form prevails over matter, form defines life, while physical support is just a circumstance.

Some understand that the records of essential elements characterizing biological life, whether of a Human Being, a mouse, or a blue whale are identical to the records produced by artificial beings, when plotted on a graph so that in the search for extraterrestrial life what should be researched is records similar to these and when found, it is considered that one is facing life, although it is neither biological or, even if it is biological, structured in a way different from that known on Earth, around the DNA.

---

[264] *Ibidem*, p. 231.

4 BRIEF TECHNICAL
UNDERSTANDING OF ROBOTICS

4.1 Cybernetics

It is quite accurate the origin of the term cybernetics. Stafford Beer[265] states that

> *Cybernetics had its origins in the early 1940s, when a group of distinguished scientists was gathered together in Mexico to deal with various assignments associated with the Second World War. It is well-documented how they discovered that — precisely because of their eminence in different fields — they found it difficult to talk to each other about anything serious. So, they decided to choose a topic that was nobody's specialty, but of interest to everyone. And their eminence was really important for another reason: they had nothing to prove. They decided to discuss the nature of control.*

They understood that control was a constant element in any system of any nature. Among these scientists was a mathematician named Norbert Wiener. He was the one who named the new area of knowledge. Its inspiration came from the ancient Greek ships that faced the most diverse meteorological conditions, many of these totally unpredictable. However, its trajectory was controlled by the responsible for the rudder which, keeping his eyes focused on the lighthouse, controlled the tiller, to continually adjust the direction of the ship to reach the lighthouse. From the time of Homer, the Greek word for this person responsible for the helm was *kubernetes*, which, translated into English, would turn *cybernetes*. In the same sense, in Rome, the same word in Latin became *gubernator*, which

---

[265] Beer, S. *What is cybernetics?* Lecture given at the University of Valladolid at the end of 2001. Retrieved from: <http://www.nickgreen.pwp.blueyonder.co.uk/beerWhatisCybernetics.pdf>. (pp. 4). Last access date: February 13, 2009.

means governor. In this way, the word cybernetics means control, governance.[266]

Wiener, recalls Beer, reffered to the definition of cybernetics to animals and machines, which is quite appropriate in this work.

Cybernetics, by Norbert Wiener, is one of the seminal works in information technology. This work inaugurated a new science and guided all studies in computer science since then, spreading even to the most diverse branches of knowledge, because it is, inherently, inter or transdisciplinary.

Published in 1948, it was updated in 1950 under the title: The human use of human beings: Cybernetics and Society. The author states that:

> *The thesis of this book that society can only be understood through a study of the messages and the communication facilities which belong to it; and that in the future development of these messages and communication facilities, messages between man and machines, between machines and man, and between machine and machine, are destined to play an ever-increasing part.*
>
> (...)
>
> *It is the purpose of Cybernetics to develop a language and techniques that will enable us indeed to attack the problem of control and communication in general, but also to find the proper repertory of ideas and techniques to classify their particular manifestations under certain concepts.*[267]

The MIT — Massachusetts Institute of Technology — professor states that he was influenced in the making of the book by the ideas of Leibniz, who was interested in computing by machines and automatons, but that the conceptions of the book are not Leibnitzian.

The book does not overlook a characteristic of Law that allows it to be characterized as a cybernetic system, discussed below.

---

[266] *Idem.*

[267] Wiener, N. (1993) *Cibernética e sociedade: o uso humano de seres humanos*. [The Human Use Of Human Beings: Cybernetics And Society]. (J. P. Paes, Trans.). (9th ed., pp. 16-17). São Paulo: Cultrix.

4.2 Law and Communication

Law can be defined as an ethical control applied to communication, and language as a form of communication, especially when such a normative aspect is under the command of some authority powerful enough to give to their decisions the character of sanction or effective social decision.

The nature of our legal system is based on conflict. It is a conversation in which at least three participants intervene — for example, in a civil case, the author, the defendant, and the legal system, as represented by the judge and the jury. This is a game, in the full sense of Von Neumann.[268]

It is also interesting to know Wiener's three premises:

1) The paradigm shift from energy to information, the real engine of cybernetic machines;

2) Analog computing is substantially cheaper than digital, which comes in handy in massively parallel systems such as the brain and

3) Newton's time is reversible because, if we run the world of the Newtonian way back in time, it will continue to follow Newton's laws. Computation, as a rule, is not reversible in time, but there are two kinds of computational transformations, one in which information is preserved — and therefore reversible — and another where it is destroyed.

4.3 Artificial Intelligence

4.3.1 Introduction

Long before the advent of electronics, Man has tried to create intelligent machines. This historical account is quite summarized and does not cover all attempts and projects that sought an artificial

---

[268] *Ibidem*, p. 167.

form of intelligence. Therefore, here there is only a sampling of the evolution of these devices and their creators.

Blaise Pascal (1623-1662) is considered to have been the pioneer in building his calculating machine which mechanically effected additions and subtractions.

Gottfried Wilhelm Von *Leibniz* advanced a little further because he conceived a machine of reasoning, considering that thought is reducible to calculation, and hence the forerunner of artificial intelligence. His solution was to design logic.

Advancing in time, comes the 19th century, when Lord Charles Babbage, built in 1833 a calculating machine. In fact, he made a differential machine, capable not only of performing the four elementary arithmetic operations alone but also sequences of operations. His genius conceived of something more sophisticated the following year: a new machine to simultaneously perform arithmetic calculations with numbers and manipulate formal expressions, that is, an analytical machine, though he has not been able to build it.

George Boole (1815-1864) collaborated greatly for artificial intelligence, creating Boolean logic.

However, only with the ideas of Alan Turing[269] describing his universal machine, capable of representing any other machine that could be mathematically formalized and to solve any computable problem, as long as he had sufficient time and memory. It was from there that the problem of artificial intelligence came to be approached by modern methods. He proved also that

> *The behavior of a machine is often so unpredictable that it does not reveal the succession of the elementary instructions that gave rise to it. Thus, even if the activity of a machine results from what has been ordered, even if it is the faithful reflection of it, the speed of calculation and the multiplicity of the operations performed make us unable to reconstitute, only from the observation of its behavior, the sequence of instructions to which a machine obeys. In a way, this means*

---

[269] Ganascia, J. G. (1997). *Inteligência artificial* [Artificial Intelligence]. (R. C. C. de Moraes, Trans.). (pp. 31). São Paulo: Editora Ática.

that there is something else in what results from a machine, beyond what has been supplied to it.[270]

So, even if the result always results from the precise application of precise instructions and data not supplied by the machine itself. It simply means that, given the high number of operations performed in a given period of time, Man is unable to mentally reconstitute its chain.

His second proof: the human difficulty of determining the origin of the behavior of the machines constitutes an obstacle for the men in charge of programming them.

For Turing, an intelligent machine is one that behaves intelligently in the eyes of men. In order to do so, he conceived a test in which a person or machine is put to the test, so that another person discovers that it is a Man or a computer, without physical or visual contact with it, only in the light of answers given by written questions also written formulated. This test is unanimously known as the Turing Test.

It must be agreed with Kurzweil[271] that if the computer passes the Turing test it is evidence of intelligence, on the other hand, the contrary would not characterize the lack of intelligence.

Technically artificial intelligence can be defined as the ability of a device to perform functions that are normally associated with human intelligence such as reasoning, learning, and self-improvement.[272]

As language is characteristic of human intelligence and so we must now learn a language common to men and machines, "The intelligent machine would then be the one with which we could communicate through written language."[273]

Kurzweil considers that

---

[270] *Ibidem*, p. 33.
[271] Kurzweil, R. (1999). *The age of intelligent machines.* (3rd reprint, pp. 117). Cambridge, Mass.: MIT Press.
[272] Rosenberg, J. M., *op. cit.*, p. 10.
[273] Ganascia, J.G., *op. cit.*, p. 31.

> *Probably the most durable definition of artificial intelligence, and the most often quoted, states that: "Artificial intelligence is the art of creating machines that perform functions that require intelligence when performed by people".*[274]

Or, still, "Artificial Intelligence is the study of computer problems that have not yet been solved".[275]

In Brazil, one of the pioneers in the study of modern artificial intelligence from a legal point of view is Aires José Rover. In the author's view, artificial intelligence systems contribute to overcoming the inability of the human mind to store and evaluate all possible variables in a given problem-situation in Law.[276]

Rover[277], in consonance with Marvin Minsky, defines artificial intelligence as the

> *Science of building machines that do things that would require intelligence if they were made by men. On the other hand, it is the study that seeks to simulate intelligent processes or learning processes on machines or that tries to make computers perform tasks in which people are better at the moment. This includes tasks such as behaving as a specialist, understanding and speaking a natural language, recognizing patterns such as writing.*

In an interesting work on the construction of the legal treatment of artificial intelligence, Sam N. Lehman-Wilzig discusses the capacities of machines equipped with artificial intelligence, which for him are briefly:

(1) Imitate the behavior of any other machine.

---

[274] Kurzweil, R. (1999). *The age of intelligent machines*. (3rd reprint, pp. 14). Cambridge, Mass.: MIT Press.

[275] *Ibidem*, pp. 14.

[276] Rover, A. J. (2000). *Direito, sociedade e informática: limites e perspectivas da vida digital*. [Law, society and information technology: limits and perspectives of the digital life]. (pp. 107-112). Florianópolis: Boiteux.

[277] Rover, A. J. *O Uso de técnicas computacionais inteligentes no domínio do direito: uma introdução* [The use of intelligent computational techniques in the field of law: an introduction.]. Retrieved from: <http://www.infojur.ufsc.br/aires/arquivos/porto%20IA%20introducao.pdf>. (pp. 1). Last access date: February 13, 2009.

(2) Exhibit curiosity (i.e. are always moving to investigate their environment); display self-recognition (i.e. react to the sight of themselves); and manifest mutual recognition of members of their own machine species.

(3) Learn from their own mistakes.

(4) Be as 'creative' and 'purposive' as are humans, even to the extent of look[ing] for purposes which they can fulfill.

(5) Reproduce themselves, in five fundamentally differ- ent modes, of which the fifth – the "probabilistic mode of self-reproduction" – closely parallels biological evolution through mutations (which in the case of M. Sapiens means random changes of elements), so that "highly efficient, complex, powerful automata can evolve from inefficient, simple, weak automata".

(6) "Can have an unbound life span" through self-repairing mechanisms[278].

He then considers that robots form a race that can see, read, speak, learn, and even feel [emotions].

Artificial intelligence presents itself to the general public as be- coming. As something that has not yet materialized, that has not lost its mystical aura. As something whose operation is not yet known. This is because everything that was once attributed to the field of artificial intelligence, after it was accomplished by artificial intelligence, has now been discarded as such. It seems that man must believe in something mysterious to support himself in the concrete world. Before people thought of gods or God. Now in the technological world, in the future human creation, unexplained and desirably inexplicable, for what has already been understood belongs to the kingdom of men and does not hold the transcenden- tal mystery that will lead to eternity.

In fact, artificial intelligence surrounds us in the present world[279],

[278] Lehman-Wilzig, S. N. *Frankenstein Unbound: towards a legal definition of artificial intelligence.* Retrieved from: <profslw.com/wp-content/uploads/academic/40._Frankenstein_Unbound.Towards_a_legal_definition...pdf>. (pp. 444). Last access date: February 22, 2009.
[279] Levy, S. (2011, January) Artificial intelligence is here. In fact, it's all around

but is not always visible or perceived as such[280], since its development has led to systems[281] that often depart from the collective imaginary.

However, Kurzweil recalls, such behavior also occurs when one discovers how an expert operates and if one understands his basic methods and rules, what once seemed intelligent would appear to be less.[282]

The reasoning is developed by Kurzweil[283]:

> In fact, artificial intelligence research made tremendous progress in just a few decades, and because of that speed, the field has acquired a bleak reputation! This paradox resulted from the fact that whenever an artificial intelligence research project made a new discovery useful, it often developed rapidly by forming a new scientific or commercial specialty under its own name. These name changes led outsiders to ask why we see so little progress in the central field of artificial intelligence? Here are some specialties that originated at least in part from artificial intelligence research, but later separated into different fields: robotics, pattern recognition, specialized systems, proofs of automatic theorems, cognitive psychology, word processing, machine vision, knowledge engineering, the symbolic applied to mathematics and computational linguistics.

Kurzweil[284] brings to light the elements collected by Allen Newell for a system to be considered intelligent: it operates in real time; explores vast amount of knowledge; tolerates unknown and unexpected actions; uses symbols and abstractions; communicates using some form of natural language; learns from the environment and exhibits adaptive behavior focused on a goal.

---

us. But nothing like we expected. *Wired.* (pp. 87-89). New & Improved.

[280] Brown, J. (2011, January). Drivers not wanted. *Wired.* (pp. 94-97). New & Improved, p. 94-97.

[281] Salmon, F. et Stokes, J. (2011, January). Bull vs. bear vs. bot. *Wired.* (pp. 90-93). New & Improved.

[282] Kurzweil, R. (1999). *The age of intelligent machines.* (pp. 16, 3rd reprint). Cambridge, Mass.: MIT Press.

[283] *Idem.*

[284] *Ibidem*, p.18.

Unlike human intelligence, machine intelligence has developed and improved rapidly. The evolution of the machines is estimated to be ten million times faster than the biological one.[285]

It should be remembered that, therefore, if man is intelligent as he is supposed to be, he would have arisen from a process that seems to be objectively unintelligent which is evolution and its long course, given that intelligence is usually related to the ability to solve problems quickly. So much so that it is considered more intelligent who solves a given problem in a matter of minutes than the one that solves it in weeks, months or years!

However, being a process intrinsically not intelligent, evolution has generated humans, who are considered intelligent. So, again, a process that is not intelligent or even considered intelligent can generate an intelligent or even more intelligent product, which opens the door to the possibility of creating computers that are smarter than Men, as Kurzweil understands.[286]

4.3.2 Brief History of Artificial Intelligence

The development of artificial intelligence was not linear or pro-grammed. Here it is not a long history, but only the information about the main periods by which it passed.

Although studies had already occurred for years, only in 1956, John McCarthy proposed to create a new discipline, which would be called *artificial intelligence.*

From there, four periods of artificial intelligence can be seen: I) the first of euphoria, the opportunity in which all qualities were attributed; II) the second period begins in 1966, when the ALPAC report, drafted at the request of the US State Department, high-lighted the limitations inherent in this approach, with an immediate reduction of official funds. Even so, many advances and practical

---

[285] Moravec, H. *Interview given to Robot Books.com*. Retrieved from: <http://www.robotbooks.com/Moravec.htm>. Last access date: February 27, 2009.
[286] Kurzweil, R., *op. cit.*, pp. 20-25.

results have occurred at this stage; III) in 1976 is the beginning of the third period, which could be described as the "expert systems" period; IV) the fourth, of maturity and commitment, which persists to this day.

4.4 The Robot

Let's think of this situation: an entity arose from a legal fact. This fact results from a human being will, either by himself or through a legal entity (a company for example). This advent is not a result of legal acts but conceived from a physical or logical event that happened in the world independently of any will of a human act. I mean, the cause was a human act but the resulting creature in its wholeness was not. Would this resulting legal entity deserve the same legal status as its creators?

This can be explained. What *status* will a machine have, endowed with intelligence similar or superior to the human? This machine is the result of logical interactions in an artificial intelligence program, the result of which, therefore, is not aprioristically and minutely determined but generically, though with all coherent steps, as the sequencing of human DNA that will result in a Human Being.

The specific characteristics of that being cannot (yet) be predicted, only the generality of what makes us physically human, like: two eyes, nose, hands with five fingers, etc.

We have already dealt with the robot generated by a legal act. Here we look at the robot that emerged from a legal fact.

The human being, according to the Darwinian theory, did not arise from the divine will, but from an evolutionary process. What about an entity that arises from an artificial intelligence program that uses genetic algorithms, adaptive to the surrounding environment, as they already exist, that is, from an evolutionary process?

For biological beings to remain alive, i.e. functionally operative, with the systems and subsystems in operation, they need to extract energy from elements of nature, breaking down molecules, usually organic ones, to obtain chemical reactions that produce usable energy.

What about human-designed systems that draw energy from similar or identical processes to the breakdown of certain molecules by enzymes to obtain the energy necessary to maintain their functioning and subsystems?

We are used to call biological life the one resulting from carbon structured molecules, but how would we call similar entities that have a non-carbon molecule structure? What about machines designed to use systems based entirely or partially on molecules structured by carbon? How to conceptualize processing systems based on bacteria?

> *Scientists have managed to perform logical functions with DNA molecules, turning a tube full of DNA into an enormous number of computers, about 10^{23} of them. That's a lot. Because they communicate with each other slowly, the easiest way to use them is like a lottery, preparing all possible answers to a problem and then checking to see which molecule has the winning solution.*[287]

If what distinguishes humans is the **consciousness** of their individuality, how to refuse personality to systems or machines that can recognize their individuality in the face of other machines and beings?

It is considered that, in the legal scope, the concepts of person and legal personality are normal. The status is considered as normal, the way of being stable, according to Telles Junior[288]:

> *This is characterized by the preponderance of normal procedures. It is the state of the body or mind, an atom or a galaxy, a social grouping, or a nation, in which the procedures do not contradict the dominant beliefs about how things should be, can be, or how things are necessary.*

In contrast, the abnormality occurs when normality is disrupted, always on an exceptional basis.

---

[287] Gerschenfeld, N. (1999). *When things start to think.* (pp. 157). New York: Henry Holt and Company.
[288] Telles Júnior, G., *op. cit.*, p. 190.

However, alongside the exceptionality of normality, there are apparent abnormalities, which diverge from erroneous conceptions in force, and which, when misunderstandings are dissipated by new ideas, they become normal.

It seems that is the quality of thinking that develops in this work on the legal personality of the robot.

In any case, it is understood that, in addition to the possibility of the rise of an intelligent robot by human work — result of a legal act, characterized as a person, by the attributes that it may come to have — what seems most likely is that robotic people arise due to a legal fact, represented by the appearance of the first intelligent robot by virtue of the developments not purposely programmed or planned in a given system.

This cybernetic Adam, the result of the evolution of the system, will be born as the Man of an event without interference from an external will, of an exogenous consciousness or a strange intelligence.

It's the technological singularity!

But, after all, what is a robot?

4.4.1 Brief History of the Robot

First of all, it is convenient to bring a historical summary of the robots, which only gained that name, it will be seen, in 1920. Clarke teaches that "The Egyptian, Babylonian and Sumerian legends that existed 5000 years ago reflect the widespread image of creation, with god-men blowing life in images made of clay."[289]

Asimov[290] recalls that in the eighteenth book of Homer's Iliad it is seen that Hephaestus, the Greek god of the forges, had as helpers two maidens made of gold but who were just like living girls who

---

[289] Clarke, R. *Asimov's Laws of Robotics: Implications for Information Technology*. Retrieved from: <www.anu.edu.au/people/Roger.Clarke/SOS/Asimov.html>. Last access date: February 12, 2009.

[290] Asimov, I. (1994). *Visões de robô* [robot's visions]. (R. S. de Biasi, Trans.). (pp. 12). Rio de Janeiro: Record.

could think, speak and use muscles, besides being able to spin and weave.

From Greece, we still have the legend of Talos, the bronze giant of Crete, who patrolled the coast incessantly looking for invaders.

Of all the medieval stories about robots and automatons, what has come most alive to this day is that of Rabbi Loew of Prague, in the sixteenth century, which made an artificial man of clay, a golem (a substance not formed, in Hebrew), without life. However, the rabbi, using the name of God gave life to the dummy and made him protect the Jews.

In the eighth century, automata proliferated, like soldiers and toys birds, etc., presented to nobles and wealthy people and exhibited in public to the general astonishment.

Due to Luigi Galvani's discovery in 1798 that dead muscle tissue reacted to electricity, the idea of creating artificial life, like Frankenstein by Mary Shelley of 1818, was sharpened in the minds.

It is interesting to note that, maybe for fear of hurting divine or religious susceptibilities, in almost every story, the autonomous ran away from control and threatened their creators and others, and it was necessary to destroy them.

Only in 1920, Karel Capek wrote R.U.R. (Rossum Universal Robots)[291], in which Rossum, an Englishman, made artificial men in series to serve as slaves.[292]

From there the word robot has gained the *status* it has and is used to refer to these machines.

For the purpose of this book, robot, computer, artificial intelligence system, android and cyborg are considered as synonyms, because what matters here is not the concern with form, but, with the functional aspect, with the practical result of knowing if, certain conditions being fulfilled, one would face the hypothesis of a nonhuman subject of rights or an object of law, as currently, everything animate or inanimate which is not human.

Thus, an artificial intelligence software running on any kind

---

[291] Capek, K., *op. cit.*
[292] Asimov, I., *op. cit.*, p. 15-16.

of equipment, whether it be computers that exist today, super-computers occupying refrigerated rooms, treated as weapons of war, large mainframe computers, medium-sized corporate or departmental servers, desktops, laptops, ultrabooks, netbooks, pocket pcs, smartphones etc. or a wearable or edible computers, with autonomous movements or a real cyborg, whether or not it depends on physical substrate or in a defined way, they are, for the purposes of this work, considered as robot or simply machine or computer.

However, as the doctrine has created distinct categories to refer to several of these machines, for didactic purposes define what is at least, computer, robot, and cyborg.

4.4.2 Robot Concept

For Isaac Asimov[293], who conceived the laws of robotics, a robot is

> an artificial object that looks like a human being; [or] machines performing certain special functions. A robot is a computer machine capable of performing tasks that are too complex for any living brain other than man's, and of a type that no non-computer machine can do. In other words, robots can be defined by the equation: robot = machine + computer[294].

This is the classic view of the robot, attained since the first appearance of such characters in world literature, in R.U.R. (Rossum's Universal Robots) by the Czech writer Karel Capek[295]. Robota means forced or bonded worker in Czech.[296]

However, Asimov himself in the above-mentioned work suggests abandoning the criterion of appearance to deal with the function, explaining that a robot is a creature capable of doing what the human does, more quickly and efficiently, concluding that, any

---

[293] *Ibidem*, p. 11.
[294] *Idem*.
[295] *Ibidem*, p. 11.
[296] Capek, K., *op. cit.*

machine or many machines could be defined as robots, such as a sewing machine.

It should be emphasized that the term should be reserved for computerized machines that perform certain special functions, too complex for any living brain except that of man, and which no other machine is capable of performing. Robot for Asimov would be the machine and computer junction.

Clarke[297] sees the robot as "a reproducible multifunction device designed to handle and / or carry materials through variable movements programmed to perform a variety of functions." Thus, on the basis of this definition, it distinguishes three key elements, without which, one cannot talk about robots:

a) programmability, whether computational or symbolic — manipulative capabilities that the builder can combine in any way he wants (the robot is a computer);

b) mechanical capacity, allowing it to act in its environment rather than acting as a mere data processor or computing device (the robot is a machine);

c) flexibility, being able to act using a range of programs and handling and transporting materials in various ways.

He also does not admit to differentiating a computer and a robot: "We can then conceive a robot as an improved computer machine or as a computer with sophisticated input and output devices."[298]

Thus, there are no vital differences between computers and robots.

---

[297] Clarke, R., *op. cit.*, p. 12.
[298] *Ibidem*, p. 5.

4.4.3 Examples of Smart Robots

Dealing with any mention of the possibility of robots or any machine having a resemblance, other than merely physical with Man, immediately provokes reactions that are often fervent.

At least in Judeo-Christian civilization Man is created in the image and likeness of God, who holds the monopoly of creation in its biblical sense. Thus, any attempt to create a human-like entity gives rise to a culturally ingrained sense that Man is playing God.

However, this cannot and should not be considered. Firstly, because one does not try to move into a religious field, but rather in technical and scientific terms. Secondly, because the interest that drives scientists in robotics and artificial intelligence is not that of creating souls or men, but intelligent machines, although machines, even if machines are considered living beings and people and humans can be defined as machines.

The reason for wanting to create machines of this nature seems to be simple, although it involves several factors and causes, among which the following stand out: i) the possibility of doing so; II) the challenge of doing so; III) the economic and political interest involved and IV) the need.

In fact, it is possible to say that there are already intelligent machines, or otherwise, that perform tasks that were judged or thought to be intelligent and that therefore could and could only be done by someone or something with intelligence. The examples are numerous and growing. Here are some:

EWA-1, produced by Environmental Robots, had sufficient strength to participate in the Human X Robot Arm Wrestling Competition, which NASA's Jet Propulsion Laboratory (JPL) held in 2005. Its strength comes from six internal conductive graphite fibers that contract when a 120v current hits them and produce reactions to the chemicals in them.

The interesting thing about this robot is that it has the functional equivalent to muscles, something essential to a humanoid robot.

Some robots produce dozens of movements similar to those of the human hand. There is a robotic finger with a configuration similar to the bone and joints of a human finger that moves as a result of signals that emulate the neural commands of the human brain.

It is important to emphasize here that Man used the experience accumulated by evolution to position the thumb in the evolved human form. Thus robots — applying the Law of Accelerating Returns — do not have to wait for the same evolutionary time of the human being to acquire this tool.

A robot called WE-4R, created by a team from Waseda University in Japan can demonstrate facial expressions of fear, anger, surprise, joy, and sadness or even a zen expression of tranquility. He can also see, hear, touch and smell.

All these characteristics belong to Man.

Partner is the name of a robot created by Toyota to play the trumpet, an instrument that requires many lip movements and different types of blows of the musician in its performance since it does not have internal structures to produce the different notes. Professional jazz musician Paul Hogson has created a software based on artificial intelligence called the Improviser that performs, as the name implies, jazz **improvisations** in real time, following the style of Charlie Parker.

It should be noted that this is a true production of unpublished and creative music, something that only Man supposedly could do next to some cetaceans.

KRT-V.3 is a robot, created by Hideyuki Sawada, who mechanically speaks some words in Japanese with artificial vocal cords almost naturally.

The important thing in this robot is that the sound is not provoked like in other electronic equipment, but, by vocal cords, similar to human ones.

This is an important step in giving a human voice to the robot. The machine will be able to speak like a human.

Vera, created by David Hanson of the University of Texas at Dallas, has a man-made textured skin similar to human skin, made of a special silicone, producing facial expressions with 1/20 of the strength required by previous synthetic skins. With this, the robots approach to have a face identical to the human.

And not only, but Vera also has the equivalent of the largest human organ, which is the skin, very similar to ours, opening the door to the creation of robots that look very similar to the human.

The International Institute for Advanced Research in Telecommunications of Japan has developed ROBOVIE IIS, whose skin is sensitive. Metallic piezoelectric films on his artificial skin generate a voltage when touched. If someone gently touches him, he replies, "Yes?". If someone hits him or touches him harder, he produces an English onomatopoeia expressing pain.

That is to say: one of the human senses of vital importance for survival already has its robotic version.

Jerry, developed by MIT, imitates the way humans use contextual clues to make quick and precise visual conclusions. He can identify, for example, the distance from the horizon, the surroundings and decide if what blocks his passage is, for example, a car or a sofa, making it easier for him to get around.

Thus the ability of animal georeferencing, is already available in machines, allowing its autonomous displacement.

Other examples of robots with auditory, olfactory, near human and animal mobility, etc., can be found in the July 2004 issue of Wired Magazine, referred to in my work.[299]

> *The robot called Kismet, which uses sight and speech as its main input, carries on conversations with people, and is modeled on a developing infant. Though not quite the centered, reliable personality that was portrayed by HAL, Kismet is the world›s first robot that is truly sociable, that can interact with people on an equal basis, and which people accept as a humanoid creature. They make eye contact with it; it makes eye contact with them. People read its mood from the intonation in its speech, and Kismet reads the mood of people from the intonation in their speech. Kismet and any person who comes close to it fall into a natural social interaction. People talk to it, gesture to it, and act socially with it. Kismet talks to people, gestures to them, and acts socially with them. People, at least for a while, treat Kis-*

---

[299] Castro Júnior, *op. cit.*

met as another being. Kismet is alive. Or may as well be. People treat it that way.[300]

Thus, the creation of important elements of the human psychological personality in robots has been carried out.

Brooks recalls that

> *Professor Sherry Turkle visited our lab. Sherry has always been something of a critic of the claims of artificial intelligence research. [...] Cog "noticed" me soon after I entered its room. Its head turned to follow me and I was embarrassed to note that this made me happy. [...] My visit left me shaken - not by anything that Cog was able to accomplish but my own reaction to "him". [...] Despite myself and despite my continuing skepticism about this research project, I had behaved as though in the presence of another being. [...] The students who work with Kismet report the same sort of effect.[301]*

The technology built into Kismet is so advanced that even unbelieving *experts* at the possibilities of artificial intelligence are surprised by it. It is interesting to see Turkle's[302] experiences, including children and computers and the perspective of the new generations concerning machines.

Brooks[303] states:

> *We would probably be surprised if our dog suddenly started to act the same way as Kismet during the calibration. [...] Should we agree to designate Kismet the status of being? Or will Kismet be just a machine that occasionally is switched on? We may consider Kismet as something thinking because if the Kismet of the present day does not qualify as worthy of having the status of being, a person could ask himself three other questions [...].*

---

[300] Brooks, R. A. (2002). *Flesh and machines: how robots will change us.* (pp. 65). New York: Pantheon Books.

[301] *Ibidem*, p.149.

[302] Turkle, S. (1997). *A vida no ecrã: a identidade na era da internet.* [Life on the Screen: Identity in the Age of the Internet] (P. Faria, Trans.). (pp. 111-148). Lisbon: Relógio D'Água Editores.

[303] Brooks, *op. cit.*, p.151.

When Honda introduced P2 to the world in 1997, succeeded by P3 in 1998, followed in 2001 by the ASIMO model, the robots looked like people wearing spacesuits. These are the first examples of bipedal robots with almost natural human walking.

Moravec[304] also mentions an example of a robot that brings artificial intelligence to another level:

> [...] In October 1995 an experimental vehicle called Navlab V crossed the U.S. from Washington, D.C., to San Diego, driving itself more than 95 percent of the time. The vehicle's self-driving and navigational system was built around a 25-MIPS laptop based on a microprocessor by Sun Microsystems. The Navlab V was built by the Robotics Institute at Carnegie Mellon University, of which I am a member.

> [...] Dramatic progress in this field became evident in the DARPA Grand Challenge contests held in California. In October 2005 several fully autonomous cars successfully traversed a hazard-studded 132-mile desert course, and in 2007 several successfully drove for half a day in urban traffic conditions.

Siemens launched on the European market in 2004, at the price of € 1,399 (one thousand and three hundred and ninety-nine euros), the robot Dressman, whose system uses hot air to dry and pass the shirt at the same time. The robot has the shape of a mannequin, simply wear the clothes washed in it and activate one of the 12 programs it has for different fabrics.

The Watchman robot already exists in Brazil, able to monitor environments and transmit information (including audio) in real time to an External Monitoring Center as well as send images via the internet.

The robot can patrol through several rooms and has sensors that allow detecting any changes in the environment, which will be communicated directly to the Command Center.

---

[304] Moravec, H. (2008). A Ascensão dos Robôs [Rise of the robots] *Scientific American Brasil*. Seu futuro com robôs: as máquinas inteligentes que vão transformar o mundo. [Your future with robots: the intelligent machines that will transform the world.] (Special edition n. 25, pp. 16). Editora Duetto.

The machine can also be used to investigate the alarm trigger cases, verifying if it is an attempted invasion or mere accident.

Another example of a robot, this one of daily use by millions of people around the world, is the search robot[305]. It is the artificial intelligence system behind every search tool, whether it is the gigantic Google, or other, smaller, like Goshme, developed by young Bahians. These systems scan vast databases in fractions of a second to present to the interested party the result of their search in a consistent and useful way.

However, such systems do much more than just research. They seek to learn from the universe of searches they have dealt with since its inception, suggesting results that may even be related to a given context.

In addition, they have their own tools to avoid being deceived by little relevant sites that try to use techniques that allow them greater visibility, among other functionalities, whose treatment is not allowed here.

There is the example of RAP (Robotic Action Painter) a visual artist robot created by *also* visual Portuguese artist Leonel Moura, who creates his works without any external intervention.[306]

---

[305] Rover, A J. *Dados e informações na internet: É legítimo o uso de robôs para formação de base de dados de clientes?* [Data and information on the internet: Is it legitimate to use robots to build customer databases?] Retrieved from: <http://www.infojur.ufsc.br/aires/arquivos/manole2aires.pdf>. Last access date: February 13, 2009.

[306] Kato, G. *Eu Robô* [Me robot] Retrieved from: <http://bravonline.abril.com.br/conteudo/artesplasticas/artesplasticasmateria_292516.shtml>. Last access date: January 05, 2009. p.1-3. "The Portuguese artist Leonel Moura is the creator of the robot known as RAP (Robotic Action Painter), **born** in 2006. His movements resemble the movements of an ant, have eyes that work as sensors and equipped with six colored pens, is capable of creating paintings in the style of Jackson Pollock (1912-1956; prominent of expressionism in the USA). There are three robots like this, and although they were created at the same time, Moura says that each one has a distinct behavior, for example, one of them uses much more the color red.

Leonel Moura assures that his robot does not obey rules predetermined by him. According to him, "the program gives the robot full autonomy to choose where to circulate, what to do and when to stop." "It's almost an anti-program." Thus,

These modern devices bring built-in artificial intelligence systems that behave, in whole or in part, like their biological counterparts.

However, intelligent or biological behavior is not an advent of the state of the art technology. Wiener[307] and other researchers cited by him, such as Ashby and Walter, already designed such machines in the fifties of the last century:

> *[...] some earlier machines of Dr. Walter[308] somewhat similar to my "moth" or "bug," but which were built for a different purpose. For these phototropic machines, each element carries a light so that it can stimulate the others. Thus a number of them put into operation at the same time show*

---

the RAP has autonomy to decide when to start a painting and when its work will end.

In this way, one wonders if what RAP does is art. Leonel Moura guarantees that yes and in doing so, he would be breaking the concept of art consolidated in the early 20th century, which is linked to the intention of the artist and his art (author's power over his work) (paradigm established by Marcel Duchamp in 1913). Moura questions these values: "I identify art associated with creativity, with doing something that did not exist before. No drawing or painting of my robot repeats itself or copies something already seen. **He** does not submit to a set of instructions. **He** creates". Thus, for Moura, any being (human or not) would be able to make art, as long as it has creativity (this being may be artificial). What matters is the content and not who created it. (bolded emphasis added)

Leonel Moura, in his atelier in Portugal, works with a team of twenty robot-painters and the works signed by him already have market acceptance. A screen costs $ 10,000 while a drawing comes out at half the price. Leonel says experts in fine arts do not distinguish between the screens made by humans and those made by robots.

The São Paulo artist Rodrigo Andrade disagrees with the Portuguese artist. He does not agree with the existence of a machine with freedom of choice. He sees the robot as an instrument of the artist. Giselle Beiguelman, from São Paulo, comments: "It's a brilliant idea. With the robot, it alerts us to this increasingly hybrid frontier between man and machine." But regarding the robot's signature, he says: "When the robot finishes the drawing and goes to the corner of the paper, it again operates within the restrictions imposed on art today by the Cartesian culture."

[307] Wiener, N. (1989) The Human Use Of Human Beings: Cybernetics And Society. (9th ed., pp. 172) London: Free Association Books, 1989.

[308] *Ibidem*, p. 22. "For us, the machine is a mechanism capable of transforming received messages into emitted messages."

*certain groupings and mutual reactions which would be in-
terpreted by most animal psychologists as social behavior if
they were found encased in flesh and blood instead of brass
and steel. It is the beginning of a new science of mechanical
behavior even though almost all of it lies in the future.*

In the early days of computing, the genius of Wiener[309] thus
reverberated, further advancing in predicting the possibilities of
artificial intelligence:

*We now come to another class of machines which possess
some very sinister possibilities. Curiously enough, this
class contains the automatic chess-playing machine. [...] it
is hopeless to try to make a machine to play perfect chess
for such a machine would require too many combinations.
Professor John von Neumann of the Institute for Advanced
Studies at Princeton has commented on this difficulty. However, it is neither easy nor hopeless to make a machine
which we can guarantee to do the best that can be done for
a limited number of moves ahead, say two; and which will
then leave itself in the position that is the most favorable in
accordance with some more or less easy method of evaluation.*

*The present ultra-rapid computing machines may be set up
to act as chess-playing machines, though a better machine
might be made at an exorbitant price if we chose to put
the work into it. The speed of these modern computing machines is enough so that they can evaluate every possibility
for two moves ahead in the legal playing-time of a single
move. The number of combinations increases roughly in
geometrical progression. Thus the difference between playing out all possibilities for two moves and three moves is
enormous. To play out a game-something like fifty moves is
hopeless in any reasonable time. Yet for beings living long
enough, as von Neumann has shown, it would be possible;
and a game played perfectly on each side would lead, as a
foregone conclusion, either always to a win for White, or always to a win for Black, or most probably always to a draw.*

[...]

*How much this would slow the game, lengthening each
move beyond the legal limit, I do not know; although I am*

---

[309] *Ibidem*, p. 172 e 175.

not convinced that we can go very far in this direction without getting into time trouble at our present speeds.

[...]

Its game would be stiff and rather uninteresting, but much safer than that of any human player.

[...]

Though we have seen that machines can be built to learn, the technique of building and employing these machines is still very imperfect. The time is not yet ripe for the design of a chess-playing machine on learning principles, although it probably does not lie very far in the future.

[...]

The best way to make a master machine would probably be to pit it against a wide variety of good chess players. On the other hand, a well-contrived machine might be more or less ruined by the injudicious choice of its opponents. A horse is also ruined if the wrong riders are allowed to spoil it.

In the learning machine, it is well to distinguish what the machine can learn and what it cannot. A machine may be built either with a statistical preference for a certain sort of behavior, which nevertheless admits the possibility of other behavior; or else certain features of its behavior may be rigidly and unalterably determined. We shall call the first sort of determination preference, and the second sort of determination constraint. For example, if the rules of legal chess are not built into a chess-playing machine as constraints, and if the machine is given the power to learn, it may change without notice from a chess-playing machine into a machine doing a totally different task. On the other hand, a chess-playing machine with the rules built in as constraints may still be a learning machine as to tactics and policies.

The creator of cybernetics reminds us that Father Dubarle wrote a review of his book in the edition of the Le Monde, December 28, 1948, with a very convincing conjecture worthy of transcription, almost in its entirety by the actuality of his content:

One of the most fascinating prospects thus opened is that of the rational conduct of human affairs, and in particular of those which interest communities and seem to present a certain statistical regularity, such as the human phenomena of the development of opinion. Can't one imagine a machine to collect this or that type of information, as for example information on production and the market; and then to determine as a function of the average psychology of human beings, and of the quantities which it is possible to measure in a determined instance, what the most probable development of the situation might be? Can't one even conceive a State apparatus covering all systems of political decisions, either under a regime of many states distributed over the earth, or under the apparently much more simple regime of a human government of this planet? At present nothing prevents our thinking of this. We may dream of the time when the machine à gouverner may come to supply — whether for good or evil — the present obvious inadequacy of the brain when the latter is concerned with the customary machinery of politics.

A machine to treat these processes, and the problems which they put, must, therefore, undertake the sort of probabilistic, rather than deterministic thought, such as is exhibited for example in modem computing machines.

This makes its task more complicated, but does not render it impossible.

The prediction machine which determines the efficacy of anti-aircraft fire is an example of this. Theoretically, time prediction is not impossible; neither is the determination of the most favorable decision, at least within certain limits. The possibility of playing machines such as the chess-playing machine is considered to establish this. For the human processes which constitute the object of government may be assimilated to games in the sense in which von Neumann has studied them mathematically. Even though these games have an incomplete set of rules, there are other games with a very large number of players, where the data are extremely complex. The machines à gouverner will define the State as the best-informed player at each particular level; and the State is the only supreme coordinator of all partial decisions. These are enormous privileges; if they are acquired scientifically, they will permit the State under all circumstances to beat every player of a human game other than itself by offering this dilemma: either immediate ruin, or planned co-operation.

Despite all this, and perhaps fortunately, the machine à gouverner is not ready for a very near tomorrow. For outside of the very serious problems which the volume of infor-

mation to be collected and to be treated rapidly still put, the problems of the stability of prediction remain beyond what we can seriously dream of controlling.

As far as one can judge, only two conditions here can guarantee stabilization in the mathematical sense of the term. These are, on the one hand, a sufficient ignorance on the part of the mass of the players exploited by a skilled player, who moreover may plan a method of paralyzing the consciousness of the masses; or on the other, sufficient good-will to allow one, for the sake of the stability of the game, to refer his decisions to one or a few players of the game who have arbitrary privileges. This is a hard lesson of cold mathematics, but it throws a certain light on the adventure of our century: hesitation between an indefinite turbulence of human affairs and the rise of a prodigious Leviathan. In comparison with this, Hobbes' Leviathan was nothing but a pleasant joke. We are running the risk nowadays of a great World State, where deliberate and conscious primitive injustice may be the only possible condition for the statistical happiness of the masses: a world worse than hell for every clear mind. Perhaps it would not be a bad idea for the teams at present creating cybernetics to add to their cadre of technicians, who have come from all horizons of science, some serious anthropologists, and perhaps a philosopher who has some curiosity as to world matters.[310]

The alert given by the Father has never been so current, because it is thought that the NSA — National Security Agency, according to information published by a former collaborator, Edward Snowden, through the Wikileaks website, would have used his enormous computational arsenal and telematics to snoop around citizens, businesses and authorities around the world.

My Real Baby was a doll launched in the United States around 2002 that was endowed with artificial intelligence and behaved like a real human baby, crying when she was tired, alone, hungry, dirty or irritated; sleeping when she was tired, eating when she was hungry, burping, flatulating, smiling, showing her "emotions" with lots of realistic facial expressions, babbling, at first, baby sounds and learning words over time, to the point of uttering

---

[310] Dubarle *apud* Wiener, *op. cit.*, p. 176-178.

phrases with up to four or five words. Tickling her feet or face, she laughed. When left alone, she cried for attention. None of this was pre-programmed, but it was learned by the doll over time. Its stay on the market was short-lived, officially due to production problems and advertising errors. Copies of this toy currently reach high values in the secondary market for being considered a rare product, being disputed by collectors and researchers of robotics. It was an extremely complex, baby-like robot, thanks to hundreds of competing programs that produced the doll's general behavior and advanced electronics for the time when the software worked, felt, and acted.

Knowing its existence, I managed to buy a new, unused copy at auction on the eBay site, and presented it to my daughter Maria at the age of three at the time. Like any new toy, My Real Baby caught her eye at first and then was dropped. After being questioned, my daughter said that the doll was boring because it had to be fed, lullabied, put to sleep, cleaned, and it seemed like her little cousin — the other dolls did not demand so much care.

I realized that the little "mama" of the doll still had a lot to enjoy in life and could not dedicate herself to motherhood at such a young age, confined to the sophistication of this robot, treated like a real human baby!

Regarding my youngest daughter, Rafaela, who was 3 to 4 years old, some 7 to 8 years later, it happened a bit differently, as she more easily accepted the doll. I could not say whether because she had had other toys, so to speak, smarter than those available to her older sister, or if, since all these years, technology of that nature is becoming more common or more natural for the children, although, in 2017, there was no news of another doll with the same capacity as My Real Baby.

The example that was reported by the newspaper A Tarde[311] tells of two robots that "can reason, formulate theories and discover scientific knowledge on their own [...]". This fact is still published in

---

[311] Robô-cientista consegue raciocinar e criar teorias [Robot-scientist can reason and create theories.] *Jornal A Tarde.* Caderno 4, p. 7, Salvador. April 5, 2008.

the journal Science[312] and opens new frontiers for the applications of artificial intelligence, demonstrating that a robot smarter than humans is increasingly closer and more feasible.

Nowadays, the chips are embedded in almost everything: television, Blu-ray, phone, airplane, clothes and in the robots, that appear in the most varied sizes, forms, and utilities. Several are in factories, taking the place of human workers in heavy or repetitive functions; others perform functions quite dangerous or impossible to humans, such as entering volcanoes, disarming bombs or navigating the sea depths; or on another planet there are still those who help with household chores or, like pets, amuse who owns them.[313]

With nearly two million copies sold by the end of 2005, *iRobot's* Roomba in the United States, owned by Rodney Brooks of MIT, is a success. Functionally similar to the cartoon maid, from *The Jetson*, Rosie, in a much simpler version, Roomba uses artificial intelligence to vacuum the floor of the house. Standalone, deviate from obstacles and differentiate types of floors and carpets. Thanks to this ability, it is not necessary to program in its memory the disposition of the furniture and carpets of the whole world before selling it, something impossible. The latest versions allow it to be programmed to self-tap and clean the house, which does not even require the presence of the owner or to push the power button. Also, when they notice that the battery is running out, they return to the charging dock. Roomba was decorated with flashing lights, as many buyers were amazed to see the robot work. *IRobot* also has other models, such as Scooba, which removes dust, scrubs the floor with water and cleaning products, and then dries it.

There are several other autonomous vacuum suctioning robots, such as Trilobite from the Swedish company *Electrolux* and

---

[312] *The automation of science.* (2008, April 6). Retrieved from: <http://www.sciencemag.org/cgi/content/abstract/sci;324/5923/85?maxtoshow=&HITS=10&hits=10&RESULTFOMAT=&fulltext=robot++ross+king&searchid=1&FIRSTINDEX=0&resourcetype=HWCIT>. Last access date: April 06, 2008.

[313] Many examples have been taken from the book Shimizu, H. (2006). *Robô, o filho pródigo* [Robot, the prodigal son.] São Paulo: Editora Terceiro Nome; Mostarda Editora.

Dyson from the English company of the same name. A popular model of *Electrolux* is Automower. This quiet model cuts the grass alone, can work for 24 hours, regardless of the sun or rain, and the small pieces into which the leaves are transformed serve as fertilizer. One of its competitors, Robomow, of the American *Friendly Robotics*, can trim in three hours five hundred square meters of grass.

Japan's *Fujitsu* has created Maron that controls television and DVD players, for example, and can be programmed to circle around the house and see if everything is in order. In case Maron notices an invasion, an alarm is triggered and, through a built-in cell phone, the owner is alerted. Measuring about one foot and weighing eight pounds, it can also send photos. Another model of the same company is the Papero. He circulates around the house, crosses obstacles, expresses emotions, dances when he is happy and understands about three thousand sentences relating to different situations, which allows us to talk to him. Everything new that he learns, Papero stores in his memory and, thus, behaves differently with each owner.

However, it's the Witsamaru model from *Mitsubishi* which comes closest to Rosie. With humanoid form and female voice, it was created especially to dialogue with its owners. She understands about 10,000 words in Japanese, recognizes the faces of the people, wakes up the owners in the morning, informs the main news and the weather forecast, received from the internet. When the owners are absent, it communicates them in case of an invasion through a cell phone. Its main purpose, however, is to serve as a companion for children or the elderly.

The Japanese *ZMP* launched a robot that sings, dances and understands voice commands. At a distance, on the cell phone, the owner can order him to go around the house and send pictures taken by a digital camera.

Asimo, manufactured by *Honda*, and named after the writer Isaac Asimov, is one of the most fabulous examples of robotics. The size of a child, it has arms and legs and moves fluidly, which in no way resembles the "robotic" movements of other robots; he is able to run and descend or climb stairs.

K-Team, a Swiss company, has launched a model that acts as a jockey on camel races through voice commands received by radio, replacing humans. Its main purpose is to prevent many children from performing the task, often being sold by their families, as has already been reported.

In 2005, Bruce Donald, Edward Foley and their team introduced their microrobots, the smallest ever built. Measuring around 250 micrometers — a thousandth of a millimeter — they have battery, locomotion and communication systems, which allows them to be controlled from a distance. The US team has thought of quite a variety of applications, such as repairing electronic circuits or manipulating human cells and tissues.

The Predator is an autonomous aircraft that photographs enemy camps and launches missiles at certain targets on the ground. Other models are used to install land mines or in tanks. There are several other military robots available nowadays.

IRobot's Packbot has been used to find bombs in countries in armed conflict. It can operate autonomously or controlled by a computer with wifi wireless connection.

The US Department of Defense hopes that a third of all military vehicles will soon be robotic and will not need human soldiers. Some infantry models tested obey commands from a distance, such as in a video game. For Vijay Kumar, a professor in the Department of Mechanical Engineering at the University of Pennsylvania, the robots will be the soldiers of the future. They will fight like in a game, quite expensive, it is true, but it saves human lives.

NASA coordinates a very advanced robotics project. Robonaut has very clever hands and arms. Equipped with thermal and tactile sensors, motion and power controllers, it can lift heavy or very delicate objects and adapt to the most extreme temperature situations. Being able to function remotely or autonomously, its main purpose is to be sent to the Moon and Mars, replacing humans in risky procedures.

Japan's Matsushita, along with Shiga University, has launched a robot that takes medical tests around the hospital. Based on site maps, he receives the medical tests of employees, who say where to deliver them.

RoTa (Robotic Aid Travel) has been developed by Yamanashi University, in partnership with private companies and the Ministry of Education of Japan. Its purpose is to guide visually impaired people through the streets, identifying objects and traffic signs. Equipped with a voice recognition system and a cell phone to contact a control center if something goes wrong.

In Germany, the Fraunhofer Institute develops Care-O-Bot. It helps the elderly with medication schedules, in their locomotion, changes television channels and keeps company, as it is programmed to answer simple questions.

US-based Intuitive Surgical has launched its da Vinci surgeon robot, which has been tested by more than 50 research institutes worldwide for extremely delicate surgeries. Due to its therapeutic nature, Computer Motion's da Vinci and Zeus have been approved by the US Food and Drug Administration (FDA), which oversees medicines and foods (2008 data).

According to 2006 data, approximately 10% of 60,000 prostatectomy surgeries carried out annually were performed with the aid of robots. According to participating researchers, the accuracy achieved is much higher than that of a human. In 2001, the whole world was astonished when a patient in Strasbourg, France, was operated by a New York medical team, using signals emitted by fiber optic networks for a robotic arm in the operating room, at a distance of almost six thousand kilometers. The procedure lasted 54 minutes and was successful.[314]

Brazilian researcher Miguel Nicolelis reports several experiments with robotics arms and monkeys, proving the pos-

---

[314] Available on: <http://www.davincisurgery.com/>. Last access date: August 31, 2010.

sibility of brain interface with machines. In his latest book he goes beyond and teaches about further possibilities of brain / computer interfaces[315].

The Repliee Q1, developed by Osaka University and built by Kokoro Company Ltd., was a sensation at the 2005 World Expo in Nagoya, Japan. Also known as Actroid, when it was launched it was the most realistic humanoid ever built. She is able to locate the eyes of the interlocutor, turns around to be called, realizes great amount of movements and seems to breathe, due to the 42 joints on her face, controlled by air compressors. The project's lead scientist, Hiroshi Ishiguro, says people, in the first contact, interact with it as if it were human, in addition to showing surprise.

The release of a happy puppy-like robot, Sony's Aibo, transformed 1999 into the year that robots physically gained mass culture. From the world of fiction or industrial isolation, they now enter homes. More than a sales success because of its high cost, it was a success of popularity, because in a short time the whole world knew the novelty.

Autonomous, which means that it works without remote control, Aibo can perform several movements — run, walk, sit —, bark and even talk, it understands voice commands and learns new things. Equipped with a vision system, it can identify people and objects and take digital photos. Its operating system, Aiboware, has several modules. In one of them, the "life", the dog grew and matured. For those familiar with computer science, it is possible to program it for other activities, such as speaking with an English accent. He is also a participant in RoboCup, the world cup of robot soccer, in a category of his own. Its rather complex and relatively low-cost software has made Aibo more than just a toy, being a platform for studies at various universities. Until today it is much sought after in the used market or by collectors and researchers.

---

[315] Nicolelis, M. (2011). *Muito além do nosso eu: a nova neurociência que une cérebro e máquinas — e como ela pode mudar nossas vidas* [Far beyond our self: the new neuroscience that unites brain and machines — and how it can change our lives]. São Paulo: Companhia das Letras.

Another robot from Sony is the Qrio, whose name comes from "curious". In a humanoid form, it stores information about the environment around as it explores it. When walking, if it falls, it can stand up on his own. It looks like a simple action, but it represents a huge breakthrough when it comes to a robot. At its launch, Sony believed that in 2010, every Japanese home would have at least two robots, just for fun, which did not happen until the current year of 2018.

In early 2006, Sony reported that it would no longer produce Aibo and Qrio. Curiously, the news came a week after a study by researchers at Purdue University in the United States showed that robotic pets offer the same emotional benefits to owners as real animals.[316]

For those who prefer cats, the solution is NeCoRo, from the Japanese Omron. Kind of skittish, typical of his feline personality, he is happy to gain affection and brave when being mistreated. He sleeps, purrs and does not need to be fed.

Several other animals became robots, such as Paro, of the Japanese company Intelligent System. In the shape of a baby seal, it expresses contentment by being petted and is intended for the elderly, as it is a nice companion without demanding the care of a real pet, although you cannot expect a seal to behave in this way.

For lovers of prehistoric animals, the Chinese Wow Wee Toys launched the Roboraptor, a mechanical dinosaur that walks and reacts to outside stimuli, and Robosapien, able to dance and fight karate.

Lego's Mindstorms line attests to the popularity of robots among children and teenagers. Developed in conjunction with MIT, the models include plastic blocks with built-in programmable chips. These blocks, which are called RCX, are capable of communicating with a computer or other robots by exchanging data through infrared. The line also has electric motors, sensors, wheels and pneumatic devices. Much more than a sensational toy, Mindstorms is an educational

---

[316] Technologic innovation. Sony stops production of AIBO and QRIO robots. Retrieved from: <http://www.inovacaotecnologica.com.br/noticias/noticia.php?artigo=010180060131>. Last access date: October 3, 2010.

tool used in several fairs and robotics competitions in Brazil and the world, such as the First Lego League.

Several companies in the world have robots for educational purposes. Many of these robots can be seen in competitions such as First, which was designed by the American Dean Kamen and brings together thousands of students from various countries. The intention is to encourage knowledge of robotics through challenges to build models involving varied knowledge such as engineering or design.

RoboCup is the world cup of robot soccer. Held for the first time in 1997 in Nagoya, Japan. The games had researchers from 31 centers in ten countries and players were divided into different categories, depending on the size. It happens annually and has already been headquartered in several countries, such as France, Sweden, Australia, United States, among others. The big promotion was one of the responsible for the gigantic increase of participants. In 2005, back in Japan, in the city of Osaka, this event had 330 teams from ten countries and about two thousand participants. The big highlight was Team Osaka, who participated in the most complex category, the humanoids, and outclassed opponents.

Artificial intelligence is the great highlight, as players need, in each situation, to figure out what to do. Also, they must see the ball and its companions, which requires a sophisticated system of computer vision. They need to be agile and light because of the complexity of the movements.

Hiroaki Kitano, responsible for RoboCup, admits that this competition and similar ones have boosted the great development, but its goal is to create a team capable of winning the Soccer World Cup in 2050, the World Cup! The endeavor is difficult but quite possible. His only challenge is who would want to do it and pay for it.

Examples of intelligent robots are becoming more frequent in the news, being just mentioned a few of them, some are terrifying, like the Big dog, with which this list ends.

4.5 Human treatment for machines

The doctrine has considered that there is an increasingly favorable environment for the humanization or anthropomorphization of machines since Men attribute to them typically human characters.

Thus, for example, reports of computer and machine assaults are reported because of the feeling of anger, disillusionment or disappointment with the behavior of the equipment, such as when, for example, a machine receives the money but does not deliver the beverage can or when a computer crashes, looping in the eternal and stupid attempt to solve a non-computable problem, showing in the Windows operating system the famous and dreaded blue screen (BSOD) or even when the ATM does not deliver the money or makes it smaller or "swallows" the card.

In such cases, the human reaction is similar to or worse than that which could occur if the person responsible for the unfavorable acts was another Human Being. It is as if we could be angry with something that would be endowed with self-will and that would be acting against us.

Other times, human humor, action or anatomy is attributed to machines, as in the example of the hourglass icon indicating that the computer is "thinking" as if it had a brain — formerly called electronic brains — or when the drive or the computer itself is not willing to read a file or a media or a software does not want to run or when it is said that a computer has deleted or hid a file. Other times, Yorik Wilks and Afzal Ballim remember, saying "What the color chip is saying is that it is in the background mode", and they add: that there is no difference to what is said of the human body or its parts.[317]

This phenomenon has not gone unnoticed by Professor Rover[318]:

---

[317] Wilks, Y.; Ballim, A. Liability and consent. In Narayanan, A.; Bennun, M. (ed.). (1991). *Law, computer, science and artificial intelligence.* (pp. 118). New Jersey: Ablex Publishing Corporation.

[318] Rover, A. J. *Para um direito invisível: superando as artificialidades da inteligência* [For an invisible Law: overcoming the artificialities of intelligen-

*The psychological dimension of the human being to attri-
bute humanity to his creatures seems even more important.
Let us remember the old Tomagochi, so small and so rude,
but with a power of indecipherable unity with whom the human being takes as a guardian.*

For Negroponte[319]:

*What seems to trouble people most is their own self-con-
sciousness about talking to inanimate objects. We are perfectly comfortable talking to dogs and canaries, but not
doorknobs or lampposts (unless you are totally drunk).
Wouldn't I feel stupid talking to a toaster? Probably no more
so than you used to feel talking to an answering machine.*

Also, in this respect, it is convenient to repeat Sherry Turkle's
studies with the perception that children have of human elements
in computers, denoting a change or beginning of a psychological
paradigm shift. It is interesting how the submission to the current
paradigm is happening with their growth.[320]

---

ce.] Retrieved from: <http://www.infojur.ufsc.br/aires/arquivos/direito%20
invisivel%202005.pdf>. Last access date: February 25, 2009.

[319] Negroponte, N., *op. cit,* pp. 145-146.

[320] Turkle, S., op.cit., pp. 68-73: "So I chose six children, seven to nine years
old, who have been working with computers for several years, but who have
assured me that they have not read anything about an old or more recent work
by Wittgenstein.

I told each child (one at a time) that I would ask several questions and that there
would be no right or wrong, I just wanted their opinion. The questions were: Can the
computer remember? Does the computer learn? Computers think? Do computers
have feelings? Do you like computers? Do computers like you?

For the first two questions, the children answered affirmatively: Computers remember and learn. The third question required a few moments of reflection, and all but
two children concluded that yes, computers think. Apparently, an important tip for
the ability of computers to think for children was the fact that when children ask the
computer to do something, the computer responds immediately or sometimes takes
time while the computer apparently "thinks" about the task before answering. This,
in the opinion of children, is quite similar to the way they answer to the issues.

The fourth question — Do computers have feelings? — it was not only answered in the negative, but also it generally resulted in laughter when asked. Do
elephants fly? Laughter, according to Freud, sometimes results from a juxtaposition of two concepts that should not be together, which may derive from the fact

I had a similar experience with my daughter Maria, then at age four, obtaining similar results. Try it, too.

The way children see computers would be, for Kurzweil, a change of perspective that opens up to the possibility of lifeless consciousness, that is, the idea of an artificial consciousness.[321]

More than that. To the extent that younger children recognize typical human-like emotions in computers, hence the reason they are considered alive, when they grow up a little more, they recognize that computers are somewhat alive because they have intelligence, but they distinguish them from people just because the late have feelings. Thus, children identify with computers by psychological bonds, generating the possibility of confronting Man with the Aristotelian conception of rational animal, to consider people as emotional machines.[322]

This in itself does not confer any legal effect, say Wilks and Ballim, but it certainly constitutes a necessary precondition for the attribution of legal or other responsibility. They note, however, that these are real changes for anyone with Dennestist's tendencies.

> *A Dennetist tendency in philosophy — if we may use that word to refer to one who gives theoretical priority to successful explanatory vocabulary rather than underlying or direct ontological evidence — machines*

---

that the two concepts are never related before or a social taboo. Possibly the two motives caused laughter in this case.

In the fifth question, the children say yes, they liked computers. They all thought the last question was silly, that computers have no taste or aversion.

The children were, of course, answering questions based on understanding the terms employed. Their understanding is based on rich and diverse associations that our civilization posed in terms like "think" and "feel," but was not influenced by attempts by adult philosophers to establish precise definitions. What children seem to be saying is that computer analytical processing can be seen as thinking, but that feeling and liking, both involve a conscious active agent, are not characteristics perceived in a computer. In other words, "computers, or at least the computers with which these children have experience, are not aware, but they think, and therefore thinking does not require consciousness."

[321] Kurzweil, R. (1999). *The age of intelligent machines*. (pp. 71, 3rd reprint). Cambridge, Mass.: MIT Press.
[322] *Idem.*

may therefore now have certain key human character-
istics. If that is so, then it may be the peg on which to
hang any possible legal responsibility of machines or
programs.[323]

From this precondition, it is emphasized, Wilks and Ballim establish a gradation. They explain that in Common Law at least, there would be an established precedent, which deals with entities that are neither human nor totally irresponsible, which are animals like dogs, which would be different from *ferae naturae* such as tigers: if you create a tiger and this does something wrong, you are responsible because they are considered mere machines in your possession.

> *With dogs the situation is more complex and normally, though inaccurately, summed up in the cliché "every dog is allowed one bite"; the point being that a dog is not deemed savage simple because it bites someone once. It may, like us, be acting out of character. Whereas to be a savage dog is to be a habitual biter and, in particular, to have a savage character known to its owner. Tigers are not to be thought of as having characters to act out of: They are just machines that bite. This notion of having a character one could act out of is tightly bound up with the notions of moral and legal responsibility and blame.*

> *Dogs are blamed and punished in analogous ways to people — in some countries both can be executed — and that is only because they share very similar (though importantly different) physiological structures. The problem with machines and their programs, even if we were to squeeze them into the same category as dogs, would be how to blame and punish them.*[324]

The authors consider that this difficulty can always be avoided, always identifying the humans behind the machines and programs to take the blame, in the sense that for them there will always be real humans behind agents and companies with their own legal personalities, which today would not be difficult to do.

---

[323] Wilks, Y.; Ballim, A., *op. cit.*, p. 118-119.
[324] *Ibidem*, p.119.

However, things can become more complicated over time and with the simple replacement of the people responsible for delinquent machines. They cite two practical and current examples of these difficulties: first, there are sophisticated systems that are the results of the activity of several individuals, who have been constantly editing and updating their codes over the years, and today may not have any adequate documentation, as it happens, for example, with some open source applications. Those who might have written the documentation may even be dead. Great systems have reached a point where it becomes difficult and expensive to replace them. However, those who work with them are often unsure about the reasons why they do what they do, or what they can do in the future. Errors made by such software can hardly be attributed to the individuals currently responsible for them.

Second, they say, we are a small step away from a future in which the machine will gain greater authority over its situation, its data and even its cabinet, than it holds today.

In addition, the entire program content of such a machine can be terribly long, undocumented and effectively lacking structure (predictable), as occurs with the human brain, whose programming content is virtually inaccessible to third parties, although there is a tendency to ascribe great authority, including in Judgment, to what people say about their state of mind, especially in attributing the "guilty" state of mind, the *mens rea*.

The authors conclude:

> "That movement, through impenetrable software to ultimately inadequate diagnosis, is, we think, the progression by which blame (for machines) might creep in, despite the attempts by advocates of more perspicuous programming styles to keep it out."[325]

---

[325] *Ibidem*, p. 120.

4.6 Some technical requirements for The Attainment of Technological Singularity

4.6.1 Superconductivity

The adoption of superconductors or topological[326] insulation materials can provide, when they are available for use at viable temperatures, the appearance of a new generation of processors that are much more powerful than the current ones, or even the generation immediately before it. The explanation for both is plausible. Superconductors do not generate energy losses in the form of heat, conducting virtually all of the electricity that applies to them. Since they do not generate heat, they can be denser than semiconductor materials. This results in that, in the same space occupied by current semiconductors, a much larger number of superconductors can be generated, thus generating more processing capacity.

Thus, for example, the first generation of processors made from superconducting materials could, instead of doubling the processing capacity of the previous generation, as it does today under Moore's Law, it could multiply this capacity by ten. This gain can be achieved in the same dimension, for example in the X-axis, if ten times more transistors can be placed in the same space occupied by semiconductor transistors. If, in addition, also on the Y-axis if the same achievement is achieved, the gain of the X and Y (X * Y) axes is multiplied, which, in our example, is ten in each axis, resulting in a gain of hundred times concerning the previous generation.

It should be noted that the transistor paradigm was used above, which can, at a certain point, be replaced by other more efficient and better components.

---

[326] Zandonella, C. (2010, December) Computação a frio [Cold computing] *Revista Info Exame*. Viva na casa do futuro hoje. [Live in the house of the future today] (pp. 80-84) Abril.

Similarly, the two-dimensional paradigm, which is a limitation currently existing in regular silicon chips, is maintained in the given example, due to thermal factors.

Nothing prevents the thermal problem due to the use of the superconductors to go on to design three-dimensional[327], processors, since the third axis (Z) would not concentrate more heat, and possible processing gains would be even greater. Thus, maintaining the ten-fold increment in the Z-axis — actually the Z value is zero, and therefore, the simple adoption of this new axis, giving three-dimensionality to the chips, would result in a superlative gain, although mathematically being zero the Z-axis value, any multiplication of it would result in zero. However, it is not a matter here of multiplying, but if we add a new axis that will multiply the result of the multiplication of the previous axes — we would have the following equation (X * Y * Z), with each axis being valid 10, resulting in a thousand-fold increase.

Now, you can get out of double gains for gains of ten, a hundred or a thousand or more!

This will cause an assumed graph of the computational capacity increase (horizontal axis A) on a time scale (vertical axis B) to consistently grow in the form of an ascending horizontal line, to be represented by an ascending line which, at any given moment, would become vertical, because the exponential scale of growth would burst.

---

[327] Intel anuncia transistores 3d.[Intel announces 3d transistors.] Retrieved from: <http://www.oficinadanet.com.br/noticias_web/3812/intel-anuncia-transistores-3d>. INTEL ANUNCIA TRANSÍSTORES TRIMENDICIONAIS, E DEMONSTRA IVE BRIDGE. Retrieved from:
<http://www.hardware.com.br/noticias/2011-05/intel-transistores-tridimensionais.html>. Last access date: May 05, 2011.

According to Kurzweil[328] and Vernor Vinge[329], among others, this will occur when we reach the technological singularity, an opportunity that, for the adoptive authors of this line of thought may occur on different dates, but will come.

To get an idea of the thermal problem of the processors, just see how much over clockers are dedicated to cool their CPUs for more performance.

In this direction, Rover's[330] lesson:

> *Technological evolution has the potential to reach its degree of singularity to which there would be no more explanation and logical description of this evolution, size, dynamism and overcoming stages. [...] In the short term, it is said that by 2029 home computers will have the capacity to process a thousand human brains.*

This understanding is defended by Kurzweil.[331]

4.6.2 Nanotechnology

Also, the development of nanotechnology[332] will allow producing equipment and circuits of small sizes and with special characteristics, not found in nature, potentializing the manufacture of components and, thus, the power of the equipment.

I will not go into details about nanotechnology, because, for the present work, it seems sufficient to say that it is the technology that works materials and produces machines at the atomic level.

---

[328] Kurzweil, R. (1999). *The age of intelligent machines*. (pp. 150-151, 3rd reprint). Cambridge, Mass.: MIT Press.

[329] Vinge, V. *What is The Singularity?* Retrieved from: <http://webcache.google-usercontent.com/search?q=cache:2UA--AmSFT0J:mindstalk.net/vinge/vingesing.html+singularity+vernor+vinge&hl=pt-BR&ct=clnk&cd=1&gl=br&client=firefox-a>. Last Access date: February 13, 2009.

[330] Rover, A. J. *Para um direito invisível: superando as artificialidades da inteligência* [For an invisible Law: overcoming the artificialities of intelligence]. Retrieved from: <http://www.infojur.ufsc.br/aires/arquivos/direito%20invisivel%202005.pdf>. Last access date: February 25, 2009.

[331] Kurzweil, R., *op. cit.*, loc. cit.

[332] Technology that works with objects the size of billionths of a meter (10^{-9}).

4.6.3 Quantum computing

Quantum computing will free computers from their simple binary capability, based on pattern 0 or 1, yes or no, on or off, and so on. Truly, as amazing as it is all a computer can do these days, it does this by processing binary information, that is, the computer can only deal with two stages or states, or points.

Now, between zero and one, there is an infinite number of points that the computer cannot handle simultaneously. This is a reflection of the application of classical physics to modern computing.

Thus, for example, in classical mechanics, a body cannot occupy more than one place in space at the same time. That way, if a body is in a given place it will be impossible to be in another place at that very moment, something that can be affirmed with absolute certainty in the world apprehensible by the Human Being.

However, with the advent of quantum physics, with the most accurate knowledge of atomic and subatomic particles, a new universe was unveiled. Now we know of the existence of particles that may be probabilistically in more than one place at the same time, as well as other subatomic behaviors that are impossible in classical mechanics.

Then the possibility of building quantum computers arises. The Turing machine was no longer the most sophisticated way of counting stones![333]

The need for the quantum computer arose from the incomputable characteristic of the general problem of calculating properties of a quantum system since the number of computational steps grew exponentially with the size of the studied system. "Because a quantum computer can perform all possible calculations at the same

---

[333] Galvão, E. F. (2007). *O que é computação quântica?* [What is quantum computing?] Rio de Janeiro: Vieira e Lent Casa Editorial Ltda. (pp. 7). "The word calculate comes from stone in Greek, possibly in an allusion to a rudimentary way of counting units, of calculating, of computing."

time, it can be the key to building more powerful computers."[334]

It was Richard Feynman[335] who, in 1982, showed the possibility of creating a quantum computer and thus overcoming the limitation of the binary computer.

Going a little further, David Deutsch, in 1985, described the quantum equivalent of a Turing machine, but it was only in 1994 that a real problem was discovered for which the quantum computer would be faster than the traditional one: factorization of integers.[336]

The solution was discovered by Peter Shor[337] who, using quantum steps, demonstrated that quantum computers can factor a number with a number of computational steps that grows as a polynomial of the number of digits of that number, transforming a non-computable problem into solvable in practice, as long as it is possible to construct a quantum computer.

It is interesting to add, with a special mention in Galvão, that science has not yet been able to determine the computational complexity of various problems, whether for classical or quantum computers.[338] Also, it is not known what kind of problem can be intractable in the binary computer and treatable in a quantum computer. The quantum computer, in at least three types of operation, is superior: simulation of quantum systems, factorization and search in a database. The latter can mean a tremendous increase in speed for obtaining data on the basis of gigantic proportions.

---

[334] Gerschenfeld, N., *op. cit.*, p. 158.

[335] Galvão, *op. cit.*, p.24.

[336] *Ibidem*, p. 26.

[337] Gerschenfeld, N., *op. cit.*, p. 159. "This began to change in the early 1990s. A series of results were proved by David Deutsch, Richard Josza of Plymouth University, and Dan Simon, now at Microsoft, showing that a quantum computer is more powerful than a classical computer for a series of increasingly less trivial problems. In 1994 Peter Shor of AT&T was able to use these techniques to show that a quantum computer could find prime factors in polynomial instead of exponential time. This made factoring a four-hundred-digit number almost as easy as multiplying its factors."

[338] *Ibidem*, p.31.

Moreover, not even quantum physics, or rather the phenomena it deals with, are fully or uncontroversially understood.

Do not imagine that quantum computing or quantum applications are things of the future, because there are already quantum systems in operation today, such as quantum cryptography.

Recalling quantum physics, let us remember that, unlike normal mechanics, quantum particles do not have a well-defined position, and can be in more than one place or in all places of a given interval at the same time. Their position is determined probabilistically.

By using particles and atoms with these somewhat erratic characteristics, the quantum computer can handle a greater number of data, precisely because it can be in more than one state at the same time.

For this, some characteristics of the particles must be used: quantum superposition[339] e o entanglement[340].

Therefore, there is a possibility that the use of quantum computing accelerates technological development and increases computational capacity in an extraordinary way.

Galvão exemplifies in a simple and intelligent way. In computation — stone counting[341] — traditional, in the molds of classical mechanics, the process has as computational steps a pebble and two holes. The pebble would occupy one hole at a time. Thus, in the first computational step, the pebble would be in the zero hole, then it would stay in hole one, returning to zero and so, successively alternating the hole with each computational step.

Changing perspective to quantum mechanics, instead of the pebble, we have a particle. However, it can occupy either of the two holes, zero or one or even the two holes, or any point, also

---

[339] *Ibidem*, p.44.
[340] *Ibidem*, p.52-61. Basically the entanglement is the demonstration that distant quantum particles seem to be communicating, so that the measurements of their properties reveal coordinated results between them, allowing the creation of pairs of particles.
[341] Hillis, D., *op. cit.* Interesting is the comparison made between the notches in the caves and the silicon chip that exists in this work, the reason for its title.

simultaneously, between the two holes, in the face of the superposition.

Since there is the effect of entanglement, the changes made on a particle, whether it is at any point, will affect its twin where it is.

This entanglement allows you to think about teleportation[342], encryption, telecommunications and data processing, especially for the synchronization of distant clocks, bank authentication, etc.

A complex computable task can be divided into a number of simple computational steps, occupying an X number of bits[343]. In the quantum computer, we have qbits[344], which can create states

---

[342] Wiener, N. (1971). *Deus, Golem e Cia: um comentário sobre certos pontos de contato entre cibernética e religião* [God and Golem, Inc.: A Comment on Certain Points where Cybernetics Impinges on Religion] (L. Hegenberg and O. S. da Mota, Trans.). São Paulo: Cultrix. p. 7. He understands that teleportation is possible: "The idea has already attracted my attention previously: I believe that it is conceptually possible to send a human being from one place to another via a telegraph line. I hasten to clarify that the difficulties of such a project far exceed my ability to imagine solutions to the problem, and that I have no intention of solving transportation problems by creating a telegraph carrier. Nowadays, the idea is impractical. It may remain impractical throughout the entire existence of the human race. This, however, does not make it inconceivable."

[343] Microsoft Press. (1998) *Dicionário de informática.* [Information technology dictionary] (V. Chamon, Trans.). (3rd ed.) Microsoft Press, São Paulo: Editora Campus: "*bit* – Reduced form of *binary digit*; the zero or the one of the binary numbering system. In data processing and storage, a *bit* is the smallest unit of information handled by the computer, being represented physically by a specific element – for example, an isolated pulse sent through a circuit, or a small point on a magnetic disk, capable of containing a zero or a one. Seen in isolation, a bit provides no information that a human being can consider meaningful. However, in groups of eight, bits become bytes, which are the best known form of representation of all types of information on the computer, including the letters of the alphabet and the digits from zero to nine". *See also* ASCII; binary; byte.

[344] GERSCHENFELD, Neil, *op. cit.*, p. 159. "[...] If a quantum bit is in a superposition of 0 and 1, and it interacts with a second bit, the value of the second bit will depend on the state of the first. If they're now separated to opposite ends of the universe and the first bit is measured, it is forced to decide between being a 0 or a 1. At that instant, the value of the second bit is determined. This appears to be an instantaneous action at a distance, something that made Einstein very unhappy. It is called entanglement, and it serves in effect to wire together the

that are impossible to reach with classical physics, resulting in a quantum computer not needing a number of qbits[345] as large as a classical computer would need bits to decompose a complex computable problem.

Of course, to understand what a qbit is, you need to know what a bit is. A curious description, though not a technical definition, is given by Negroponte:

> *A bit has no color, size, or weight, and it can travel at the speed of light. It is the smallest atomic element in the DNA of information. It is a state of being on or off, true or false, up or down, in or out, black or white.*[346]

This implies, in a simplified way and without allusion to the problems of quantum computing, such as decoherence[347], that is currently being faced, that a quantum computer with N qbits would be equivalent to 2n binary computers working simultaneously. If the quantum system has little entanglement, it will be easy to simulate it in a classical computer, and it is not necessary to build a quantum computer until this can be achieved by the technology.

The technology for the construction of quantum computers is in full development and has already made possible the construction of small models.

In addition, since quantum computation uses quantum physics, more has been discovered about how to control quantum systems with a few nanometers.

4.6.4 The Law of Accelerating Returns

> *«In the game of life and evolution, there are three participants: humans, nature and machines. I am firmly on the side of nature, but I suspect nature is on the side of machines."*

---

bits in a quantum computer".

[345] Oliveira, I. S. e Vieira, C. L. (2009). *A revolução dos q-bits: o admirável mundo da computação quântica* [The q-bit revolution: the admirable world of quantum computing]. (1st ed.) São Paulo: Jorge Zahar.

[346] Negroponte, N., *op. cit.*, p. 19.

[347] Phenomenon of the disappearance of overlaps.

(Darwin among the machines, George Dyson)[348]

Much was discussed and still is discussed about the pace of technological advances. There are several theories on the subject in the scientific field and futurology. In addition, the future also worries companies, who make big investments to prepare for its arrival.

Concerning the interest of companies in knowing the future today, Bruce Sterling's story is intriguing:

> *The strangest thing about my relationship with capitalism is how close the business world was to science fiction. As the years went by and my career progressed, business moved ever faster and more aggressively into my own cultural territory. Science fiction has always been a motto for the odd and the unlikely, but the turn of the century marked the first time I began to receive serious job offers from companies. Business people have begun inviting me to executive positions, to integrate advisory boards and the board of directors of corporations. It was no use telling me that I had never in my life been on a payroll, that I had no experience as an executive, that I had no interest in meeting the shareholders' expectations. They already knew all this. In fact, they liked that part. That's why they were after me. I make my living in a strange imaginary junk, and they considered it a major asset in the business world.*[349]

Many scientists have dedicated themselves to the subject as well. Paul Virilio had already taken care of the speed of change. Richard Buckminster-Fuller had already pointed out that the exponential speed of technological development had more effect on the way of living and thinking than politics.[350]

The academia also seeks to apprehend this new reality. The University Singularity, created by Kurzweil and Peter Diamandis,

---

[348] Dyson, G. *Darwin among the machines. Apud* Shimizu, H., op. cit (epigraph).
[349] Sterling, B. Tomorrow now. *O Estadão online*. Retrieved from: <http://www.oesquema.com.br/trabalhosujo/2010/12/06/bruce-sterling-julio-verne.htm>. Last access date: February 14, 2009.
[350] For further explanation, see Virilio, P. (1996). *Política e velocidade* [Politics and speed] (C. M. Paciornik, Trans.). São Paulo: Editora Estação Liberdade.

operates in some buildings of the Ames Research Center in California, near Silicon Valley, and opened its doors to the first thirty students in the summer of 2009.[351]

As mentioned above, the confluence of certain technological advances has allowed the doctrine, notably Kurzweil, to express the understanding that there is a real possibility of, in the not too distant future, really intelligent machines arise to the point of matching us or even surpass us, as a next step.

Some of these technologies, such as computing — viewed by cost-processing capability — have developed over time on a geometric rather than arithmetic scale. This means that their pace of growth is increasing.

In fact, the Law of Accelerating Returns applies not only to technology but also, to biological evolution, insofar as it is considered a phase of technology.

Since the appearance of the Universe, estimated ten or eleven billion years ago, evolution has begun. First not biological. In general terms, the emergence of life on earth took about two billion years. The same time, or almost, was spent for the first multicellular beings to appear, about 700 million years ago.

For Kurzweil[352], the goal of evolution, by natural selection, is not complexity, although it is obvious that it sets in, but seek better answers to the problem of individual and species survival and perpetuation, ie autopoietic balance. He sees in evolution an ordering of life, giving a precise meaning to order:

> *Order is not the same as the opposite of disorder. If disorder represents a random sequence of events, the opposite of disorder should be "not randomness." Information is a sequence of data that is meaningful in a process, such as the DNA code of an organism or the bits in a computer program. [...] Order is information that fits a purpose. The measure of order is the measure of how well the information fits the purpose. In the evolution of lifeforms, the purpose is*

---

[351] *Idem.*

[352] Kurzweil, R. (2005). *The Singularity is near: when humans transcends biology.* (pp. 39). New York: Penguin Books.

> *to survive. In an evolutionary algorithm (a computer pro-*
> *gram that simulates evolution to solve a problem) applied*
> *to, say, designing a jet engine, the purpose is to optimize*
> *engine performance, efficiency [...]*

Although he does not state explicitly, it seems that Gordil-ho[353] glimpses the effects of the Law of Accelerating Returns on biological evolution by defending, with a special mention in Varela that,

> *On the other hand, natural selection does not always rep-*
> *resent the perfection of the species, for nature follows much*
> *more of a proscriptive law of the type 'what is not forbidden*
> *is permitted', than a prescriptive law of the kind 'which is*
> *not allowed is forbidden', so that changes often do not oc-*
> *cur gradually **but through sudden jumps**. (our emphasis)*

From the onset of mammals, evolution began to show its acceleration. These animals came to dominate the earth about sixty-five million years ago, with the extinction of giant dinosaurs. The first primates appeared, and the time unit became a few million years. According to some estimates, the earliest hominids appeared between five hundred and three hundred and fifty thousand years ago. *Homo sapiens* dates from about one hundred and fifty thousand to one hundred thousand years.

The last glaciation occurred about ten thousand years ago. The earliest civilizations appeared about 7,000 to 5,000 years ago. Then the striking events are measured over centuries, then decades, and then years.

In the 19th century, technological progress matched the advances made over the previous ten centuries.

Progress in the first two decades of the 20th century was comparable to that of the entire 19th century. Today, significant technological transformations take only a few years to happen. Just look at the examples of the use of horses, carriages, trains, cars and airplanes in the transport segment. In communications, we start from the carved stone, for papyrus, parchment, press, radio, tele-

---

[353] Gordilho, H. J. de S., *op. cit.*, p. 83-84.

phone, television, videocassette, cellular, DVD, internet, HDDVD (already out of date) and blu-ray. Combining two of these technologies, it turns out that the internet took only five years to reach the growth of television.[354]

The pace of launching new products is staggering[355]. See the sales pace of the iPhone and iPad.[356] Most recently — within a few months — Microsoft's Kinect.[357]

Each of these inventions has reached the same number of users in a shorter period of time compared to the previous technology. Time is now counted in months or even weeks!

Take the example of Moore's Law[358] to realize that every two years, the processing capacity doubles to a chip of the same price.

Although it is thought that Moore's Law is expected to be violated in a few years[359], given the physical limit for the creation of transistor components of the chips, which cannot, in theory, be smaller than the size of an atom, alternatives are already being

---

[354] Carvalho, O. S. de. *Educação na sociedade de informação.* [Education in the information society]. Retrieved from: <www.serprofessor universitario.pro.br>. Last access date: February 14, 2009.

[355] Retrieved from: <http://www.ncbi.nlm.nih.gov/books/NBK2271/>. Last access date: December 27, 2010.

[356] *Indústria multiplica por 20 ritmo de novidades.* [Industry multiplies by 20 the rhythm of news.] Retrieved from: <http://www.anpei.org.br/imprensa/noticias/industria-multiplica-por-20-ritmo-de-novidades/>. Last access date: December 21, 2010. "Manufacturers accelerated the pace of launches: Samsung has gone from 10 to 200 new products a year, reaching full portfolio renewal every 365 days. LG, also with 10 releases at the beginning of the last decade, today presents 120 new models a year. Sony, meanwhile, among products and accessories, has almost doubled the annual volume of news, to 2,1 thousand items."

[357] *Revista Info Exame.* (2011, January). (N. 299, pp. 48). Editora Abril.

[358] Gordon Moore, who invented the integrated circuit and is one of Intel's founders, stated in 1965 that the surface area of a transistor embedded in an integrated circuit was being reduced by 30 percent every 12 months since 1958. In 1975 he reviewed this analysis by extending the time frame to 24 months. As a result, every two years, the number of transistors inserted in an integrated circuit doubles, thus doubling both the number of components in a chip and its speed, keeping the cost of production constant. Today, this span of time is estimated in 18 months.

[359] Galvão, E. F., *op. cit.*, p. 114.

sought and even created and used to escape the silicon pattern, such as studies with gallium arsenate and the construction and sale of processors made from hafnium (Hf)[360]. In addition, studies with biochips are already underway, which rely on organic capacities for computation.[361]

> *But sometime around 2020 or so everything will hit bottom. At the rate of current progress, the wires will be one atom wide, the memory cells will have one electron, and the fab plan will cost the GNP of the planet so that no one can afford to build anyway. Further improvements cannot come from the current path of shrinking silicon circuits.*[362,363]

Even in silicon, you can look for computational gains of the order of fifty times if you have already used GPUs to collaborate

---

[360] In the past two years, the Core 2 Duo has been outperformed by the Core 2 Quad, i3, i5 and i7, to be limited to Intel's desktop line processors.

[361] Welborn, S. *Race to create a "living computer"*. Retrieved from: <http://74.125.47.132/search?q=cache:GkV srFC5jvIJ:members.fortunecity.com/y2kprepare/livecomp. htm+%E2%80%9CRace+to+Create+A+%E2%80%98Living+Compute r%E2%80%99%E2%80%9D&cd=1&hl=pt-BR&ct=clnk&gl=br&client =firefox-a>. Last access date: February 09, 2009, p. 1-3. "The race to create microcomputers using organic "biochips" has already begun. Scientists are trying to create computer circuits in biology labs from living bacteria, producing microprocessors with 10 million times the memory of today's most powerful machines.

The future circuits of the "organic computer" will contain groups of organic proteins, the size of molecules, that serve as electronic memory and switch on the chips. James McLear, president of Gentronics Laboratories explains that "because of the ability of proteins to self-organize, the computer kind of would do the same." It is hoped that the biochip will facilitate the development of the computer's ability to application in daily life. The biochip will allow the computer to connect to the human nervous system to create artificial eyes, ears and voice systems. Deployed in the bloodstream, the biochip can monitor body functioning and correct imbalances.

For Forrest Carter of the Naval Research Laboratory, "at some point in the future, silicon may no longer be the choice of material to be used in semiconductor chips [...]".

[362] Gerschenfeld, N., *op. cit.*, p. 156.

[363] None of these have happened yet in 2019 (Author's note).

with the CPUs, as well as with the use of multinucleated processors.

Therefore, the search for new technologies and new materials will allow to overcome the thermal limit of the silicon, so that, in the same area, more transistors are added, without overheating due to the proximity between them and the electrons when passing between the components and tracks to meet the cycles of the processor and its internal components.

Well, starting from Moore's Law, Kurzweil[364] noted that biological and technological advances are developing at an increasing pace. In addition, computing in Kurzweil's vision embraces both technological and Darwinian evolution. He connected Moore's Law to the Law of Time and Chaos resulting in the Law of Accelerating Returns.

The Chaos Law explains that chaos increases exponentially as time decreases, also exponentially.

The Law of Accelerating Returns postulates that time accelerates exponentially as order increases, also exponentially. Its development leads to the understanding that this law is a continuation of the evolution of species, independently of the human will, being in this particular a natural law. As a result, by 2020, another computational technology, no longer human, will impose itself.[365] At that moment, the singularity will occur.[366,367]

Thus Kurzweil states:

> The introduction of technology on Earth is not merely the private affair of one of the Earth's innumerable species. It is a pivotal event in the history of the planet. Evolution's grandest creation -- human intelligence -- is providing the means for the next stage of evolution, which is technology.

---

[364] Kurzweil, R. *The Singularity is near: when humans transcend biology*. (pp. 56). New York: Penguim Books.

[365] Santos, L. G. dos. *A inteligência das espécies* [The intelligence of species]. Retrieved from: <http://www.estado.com.br/editorias/2007/09/23/cad-1.93.2.20070923.30.1.xml>. Last access date: February 04, 2009.

[366] Kurzweil, R., *op. cit.*, p.21.

[367] In 2019 it doesn't seem to be happening.

> *The emergence of technology is predicted by the Law of Accelerating Returns. The Homo sapiens sapiens subspecies emerged only tens of thousands of years after its human forebears. According to the Law of Accelerating Returns, the next stage of evolution should measure its salient events in mere thousands of years, too quick for DNA-based evolution. This next stage of evolution was necessarily created by human intelligence itself, another example of the exponential engine of evolution using its innovations from one period (human beings) to create the next (intelligent machines).*[368]

By law, as the order, whose concept was referred to above, increases exponentially, the time interval between relevant events decreases, accelerating the advances, resulting in that the returns, the products of the process, accelerate at non-linear rates. Yes, because evolution results in a better response, it creates a better complexity, although it sometimes reduces complexity.

The measure of ordination is the success of the solution engendered. Thus, the improvement of the solution increases the order. Now, once the best solution is configured, it is from this that the process follows, without having to test all the previous solutions, abandoned or overcome. This results in positive feedback that drives development. This occurs successively, resulting in gains that reduce the time between the important events of the process, causing a growing acceleration of evolution, whether it is technological or biological.[369]

Note that the previous results are not neglected. It is always built based on what has already been achieved, so development times shorten and speed increases.

Take the example of human development in early childhood. Ignoring, for purposes of exemplification, the numerous variations that exist and considering a pattern that I judged arbitrarily to be frequent, the following happens: the baby can initially only move the head and limbs. Over time, with the strengthening of members and better coordination, he starts to turn around in the crib. Then

---

[368] Kurzweil. *op. cit.*, p. 21.
[369] Kurzweil, R. *op. cit.*, p. 43.

he can lean on it and get on all fours. Then he begins to swing supported by hands and knees until he begins to crawl. The next step is to balance himself in the knees only and start looking for support to climb and try to stand up. Then he can walk on anything that supports him. Then he stands, standing autonomously, without any support, to then take the first step, fall and insistently try until he can walk. Then he walks ever firmer until he becomes the biped we are.

Note that at each stage it is no longer necessary to return to the initial stage. So, for example, it is not necessary for the baby to turn around again in the crib to move to the standing position to walk. All phases start from the previous phase, taking advantage of the gains already achieved, without having to start all over again. It is the Law of Accelerating Returns in action.

This will imply that humans may not participate in the development of the next stages of evolution, replaced by another paradigm, robocentric.

Kurzweil[370] exemplifies:

> *If I scan your brain and nervous system with a suitably advanced noninvasive-scanning technology of the early twenty-first century—a very-high-resolution, high-bandwidth magnetic resonance imaging, perhaps—ascertain all the salient information processes and then download that information to my suitably advanced neural computer, I'll have a little you or at least someone very much like you right here in my personal computer. If my personal computer is a neural net of simulated neurons[371] made of electronic stuff rather than human stuff, the version of you in my computer will run about a million times faster. So an hour for me would be a million hours for you, which is about a century.*

---

[370] Kurzweil, R. *In*: Bressane, R. *Morrer datou* [Dying is outdated]. Retrieved February 14, 2009 from: <http://impostor.wordpress.com/2008/11/01/morrer-da-tou/>.

[371] Dawkins, R., *op. cit.*, p. 111. "The author understood that the individual neuron is a data processing unit much more sophisticated than the transistor, although slower, since in one of these cells there may be tens of thousands of connections, whereas in the semiconductor there are only few connections. In addition, the cell has a much higher level of miniaturization".

Similarly, in 1990, given the rate at which it occurred, critics predicted that it would take thousands of years to decipher the genome because a tiny percentage of the code had been known. Even by the calculations of 2003, the time actually spent was insignificant. Amazingly, everything else was deciphered in the remaining time. The cost of sequencing decreased from $ 10 a pair deciphered to a few cents. It took 15 years to sequence the DNA of the HIV virus and 31 days for the same task targeting the bird flu virus. The average American's life expectancy was 37 years in 1800, 48 years in 1900 and 78 years in 2002.[372]

It is interesting to note that Kurzweil's predictions have been realistic, and even his detractors respect them. An example of this was the prediction made in 1990 that a computer would defeat the human chess champion in 1998.[373] He missed the prediction for a year, because Deep Blue defeated Gary Kasparov in 1997.[374]

Let's not focus only on technological examples. Human bodies are undergoing accelerated transformations. Just over a century or two ago, humans had on average three molars, sometimes four.

Currently, the number of people who have third molars has decreased and those who have four molars are rare. Another more striking and visible example is the average height. A quick reminder is enough to see the average height of men of the early 20th century for the difference in the average height of adolescents today, early 21st century.

---

[372] Kurzweil, R. *How technology's accelerating power will transform us*. Video lecture. Monterey, California: filmed in February 2005, posted in November 2006. Retrieved from: <http://www.ted.com/index.php/talks/ray_kurzweil_on_how_technology_will_transform_us.html>. Last access date: February 22, 2009.

[373] *Idem*.

[374] *Game over: Kasparov and the machine*. The ultimate battle of man vs. machine. Vikram Javanti (dir.). Canadá: Gambit Films Limited/ BBC/ UK Film Council/ National Film Board of Canada. 2003. 85 minutes. DVD.

Yes, human evolution has been striding, exponentially. This is still a controversial and recent subject in the scientific doctrine, but that already begins to occupy a prominent place in the specialized publications.

Recently, the US magazine Discovery[375] published a story under the title "Are We Still Evolving? Our story is far from over: humans are actually changing faster than ever."

It is reported that a group of researchers observed numerous adaptive mutations present in the human genome; some of them have occurred faster and faster, like an avalanche. Statistical data shows that human evolution has occurred at a rate 100 times faster in the last 10,000 years than at any other time in our history.

There are some 2,000 (two thousand) genetic adaptations related to the brain, digestive system, life expectancy, immunity to pathogens, sperm and bone production — in short, practically all aspects of human functioning.

Many of these DNA variations are limited to the continent of origin, with certain provocative implications. Anthropologist Henry Harpending of the University of Utah, the co-author of an important book on human evolution, analyzes: "It is possible that the human races are evolving in ways different from each other." He further states that "We are not equal to the people who lived a thousand or two thousand years ago."[376].

Even today's skeptics admit that at least some human traits are evolving rapidly, challenging once-crystallized beliefs, including that human evolution, would have stalled.

Not only environmental causes, but cultural causes are fastly changing our bodies, according to Daniel Lieberman.[377]

---

[375] Mcauliffe, K. (2009, March). Are we still evolving? Our history is far from over: humans are actually changing faster than ever. *Discover Magazine*. (pp. 50-59). 2009.

[376] *Ibidem*, p. 51.

[377] For an intriguing and well written book about our body's story I recommend The Story of the Human Body: Evolution, Health, and Disease by Daniel Lieberman.

John Hawks,[378] of the University of Wisconsin notes that: "You do not have to try hard to see that the teeth are getting smaller, the size of the skull is decreasing, the stature is being reduced." (As for the latter, as we have seen above, it cannot be agreed, except, perhaps, if the time sample is long enough).

Hawks' theory of accelerated human evolution was influenced by newly formulated genetic data. Due to advances in DNA sequencing and decoding in recent years, scientists have begun to discover, one by one, genes that drive the evolutionary race. These variants emerged in the Stone Age and appear to help populations fight off contagious organisms more efficiently, survive inhospitable temperatures, or adapt to local conditions. And these variants have come up with a high frequency.

Hawks and Gregory Cochran,[379] a physicist and associate professor at the University of Utah, discussed the matter on the telephone. Hawks recalls: "We both realized at the same time that there are a lot more people on the planet recently". "In a large population, you do not have to wait so long for the rare mutation which boosts brain function or does anything else desirable".

Ten thousand years ago, there were less than 10 million people on Earth. That number rose to 200 (two hundred) million at the time of the Roman Empire. Since 1500 the global population has increased exponentially, surpassing 7 billion. Cochran[380] notes: "Darwin himself emphasized the importance of maintaining a large herd for selecting favorable traits." Interesting is that there is a variation of human DNA of less than 0.5% (half percent) from one man to any other on Earth.

Researchers have found that 7% (seven percent) of human genes fit into the recent adaptation profile, with most of the changes occurring between the last 40,000 years and the present day. These apparent adaptations occurred at the same exponential rate as the population explosion. To counter the classic view — that our evo-

---

[378] *Ibidem*, p.52.

[379] *Ibidem*, p.52.

[380] Mcauliffe, K., *op. cit.*, p. 53.

lution has occurred at a steady rate — scientists do an additional test. They simulated on the computer to observe what would have happened if humans had evolved at current rates since there was the distancing of the chimpanzees six million years ago. The test led to an absurd result: the difference between the two species to-day would be 160 (one hundred and sixty) times greater than it really is. The results confirmed that human evolution has only re-cently reached such acceleration. Just read Hawks' claim that no one on earth had blue eyes ten thousand years ago.

Also, a mutation that appeared 8,000 (eight thousand) years ago in northern Europe allowed the digestion of lactose (the main sugar in milk) by adults and this spread rapidly, allowing the rise of the dairy industry. Today, the gene for lactose digestion is present in 80% (eighty percent) of Europeans, but only twenty percent (20%) of Asians and Africans.

Malaria has been endemic in sub-Saharan Africa and other regions. People in this region have already developed twenty-five (25) new genes that protect them from malaria, including the Duffy[381] blood type, an entirely new blood group. More re-cently, resistance to HIV has arisen due to a genetic mutation present in 10% (ten percent) of Europeans. Scientists believe the variant may have evolved originally as a protection against smallpox.

Human semen may also be evolving at a high speed because of competition for reaching the egg before another sperm does. Since sperm can fertilize an ovum within 24 hours after being ejaculated in the vagina, a woman who engages in sex with two or more part-ners in a short time may be creating a competition field between sperm. Today's sperm is very different from the spermatozoid of 5,000 (five thousand) thousand years ago.

The examples are varied and impressive.

The brain may be evolving as fast as the rest of the body. Other genes that are rapidly changing — approximately one hundred —

---

[381] *The Duffy Blood group*. Retrieved from: <http://www.ncbi.nlm.nih.gov/books/NBK2271/>. Last access date: December 29, 2010.

are related, among others, to dopamine and serotonin. It is estimated that 40% (forty percent) of the neurotransmitter genes appear to have been selected over the past 50,000 years, with most having arisen in the last 10,000 (ten thousand) years.

Thus, it can be affirmed that the Law of Accelerating Returns has imprinted its effects on biological and technological evolution and concurred for the appearance of the singularity.

Regarding Man, but in the field of sociology and cyberculture, Lemos[382] had already noticed that,

From mechanics to electricity, from microelectronics to nano-technologies, technology spreads at enormous speed, infiltrating both everyday objects and the human body, in an incessant movement of miniaturization, aesthetics, automation, and self-regulation.

Therefore, not only the experimental sciences but also the human sciences have supported the idea of an acceleration in the evolutionary course.

Thus, as stated by the Law of Accelerated Returns, both biological, particularly human, and technological evolution have undergone exponential growth.

In this way, one might think that, since man is currently at the forefront of anthropologically conceived intelligence, this Man-machine disparity would be assured. This fact can indeed occur, as long as the power by which the two evolutions multiply is the same.

On the other hand, if it is true, as Moravec[383] has said, that the speed of evolution of machines is ten million times faster than that of humans, we must take into account the newly discovered human evolutionary speed to verify if this mismatch still happens. If this mismatch is smaller or larger, but remains and therefore the deadline for the technological singularity would be changed. Or, if there is no more mismatch and the two evolutions occur synchronously,

[382] Lemos, A., *op. cit.*, p. 17.
[383] Moravec, H. *Interview given to RobotBooks.com.* Retrieved from: <http://www.robotbooks.com/Moravec.htm>. Last access date: February 27, 2009.

permanently or temporarily maintaining the *status quo*.

Based on all that is happening and has been happened in recent decades, there does not seem to be a perfect human and technological evolutionary synchronism, but a mismatch in favor of technology that will guarantee, sooner or later, even with recent discoveries about human evolution, that technological singularity will take effect.

4.6.5 Machine learning

Currently, what has been most successful in the development of artificial intelligence systems is what is known as machine learning.

Instead of Man taking care of all aspects of programming in order to obtain a specialist system, it allows the computer itself to recognize patterns through algorithms that will recognize their own errors and produce better versions of themselves evolving.

Artificial intelligence systems have now achieved greater advances than those obtained by human beings.

It is not possible here to talk about machine learning or deep learning. What I want to emphasize is that in the field of development of artificial intelligence systems, the machines themselves are developing at an exponential speed and producing better results than Men.

4.6.6 Big Data

Another important breakthrough that will contribute to the attainment of technological uniqueness is Big Data, which is, in short, the ability of some algorithms to handle gigantic amounts of data that could never before be appreciated by humans or previous computer systems.

With this, a colossal volume of situations, variables, etc. can be analyzed and produce coherent results that can be used to make decisions with much more accuracy than the human capacity, opening the doors to systems of artificial intelligence that surpass us in several areas, as already occurs today.

4.7 Other factors that may contribute to the advent of technological singularity

Add to this the research developments with neural networks, parallel computing, computer virtualization and clusters of computers and servers.

Negroponte cites the studies of Mitchel Resnick in his book Turtles, termites and traffic jams, 1994, in which it refers to the possibility of orderly formation, as being "the result of a series of high-response processors that behave in an individualized way and follow harmonious rules without a commander."[384] The example quoted is that of an audience that is asked to clap hands unison and without a general organizer, with no one in particular to set the rhythm of applause, the collective in a few seconds synchronizes the rhythm. This behavior is cybernetic.

All this will contribute to the artificial intelligence developing, even more, reaching levels compatible with those of human intelligence and even surpassing it.

The attainment of the **technological singularity** with the junction of these developments is approaching in a growing rhythm. Considering the **Law of Accelerating Returns**, which foresees the potentialization of the exponential character of these developments, it is thought that by the year 2030 or 2040, it should be reached. See, by the way, the calculations elaborated by Clinton W. Kelly.[385]

4.8 The Technological Singularity

In fact, it should be said that there is a feeling, if not a general one, that is at least very recurrent among people living in large

---

[384] Resnick, M. *apud* Negroponte, N., *op. cit.*, p. 157.
[385] Kelly, C. W. *Can a machine Think?* Retrieved from: <http://www.kurzweilai.net/articles/art0214.html?printable=1>. Last access date: January 26, 2009.

cities and with access to the modern media, that time is marching faster.

This feeling has not only been noticed recently. The doctrine has been taking care of it for a considerable time, in the contemporaneity. The Russian author Volkov thus expressed that in 1967:

> *Man's history may be compared to a train which for the greater part of its long run has been moving at the speed of a tortoise, until towards the end it generated successively the speed of a pedestrian, a racehorse, a Racing car, a supersonic aircraft and, eventually, a spaceship.*[386]

But what is the technological singularity? It is a theoretical phenomenon predicted by Vernor Vinge[387] in an article originally presented at the VISION-21 Symposium, sponsored by NASA, on March 30, 1993. The first time the author used the word singularity with the current meaning was when he was speaking at the annual conference of the Association for the Advancement of Artificial Intelligence in 1982.

But what is the technological singularity? It is a theoretical phenomenon predicted by Vernor Vinge. In a similar way as the singularity of astronomy, where he theorizes about an odd, unprecedented event that produces unique effects, hence the name.

The occurrence of technological singularity will happen due to the exponential development of technology in general, which will result in the appearance of a more intelligent entity than the human being, initiating the era of post-humanity.

It is fundamental for the thesis defended in this book, because it is not possible to think about the rights of robots if they do not reach a stage of development that allows them to have at least levels of intelligence, awareness, and understanding of their situation

---

[386] Volkov, G. (1967). *Era of man or robot? The sociological problems of the technical revolution.* (pp. 181). Moscow: Progress Publishers.

[387] Vinge, V. *What is The Singularity?* Retrieved from: <http://webcache.googleusercontent.com/search?q=cache:2UA--AmSFT0J:mindstalk.net/vinge/vinge-sing.html+singularity+vernor+vinge&hl=pt-R&ct=clnk&cd=1&gl=br&client=firefox-a> . Last access date: February 13, 2009.

and dimension and the world as well, at least equal to those of human beings.

Here are some excerpts from this article[388]:

> *Within thirty years, we will have the technological means to create superhuman intelligence. Shortly after, the human era will be ended.*
>
> *What is The Singularity?*
>
> *The acceleration of technological progress has been the central feature of this century. [...] The precise cause of this change is the imminent creation by technology of entities with greater-than-human intelligence. Science may achieve this breakthrough by several means (and this is another reason for having confidence that the event will occur):*
>
> *Computers that are "awake" and superhumanly intelligent may be developed. (To date, there has been much controversy as to whether we can create human equivalence in a machine. But if the answer is "yes," then there is little doubt that more intelligent beings can be constructed shortly thereafter.)*
>
> *Large computer networks and their associated users may "wake up" as superhumanly intelligent entities.*
>
> *Computer/human interfaces may become so intimate that users may reasonably be considered superhumanly intelligent.*
>
> *Biological science may provide a means to improve natural human intellect.*
>
> *The first three possibilities depend on improvements in computer hardware. [...] I believe that the creation of greater-than-human intelligence will occur during the next thirty years. [...]. I'll be surprised if this event occurs before 2005 or after 2030.)*
>
> *When greater-than-human intelligence drives progress, that progress will be much more rapid. [...] The best analogy I see is to the evolutionary past: Animals can adapt to problems and make inventions, but often no*

---

[388] *Idem.*

faster than natural selection can do its work — the world acts as its own simulator in the case of natural selection. We, humans, have the ability to internalize the world and conduct what-if's in our heads; we can solve many problems thousands of times faster than natural selection could. Now, by creating the means to execute those simulations at much higher speeds, we are entering a regime as radically different from our human past as we humans are from the lower animals.
I think it's fair to call this event a singularity.

Von Neumann even uses the term singularity, though it appears he is thinking of normal progress, not the creation of the superhuman intellect. (For me, the superhumanity is the essence of the Singularity. Without that we would get a glut of technical riches, never properly absorbed).

Another symptom of progress toward the Singularity: ideas
themselves should spread ever faster, and even the most radical will quickly become commonplace. When I began writing science fiction in the middle '60s, it seemed very easy to find ideas that took decades to percolate into the cultural consciousness; now the lead time seems more like eighteen months. (Of course, this could just be me losing my imagination as I get old, but I see the effect in others too.) Like the shock in a compressible flow, the Singularity moves closer as we accelerate through the critical speed.

Since it involves an intellectual runaway, it will probably occur faster than any technical revolution seen so far. The precipitating event will likely be unexpected.

And what happens a month or two (or a day or two) after that? I have only analogies to point to: The rise of humankind. We will be in the Post-Human era. And for all my rampant technological optimism, sometimes I think I'd be more comfortable if I were regarding these transcendental events from one thousand years remove ... instead of twenty.

Can the Singularity be Avoided?

Well, maybe it won't happen at all: Sometimes I try to imagine the symptoms that we should expect to see if the Singularity is not to develop. There are the widely

237

respected arguments of Penrose and Searle against the practicality of machine sapience. In August of 1992, Thinking Machines Corporation held a workshop to investigate the question "How We Will Build a Machine that Thinks" (...)A minority felt that the largest 1992 computers were within three orders of magnitude of the power of the human brain. The majority of the participants agreed with Moravec's estimate that we are ten to forty years away from hardware parity. And yet there was another minority who pointed to and conjectured that the computational competence of single neurons may be far higher than generally believed. If so, our present computer hardware might be as much as ten orders of magnitude short of the equipment we carry around in our heads. If this is true (or for that matter, if the Penrose or Searle critique is valid), we might never see a Singularity. Instead, in the early '00s, we would find our hardware performance curves beginning to level off -- this because of our inability to automate the design work needed to support further hardware improvements. We'd end up with some very powerful hardware, but without the ability to push it further. [...] and there would never be the intellectual runaway which is the essence of the Singularity. It would likely be seen as a golden age ... and it would also be an end of progress.

But if the technological Singularity can happen, it will. Even if all the governments of the world were to understand the "threat" and be in deadly fear of it, progress toward the goal would continue.

I have argued above that we cannot prevent the Singularity, that its coming is an inevitable consequence of the humans' natural competitiveness and the possibilities inherent in technology. And yet ... we are the initiators. Even the largest avalanche is triggered by small things. We have the freedom to establish initial conditions, make things happen in ways that are less inimical than others. Of course (as with starting avalanches), it may not be clear what the right guiding nudge really is:

Other Paths to the Singularity: Intelligence Amplification

And it's very likely that IA is a much easier road to the achievement of superhumanity than pure AI. In humans, the hardest development problems have already been solved. Building up from within ourselves ought to be

easier than figuring out first what we really are and then building machines that are all of that.
The problem is not simply that the Singularity represents the passing of humankind from center stage, but that it contradicts our most deeply held notions of being. I think a closer look at the notion of strong superhumanity can show why that is.

For the author, the scenario has not changed since then, as the article published in the June 2008 issue of the IEEE magazine.

5 POSSIBILITY OF ACKNOWLEDGMENT OF THE LEGAL PERSONALITY OF THE ROBOT

5.1 Legal subject of Robots

5.1.1 Introduction

There has been an increasing need to legally discipline the performance of robots or their interaction with men, since they are becoming more and more present and begin to cause damage and even death. In this way, some more industrialized countries have tried to discipline the activity of robots.

In the face of the astounding speed with which technological changes are spreading across the globe, developing countries, such as Brazil, often skip development stages, receiving technology at an equal pace with more developed countries. It is not intended here to discuss the reasons for the introduction of technology at such speed in developing countries, what technologies are popularized, nor for the benefit of whom they fit in.

There is a fact, and this fact demands legal intervention to regulate the relations that surround this fact, whether preliminary, whether in its course, or later.

It is reasonable to suppose that the introduction of a new technology has consequences in the spheres of work, commerce, companies, civil society, competitiveness, consumption, among others.

In the case of effectively intelligent robots, greater consequences may even arise, and this motivates the present book, if there are new actors in the legal universe to assign rights.

5.1.2 Legislation

International legislation is still in its infancy. In Brazil, there is no news of a legal rule regulating the activity of robots. What exists is a rule potentially contrary to national interests in art. 7,

Section 27, which establishes a protection for the worker in the face of automation. Now, automation will come with this rule or without it. It seems that the Brazilian Constitution recognizes its inevitability and tries to protect the worker. The problem is not the promotion of protection, but what protection is intended, therefore, no country can be competitive if it does not automate its factories.

The employee is no match for the robot in the same function. In many cases, it is only justifiable to keep the employee in the place of a robot if he is much less paid than his counterpart elsewhere.

This constitutional norm causes concern as it may stall national development if not carefully regulated.

Karlsson and Jarrhed[389][389] provide an example of a norm for robots:

> *To increase operator safety in robotic work cells, a capacitive sensor for the detection of humans has been developed. The capacitive sensor has an antenna above the robot. The antenna covers the entire area of the robot cell. The floor of the robot cell is covered with an electrically insulated, conducting sheet. The sensor detects objects roughly in the shape of humans, placed between the antenna and the floor, and with an electrical conductivity similar to that of seawater. A person entering the cell causes a change of capacitance between the sheet and the antenna. This change is measured with a capacitance-voltage converter. The output voltage is used as a signal for human presence. The floor can be sectioned into several sheets separated from each other by guards. If the area is sectioned the sensor is not only able to give information about the presence of a person in the cell but also about the location of that person.*

The idea is to make it compulsory to use sensors such as these to avoid work accidents, disciplining the coexistence of robots and men in the factories, as studies show that the greatest risks of robot accidents occur during programming and /

---

[389] Karlsson, N; Jarrhed, J. O. (1993). *A capacitive sensor for the detection of humans in a robot cell*. In: 1993 IEEE Instrumentation and Measurement Technology Conference, Irvine, CA, USA, May 18-20, p. 164-166. Retrieved from: <https://ieeexplore.ieee.org/document/382659/>. Last access date: August 2nd, 2018. Digital Object Identifier 10.1109 / IMTC.1993.382659.

or maintenance. Usually, these accidents involve an unplanned movement of the robot, caused by equipment failure or human error.

But the robots are also killing[390], as stated before. There are several examples, of which the first case is recorded in 1971, when a Kawasaki worker, Kenji Urada[391], was killed at work. The second case resulted in a conviction of ten million dollars.[392] On March 18, 2018, Elaine Herzberg was killed by a self-driving Uber in Tempe, Arizona. At the moment of the accident, there was a driver behind the wheel but the car was in Autonomous mode.[393]

In fact, the Labor Law, or equivalent, is that has taken the lead in the discipline of robots, with news of standards in Japan, Sweden, and the United States.

5.1.3 Asimov's Three Laws of Robotics

Although one cannot attribute to them the character of Law in the legal perspective, neither as a formal law nor as a material law, it is true that one cannot intend to outline a work on robotics and related subjects without addressing the Laws of Robotics of Isaac Asimov and, therefore, the Laws of Humanics, also referred to by him.

---

[390] These references can be found in *The Economist*. Trust me, I'm a robot. Retrieved in: <http://www.economist.com/displaystory.cfm?story_id=7001829>. Last access date: August 01, 2006.

[391] *The first human killed by a robot*. Retrieved in: <http://www.thinkartificial.org/aesthetics/the-first-human-killed-by-a-robot/>. Last access date: 26 fev. 2009.

[392] "A jury has ordered the manufacturer of a one-ton robot that killed a worker at a Ford Motor Co. plant to pay the man's family $10 million. The Wayne County Circuit Court jury deliberated for 2 1/2 hours Tuesday before announcing the decision against Unit Handling Systems, a division of Litton Industries. The suit was brought by the family of Robert Williams, who was killed Jan. 25, 1979, at a casting plant in Flat Rock, Mich. It is believed to be the largest personal-injury [...]".

[393] More information can be found at https://www.nytimes.com/interactive/2018/03/20/us/self-driving-uber-pedestrian-killed.html.

However, in the present work, in addition to making it clear that these are not legal norms, it is appropriate to criticize them.

Isaac Asimov, the creator of the word "robotics", referred to the "Three Fundamental Rules of Robotics", which later came to be known as the Asimov's Three Laws of Robotics, which can be stated as follows:

> *1. A robot may not injure a human being or, through inaction, allow a human being to come to harm.*
>
> *2. A robot must obey the orders given it by human beings except where such orders would conflict with the First Law.*
>
> *3. A robot must protect its own existence as long as such protection does not conflict with the First or Second Laws.*[394]

It is interesting to note that the laws of robotics are, in fact, four, since in 1985 Asimov created the Zero Law of Robotics, considering that "A robot may not harm humanity, or, by inaction, allow humanity to come to harm. In this way, the good of humanity prevails over that of individuals."

Renato Cristofoleti[395] warns that

> *The so-called zero law, however, has the serious problem of transferring to the robot the power (possibility) to evaluate, in the face of concrete situations, whether the interest of humanity overlaps with individual interest. Such a possibility opens a dangerous breach for the dictatorship of machines, which would themselves choose the greater good, and would even be allowed to do evil to a human being (individual) if they perceive that it is better for humanity. For this reason, the so-called zero law of robotics is questioned and its existence is not a consensus.*

---

[394] Asimov, I. (2007). As três leis da robótica [The Three Laws of Robotics]. In: *Histórias de Robôs* [Robots Stories] (V. 418., Vol. 2, pp. 100) (M. Persson, Trans.). Porto Alegre: L&PM (Coleção L&PM Pocket).

[395] Cristofoleti, R. *As três leis da robótica* [The Three Laws of Robotics]..Retrieved from: <http://74.125.47.132/search?q=cache:B5Ulxx_xRTwJ:cea.eti.br/tecnologia.blog/%3Fp%3D6+lei+zero+da+rob%C3%B3tica&hl=pt-BR&ct=clnk&cd=2&gl=br&client=firefox-a>. Last access date: February 03, 2009, p. 2.

Evidently that the laws of robotics are not, in the current and anthropocentric view of law, truly laws of a legal character, notably because they do not address human beings, and we know that the current paradigm is based on the premise that laws are made by Men and for Men, while the Laws of Robotics are made by Men for Robots.

However, even though these Laws are filled with our anthropocentrism, they are for robots quite similar to the laws for Men by their imperativeness. However, these diverge by the absence of deontological character.

If it is true that the legal laws, in which the law is linked to a deontic logic and, therefore, of a cultural and social character, the laws of robotics are similar to natural, physical and mathematical laws, descriptive of nature and non-prescriptive of behaviors, their logic is ontic.

If the Laws of Robotics should be applied to robots — applied here has the sense of imposed, programmed, previously disciplinary — descriptive of something inevitable, fatal, because they would follow the programs and they could not get away, two conclusions can be reached:

a) or robots are not intelligent, or do not have artificial intelligence programs, which, by definition, cannot have their purposes predetermined and therefore do not act in the legal sphere or

b) these laws are of impossible application, because, being the intelligent robots, infallible rules of conduct cannot be embedded in them. Natural laws, like laws of gravity, physics, or any other, although they follow them by objective limitations like those that affect us as well.

Natural laws are obeyed because they cannot be transposed or overcome. When they are overcome by human inventiveness it happens immediately. Cultural laws are inculcated in common sense and can be violated, submitting the offender to the penalties therein provided, whether of religious, moral, etiquette or legal order, although they follow them by objective limitations such as those that affect us as well.

These rules were anthropocentrically thought out, as his creator made clear. One cannot fail to keep in mind that Asimov conceived his robots as intelligent, but subservient to humans, some in a condition analogous to slaves. These rules cannot be implemented infallibly in an intelligent machine because it must submit not only to natural (physical) laws, but also to deontological logic, that is, they must be programmed or "educated" with rules of conduct. But they cannot be limited, since these rules outline ideal profiles and because they are not rigidly enforced, but are thought of in virtue of human behavioral multiplicity, which admits the possibility of failure and disobedience, bring ancillary rules of control, of punishment.

The achievement of an "intelligent" conduct must be programmed based on paraconsistent logic, not excluding the law of the excluded third, as is human conduct and as robotics is expected to be, if possible.

Thus, although Man himself cannot fly, completely binding to the law of gravity, from which he cannot break free, he is subject to other orders of laws: moral, legal, religious, etc. Each law has its specific rules for cases of noncompliance, precisely because Man knows that such laws can be violated, though they should not. In this way, our intelligence or lack of it is revealed and that must be present also in the robots, in the intelligent systems, since these would not tie their effects to the programs, but to the circumstances they face, obeyed the anthropocentric paradigm or not.

The intelligent system, as well as being strictly bound to physical laws, such as those of fluid dynamics, must, therefore, be intelligently linked to a system of deontologically formulated standards where there is a possibility of deviations. Unless the possibility of deception reveals our lack of intelligence.

It is for this reason that the criticisms that Asimov himself envisaged are fully pertinent, since the conflicts and nuances on which he discusses, in addition to innumerable others, cannot be solved with ontological norms, in which the decisional freedom inherent in intelligence is not allowed.

Just take, exemplarily, any of the laws of robotics to see that they can only exist in fiction: "1st law: A robot may not injure a human being or, through inaction, allow a human being to come to harm."[396]

This leads to a number of questions, such as, for example, if a human is about to inflict harm on another human, such as an adult malefactor about to fire a gun on a baby's forehead. To do no harm to the adult is to do harm to the other human, absolutely helpless and even unaware of the situation.

This law removes the possibility of self-defense of a person, excluding crime that allows even killing to defend someone.

Only a stupid, rigidly programmed being would treat this as a non-computable problem and would find no solution by looping. Because an intelligent system would make a qualitative assessment, as humans do, and decide what is best to do: wait to see what would happen and apply violence only later; to immediately apply violence against the human in a position to cause harm to another human being that no evil can cause, nor can he defend himself; obey the first Law and not act and, in doing so, violate the second enunciation of the same law, etc.

One might think that this would be the case to apply the Zero Law, but evidently, it is not. Because humanity was not put at direct risk, but only a human being, only indirectly being affected the humanity that would lose a member at a young age and with it all his potential, without considering the values higher than the legal ones, that would be being vilified by this monstrous conduct of the aggressor. Still, the concept of humanity is not appropriate — if it is possible to establish a universally valid one, it is related to the global collectivity of human beings and not to a small group or an individual.

---

[396] Asimov, I. (1994). *Visões de robô* [Robot visions] (R. S. de Biasi, Trans.). (pp. 18) Rio de Janeiro: Record.

One cannot agree with the criticism made by Cristofoleti[397], because if the robot is intelligent, he must have, like Man, a means of evaluating the concept of Humanity, something that the average Man knows. Or one recognizes the intelligence of the machines, although from a given moment and for machines in particular, or this intelligence is not recognized. Recognizing the intelligence of machines, everything that man can, they can also. This will, theoretically, weaken the perception of this intelligence and the machines will remain as an object of law, without the power of decision. Unless intelligence is tied to an absolute and permanently straight conduct, making us all unintelligent beings.

Also interesting are the criticisms made by Clarke, applicable to the case under discussion, in which it is extremely important to be able to define lesions (slight, light, incapacitating), damage, death and mortal danger. Many times, repelling *a friendly gesture would be interpreted as causing injury. A robot that reads the mind interprets the first law as requiring it to give people not the correct answer to their questions, but rather the answers that they know they want to hear."*[398]

For example, if two Krav Maga™[399] practitioners are training strikes one another, this violent but controlled behavior could be considered dangerous or even deadly by a robot (indeed some Krav Maga™ strikes can kill or cause permanent damages) not aware that it's training.

Moreover, the very definition of a human being can be manipulated. If the robot does not have the means to instantly read the human genome and its mutations, which do not denature human nature, the mere storage of various data that would represent the human figure (skin tones and hair, bipedalism, limbs, voice characteristics, accents etc.) would be insufficient and insecure, since these elements can be changed via programming or, even though

[397] Cristofoleti, R., *op. cit.*, loc. cit.
[398] Clarke, R., *op. cit.*, p. 2.
[399] Krav Maga is a Trade Mark of South America Federation of Krav Maga.

these elements remain intact, the robot may not recognize a human that does not fit the stored patterns, such as those with physical impairments. This could make them not deserve human treatment from a robot.

Clarke[400] brings an interesting example:

> In an early story, Asimov has a humanoid robot to represent itself as a human and stand for public office. It must prevent the public from realizing that it is a robot, since public reaction would not only result in the robot losing the election but also in tighter constraints on other robots. A political opponent, seeking to expose the robot, discovers that it is impossible to prove it is a robot solely based on its behavior, because the Laws of Robotics force any robot to perform in essentially the same manner as a good human being.

Also, the definition of a human being by appearance alone would lead to robots treating humans as robots whose human appearance was perfect. The difficulty would worsen with post-human creatures like the cyborgs.

Clarke[401] himself brings an updated version of the Laws of Asimov:

> *Asimov's Robotic Laws Revised (1985)*
>
> *Meta-law*
>
> *A robot should act only when its acts are subject to the Robotic Laws.*
>
> *First Law*
>
> *A robot cannot hurt a human being or, by default, allow a human being to suffer harm unless it violates a higher law.*
>
> *Second Law*
>
> *A robot must obey the orders given to it by human beings, except in cases where such orders conflict a Law of a higher order.*

---

[400] *Ibidem*, p.3.
[401] *Idem*.

A robot must obey the orders given to it by robots of higher authority, except in cases in which such orders conflict a Law of a higher order.

Third Law

A robot must protect the existence of a robot of higher authority as long as such protection does not conflict with a higher law. A robot must protect its own existence as long as such protection does not conflict with a higher law.

Thus, it is well seen that the laws of robotics are no more than science fiction and cannot be considered as laws, strictly speaking, that is, they cannot be treated as legal norms, but can be used as examples.

5.1.4 Jurisprudence

There are in the legal treatment of the subject, news of judicial decisions that relate to computers, all extracted from Freitas Jr.[402]

In 1972, Ward v. Superior Court of California (3C.L.S.R. 206), there was the first case in which a computer was called to court for questioning because it contained information that was obtained unlawfully by its owner in another machine. Today the activity of hackers has enormously increased similar cases.

There are even cases where the decision of the computer prevails over the human, as in the divergence between the autopilot and the human pilot. Thus, for example, in Klein v. U.S. (13 Av. Cas. 18137 [D. MD 1975]), the Court decided that it evidences the negligence of the human pilot when he does not use the equipment, even if it is not mandatory for the landings. In Wells v. U.S. (16 Av. Cas. 17914 [W.D. Wash, 1981]), another court ruled over the negligence of the pilot who took command of the autopilot in a critical situation. In these cases, Man was judged negligent for not submitting to the decisions of the computer or, at least, for neglecting its orientation.

---

[402] Freitas Junior, Robert A. *The legal rights of robots.* Disponível em: <http://www.rfreitas.com/Astro/LegalRightsOfRobots.htm>. Last access date: November 15, 2000.

Robots already deserved the same legal protection of Humans in at least one judicial decision, when Judge Albert Stevens considered, in a case brought to justice by writers Ben Bova and Harlan Ellison against ABC / Paramount, which they accused of having violated the work "Brillo." The sentence considered that robots and humans must be treated identically when they are characters in literary works and therefore have the same legal protection of copyright.

A story generated by a story creation software (code generator) published in a nationwide magazine in the United States received copyright protection.

When relating legal personality with citizenship, it was necessary to make an epistemological approach to this theme that is so rich, multifaceted and with several points of contact[403]. Hence, to limit the theme and shed light on relevant issues.

5.2 Why a robotic citizenship?

It seems clear the relationship between legal personality and citizenship. Although, using the classical concept of citizenship, with its political side, it can be separated from the legal personality, allowing one to consider people who do not have citizenship but, in the modern view, these two concepts are inseparable.

The holder of rights and obligations, the individual with legal personality is concomitantly endowed with citizenship in its broader spectrum.

Thus, thinking about legal personality is thinking about citizenship. However, the construction of the concept of citizenship did not take place in the way it is currently utilized, but this has been being built for generations, with mistakes and successes — if one could talk about mistakes when referring to culture.

---

[403] Nogueira, S. (2009). Legislação robótica: cientistas querem código de conduta para aqueles que acreditam, estarão cada vez mais entre nós [Robotics legislation: scientists want a code of conduct for those they believe will be more and more between us]. *Revista Galileu*, n. 211, February.

Man had to experience his historical course, with its fluctuations and variations, in the course of which the concept and effects of citizenship were more or less enlarged, as was the case with legal personality. We realize, therefore, that the two concepts are strongly influenced by the dominant culture in a certain place and time, firmly tied to law and to the political and economic fields.

The conveniences and needs of the political and economic life — in the modern market — have dictated the pace of development and conformation of citizenship and legal personality.

However, and perhaps for this reason, one can consider a process of acquisition of robotic citizenship, as long as the robots do not control the situation, given their projected intelligence superior to the human.

It would be argued, in favor of robots or humans, with the constitutional principle of isonomy, seeking, from side to side — whether Law or some right (human, robotic, hybrid) can still intermediate this Human-Robot relationship — seeking to demonstrate that this or that element would characterize an equality between humans and machines for the purpose of the machines being citizens.

But what citizenship are we thinking about? A robotic citizenship only, with the existence of a strictly robotic right to regulate their life and activities, done by themselves and for themselves, thus recognizing the duality of legal systems in many countries, one for the humans and another to robots?

Would we think about a hybrid Law in which humans, in all biological or synthetic percentages, and machines to share decisions, by choice of parliamentary or governmental representatives of each category, with joint trials?

In any case, these two scenarios take into account the existing paradigm of social organization formulated in the course of the historical evolution of Man and which may eventually be considered inadequate, outdated or uninteresting for a society in which there are machines more intelligent than Man, stronger than Man, more intimately related than Man, and ultimately in which Man is the coadjutant or even cease to exist.

Therefore, robotic citizenship and robotic legal personality can only be considered based on the existing social, political and legal paradigms that may no longer find an echo in the future.

Only in this case of the permanence of the model, or the basic structure of the model created by Man, that it makes sense to the legal personality of the robot and its citizenship.

Once the human model of society has been overcome, one will talk about the end of Law and of society as it is known and cannot foresee how a future paradigm will be configured, since any prognosis will be tainted by the current paradigm, beyond which, a supervening paradigm doesn't need to be tied to the current one.

Thus, in the present study, in a specific way, although it is possible to consider new technical, political, juridical and social conformations, one works with the existing concept of citizenship. Based on the principle of isonomy, any machine that has characteristics that allow the Law to examine the human phenomenon as its concern dignifies it with the ownership of rights. The machine will deserve, provided it is not glimpsed and justified — and the robots accept — differences that result in unequal treatment, equal legal and political treatment, including citizenship.

Thus, the legal consequence of the technological singularity, that is the singular legal personality of robots, will automatically result in their citizenship.

Evidently, it is not unknown that certain people do not have citizenship in Brazilian law, as in the case of legal entities, hence it can be concluded that robots could be deprived of citizenship.

However, as is clear from the work, it was rightly understood that the robot can be considered as an individual rather than a juridical person, provided that it can be said that it has the characteristics of Man that the Law appropriated or used to recognize the legal personality.

It should be borne in mind that this work, when not expressly stated in the opposite direction, works with the hypothesis of a change (not necessarily substitution) of the anthropocentric para-digm and that, in these conditions, this position would not be sur-prising.

Hence, because of the importance of examining the subject of personality by overlapping it with citizenship, since, eventually, one will have to face the issue in the field of Law, its scholars must be equipped to deal with this issue.

The Law must be prepared for these issues that are to come and nothing better than the debate of ideas to formulate solutions, de-fenses or rules to be followed and enforceable.

5.2.1 The Legal Concept of Citizenship

The concept of citizenship arose in ancient Greece and rep-resented the rights of the resident in the *polis* (city). Still in its infancy, it was associated with the privileges granted to certain categories of people, thus considered citizens, establishing a re-stricted concept of citizenship. Over the centuries, this notion of citizenship has evolved to, in the Modern Age, around the eigh-teenth century, reconcile itself with fundamental rights and the concept of nation, still relying on the ideals of freedom and equal-ity enshrined in French Revolution, a reflection of American In-dependence and its Political Charter. However, in the same way, the limiting character of citizenship remained, since it depended on political rights, and these were granted to a few, excluding, for example, women and blacks.

It was a privileged citizenship, granted only to those who pos-sessed property and income, drawing a distinction of meaning between Man and the Citizen.

The citizen (belonging to the caste) would be above the com-mon man (belonging to the mass) because he holds political rights and is endowed with wealth, being able to participate in the political life of the society in which he lived.

In 1789, ratifying this distinction between man and citizen and, under the influence of the interests of the French bourgeoi-sie, came the Declaration of the Rights of Man and of the Citizen. The very title of the Charter already shows the existence of separation between Man, human being, and citizen. First, only individual rights of the first generation, based on servility, were granted, while the latter was accorded the political rights to vote and to be voted on.

This conception was gradually reformulated, and it was only in 1948 that the Universal Declaration of Human Rights emerged to consider citizens "... all those who inhabited the sovereignty of a State and received a load of the most varied duties and rights."[404] This understanding was endorsed by the Vienna Conference in 1993.

Thus, it was only with universal suffrage that the full concept of citizenship was reached, in the current molds, being attributed to all those belonging to a given Nation, regardless of the form of acquisition of their nationality, but which, as a result of it, become holders of political, social and economic rights and obligations.

According to José Meirelles Teixeira[405]: "Citizenship consists of the prerogative granted to Brazilians, by fulfilling certain legal requirements, to be able to exercise political rights and fulfill civic duties."

It follows from this definition that citizenship legally binds the individual to a particular State, whether on account of his or her birth, residence or other factors. As a result, it grants him the right to participate in the political decisions made by the State, implying recognition of the right to vote and to be voted[406].

In the face of the plexus of elements involved in the conceptualization of citizenship, this is still, according to Aras[407], very

---

[404] Aras, A. (2006). *Fidelidade partidária: a perda do mandato parlamentar* [Party loyalty: the loss of parliamentary mandate] Rio de Janeiro: Lumen Juris, pp. 27.

[405] Teixeira, J. H. M. (1991). *Curso de Direito Constitucional* [Course on Constitutional Rights] Rio de Janeiro: Forense, pp. 565.

[406] Tavares, A. R. (2003). Curso de Direito Constitucional [Course on Constitutional Rights] 2.ed. São Paulo: Saraiva, pp. 567.

[407] Aras, opus citatum, p.27.

imprecise, remembering that the constitutionalists often see a relationship of nationality and political rights with citizenship, as noted above.

That is why Aras[408] says: "It is perceived, therefore, that citizenship does not present a proper framework, being related to three basic elements and that generate their lack of definition: nationality, political rights and people".

However, it is moving towards an enlarged, multimodal, global citizenship. It seems that it is not possible to relate the concept of citizenship only by voting and being voted, with a formal citizenship, detached from effective participation in human affairs. Being a citizen is, at the same time, "to be subject and sovereign"[409]. In this field, Dalmo Abreu Dallari teaches[410]:

> Citizenship expresses a set of rights that gives the person the possibility to participate actively in the life and government of his people. Those who do not have citizenship are marginalized or excluded from social life and from decision making, placing themselves in a position of inferiority within the social group.

Basically, all the aforementioned historical landmarks have in common — in the light of the above mentioned reservations — the establishment of the idea that all men are equal before the Law, the principle of equality, and therefore everyone has the right to a dignified and full life, with minimally acceptable conditions of health, education, expression, political participation, housing, freedom, among others.

However, the modern expression of citizenship also brings with it the idea of social obligations, requiring all citizens to participate in the conduct of social affairs.

[408] Aras, A. (2006). *Fidelidade partidária: a perda do mandato parlamentar* [Party loyalty: the loss of parliamentary mandate] Rio de Janeiro: Lumen Juris, pp. 26.
[409] Covre, M. de L. M. (2008). *O que é cidadania* [What is citizenship?] 3rd ed. 16th reprint. São Paulo: Brasiliense, pp. 9.
[410] Dallari, D.de A. (1998). *Direitos humanos e cidadania* [Human rights and citizenship] São Paulo: Moderna, pp. 14.

So much so that Aras[411] draws attention to the fact that the articles 1°, II; 14 and 68, § 1, II removed from the citizenship the prerogatives of political rights or nationality.

> The citizen has become the individual to whom the Federal Constitution confers rights and guarantees, providing him with the tools necessary for his effective exercise, as well as efficient procedural means against their violation and enjoyment. A minimum core of fundamental rights and duties has been established.

Moreover, in a globalized, increasingly interconnected and interrelated world, the effects of local behaviors and postures can gain global contours in a short time. A pro-ecology manifestation at a given place for the preservation of animals or ecosystems on the other side of the world may even have more important and rapid effects than if locally coordinated.

No minimally developed and integrated country of the United Nations wants to see its image damaged by sensitive issues such as environment, civil rights, protection of minorities, protection of children, adolescents and the elderly, among others.

Thus, a campaign outside local control can amplify its effects and, due to the international or even global repercussion, produce local changes.

Political activism gains global outlines and more and more illustrious or even unknown people defending freedoms or points of view regarding local issues, not only in person, but in websites, blogs, video blogs, etc., from a remote point of the planet, which in principle would not directly affect their lives, the example of what is done with Tibet or with some indigenous people.

Obviously, an orchestration financed by governments and entities that are not very well known or whose real objectives are not very clear, involved in a pseudo-activism is not unknown, but it is a fact that the global effects of local politics and vice versa are evident.

---

[411] Aras, opus citatum, p. 27.

That is why you can no longer think small in terms of citizenship. Europe is an example of formal continental citizenship. Although the reunited countries maintain their own characteristics and identities, it is no less certain that there is a European citizenship in full consolidation and expansion.

A European constitution was discussed, norms of labor, technical, civil, criminal, etc. are standardized. European standards are valid almost everywhere on the continent, where there is a single currency and there is free transit of people and goods.

Not long ago, the entire world, although they have not voted — despite the fact that Americans across the globe are able to vote — have participated and followed the American political debate and adopted a stance in favor of the Democratic or Republican candidate.

Never before has there been such a globalized presidential campaign, with candidates making speeches not only in different corners of their country, but in the world.

In the same way, the economic effects, especially the negative ones, are felt in a global way, such as those of the financial crisis and the markets. Mistakes in the conduct of locally promoted investments, notably in large economies, affect investors and savers around the world, although to some extent the same cannot be said of their benefits.

This expanded and global citizenship has only become possible with the advent of new technologies that allow deterritorialization and dematerialization of the citizen, allowing him to take cognizance of events held almost anywhere in the world and to interact globally with people located nearby.

Technologies such as telephony, jet flights, mass communications satellites, submarine cables, mobile phones and the internet have enabled the rapid movement of information and people across the globe.

Just remember that the North American television network CNN gained global notoriety with its real-time transmissions, using portable equipment, directly from the front in the first Iraq war.

Today there is the ubiquity of photo and video cameras in almost any electronic device, allowing people not only to participate in the marvelous events, but also to transmit them live and reverberate them anywhere else on the planet.

In addition, blogs and video logs have allowed anyone with access to an electronic device and the internet to express their opinions. Share texts, images, sounds with potentially billions of other people on earth.

This, indeed, has created a global village, a world where local issues as well as general issues matter, where you do not know where the walls begin and end, the limits — if they still exist.

None of this would be possible without the massive use of technology, increasingly transparent to the user, who no longer need to know complicated programming tools, but only sophisticated and simple ones — in fact, sophistication consists of the simplicity of the interface.

Patrocínio[412], when referring to digital citizenship, teaches that:

> This constitutes a greater individual accountability of the citizen of the globalized digital technological society (the e-citizen, the net citizen, the netizen) for the construction and exercise of a cosmopolitan citizenship of the non-totalitarian universe.

With the advent of technological singularity, to which these new technologies and manifestations of cyberculture[413] contribute, this phenomenon will literally be enhanced by generating a global citizen consciousness and, eventually, a global government.

---

[412] Patrocínio, J. T V. (2004). *Tornar-se pessoa e cidadão digital: aprender e formar-se dentro e fora da escola na sociedade tecnológica globalizada* [Becoming a digital person and citizen: learning and training in and out of school in the globalized technological society] Thesis (Ph.D. in Education and Development Sciences) — Faculdade de Ciências, Universidade Nova de Lisboa, Lisboa, p. 195.

[413] Lemos, A. (2008). *Cibercultura: tecnologia e vida social na cultura contemporânea* [Cyberculture: technology and social life in contemporary culture] 4th ed. Porto Alegre: Sulina.

In this new civilization, that knows no physical boundaries, certainly new characters will exist, many of them immaterial, re-located, in the cloud. So many, physically visible and conducting a myriad of activities — many of them without any human par-ticipation, eventually giving way to a human-related or isolated, prevailing, robotic citizenship.

5.2.2 The importance of the concept of personality for citizenship

Alongside the global connection, the perception that citizen-ship has an intimate relationship with the legal personality remains clear. Truly, one cannot consider the citizenship without talking about People, that is, of holders of rights and obligations and, for that reason, can exercise them, persecute them, demand them, in-crease them, assume the resulting burdens.

Actually, the plexus of rights that compose modern citizenship is related to the rights of the personality — which are not the direct object of this study — in its various generations.

It is because of this inextricable relationship between legal per-sonality — enabling the securitization of the rights of personality — and citizenship that it is pertinent to discuss the themes here related to the Person, whether it is robotics or human.

In addition, in democratic countries and societies governed by Law there is a growing complexity of social and legal relations, with the development of personality rights of several generations, concerning their effects on the concept of citizenship and, more precisely, on the effectiveness of the citizenship that only is ac-complished with the exercise of these rights.

Thus, one cannot speak of partial citizenship, almost citizen-ship, or different degrees of citizenship, as this does not reflect the effectiveness that these rights demand. It is not enough to configure in a Political Charter a list of values or ideals if these are unattain-able or are considered as mere recommendations. Even if all the conditions for the exercise of these rights are not met momentarily, they cannot be considered as mere legal or rhetorical effects. They must be persecuted to be fulfilled, to be carried out.

The citizenship must be experienced. It is in the dynamics of social and legal interactions, in the clash of the tectonic plates of classes, of categories, of privileges, duties, rights, prerogatives and obligations that new layers emerge, that new rights arise by the exercise itself, by the gathering of ideal conditions for its effective and leading new social and legal relations.

Therefore, the legal personality manifests itself, if it is fully effective in citizenship, when it gains the maximum dignity of leading the very destiny of its holder.

One can see, therefore, that through the exercise of the rights of the personality, only accessible to those who have legal personality, is that the citizenship appears in its fullness. Therefore, the legal personality is important for the effectiveness of citizenship.

Thus, it is possible to consider that, at a time when technological singularity may arise (perhaps a little earlier), citizens can be considered not only human but also cybernetics who may or may not assume political positions like us, humans, or even, may form a new social structure, which is unthinkable for us or even unwanted.

The fact is that considering the robot of the technological singularity as a person and as a living being (the latter not so important quality as the first), it can hardly be considered denying him citizenship.

The scope of this book does not look at what effects of citizenship are anticipated for robots, nor whether the relationship between the citizenship with the territory of a nation will prevail for Men or for robots, nor yet, which criterion will define the citizenship of a robot, but only to establish that the robot with personality should become a citizen, that is, it should possess political rights and probably the related obligations.

This is the scope that is intended to be given in this book.

5.3 Robot Legal Personality

It should be recalled that there is a debate on the concept of legal personality as a positive legal or legal logic.

Several authors, such as Dray[414] and Vasconcelos[415], consider that the singular legal personality is inherent to the condition or the concept of Man, and the concept of legal personality is a positive juridical legal person.

For authors like these, the Law does not have the power to grant or refuse personality to natural persons, human beings but it is precisely the Law and the Legislation that may or may not confer the same right to legal persons.

Thus, considering the robot as a person, it qualifies with the same status as an individual. Consequently, one cannot consider disregarding their legal personality to reach whoever it is, programmers, manufacturers, distributors etc.

Firstly, because it is not a product, that allows the supplier to be held liable for defect or damage arising from it; Secondly, because the legal personality of the person is personality right, absolute, inalienable, non-transferable.

The robot can be qualified as a natural, synthetic or cybernetic person, resulting in the natural persons being subdivided into human and cybernetic or human, synthetic (as opposed to biological, natural) and cybernetic (with a robotic percentage in a human being or a human percentage in a robot).

What could happen is a robot's civil and criminal liability treatment different from that observed for the absolutely capable human being, to treat it as relatively capable. This will result in additional complications, since, by now, they will be in charge of numerous activities, including some potentially risky for third parties, as it is nowadays, with traffic control, whether by air, rail or land, medication dosage, the definition of a sentence etc.

Now, those who are in this situation can only be considered legally capable. What is proposed is that parameters or thresholds should be created so that, from a legal point of view, non-intelligent

---

[414] Dray, G. M. (2006). Direitos de personalidade: anotações ao Código Civil e ao Código do Trabalho [Personality rights: annotations to the Civil Code and the Labor Code]. (pp. 17). Coimbra: Almedina.
[415] Vasconcelos, P. P. de, *op. cit.*, p. 5.

robots continue to be subject to law, others are relatively capable, monitored and protected, whose most critical decisions require human intervention, and others, with full rights, like adult humans, without legal restrictions, besides a classification for post-humans, partially human, partially robotic.

These ideas can and should apply to both physical and immaterial robots.[416] Certainly, it will be questioned to consider as a **physical** person a robot that has no material existence. However, when we talk about the technological stage that we are thinking about here, materialization is not so important, because the system that runs on a static computer can run on another, mobile or even hominiform. This does not make sense when one considers quantum computation, as one sees in this work.

Also, since the use of writing to send telegraph messages, telephony, fax, e-mail, chat, instant message, etc., we have already experienced some extra corporeality or lack of physical presence, without — and for a few decades — greater strangeness or lack of legal effects.

It is more important, as a rule, the content than the form in the autonomous manifestation of capable will.

Hence, one cannot be surprised that in the future there will be an immaterial individual person — today, in the current circumstances, called a **physical** person.

To emphasize again: we have already experienced a certain amount of dematerialization with email, mobile telephony, and computing, wireless networks, cloud computing, decentralized systems, virtual computing, etc.

Perhaps, therefore, Rover[417] has expressed that "The invisibility

---

[416] Ganascia, J., *op. cit.*, p. 13. The author teaches that a computer allows a calculation like, for example 45 + 38 passes the other character string, in this case 83, without it being necessary to concern with the way in which these chains and operations are physically linked to the machine, and, this way, modern machines, as opposed to old ones, are immaterial.

[417] Rover, A. J. *Para um direito invisível: superando as artificialidades da inteligência*. Retrieved from: <http://www.infojur.ufsc.br/aires/arquivos/direito%20invisivel%202005.pdf>. Last access date: February 25, 2009, p 02.

of machines and devices already occurs in multiple dimensions."

Every time it matters less where the individual is because he can be anywhere to do almost anything. In the words of Negroponte:

> *Distance means less and less in the digital world. In fact, an Internet user is utterly oblivious to it. On the Internet, distance often seems to function in reverse. I frequently get faster replies from distant places than close ones because the time change allows people to answer while I sleep — so it feels closer.*[418]

Also, physical existence is not required for the occurrence of personality rights, since the deceased also has some of these rights and it is no longer possible to speak of the physical existence of the deceased, but only of his body if he has not been cremated or decomposed by the action of time. In any case, a person in the legal sense will not be bound to physical existence.

In Common Law, the approach has been somewhat different. Although the number of authors who are dedicated to the subject is very small and the doctrine still incipient, one can already foresee an approach proper to that legal system.

It is understood that a gradual approach to the subject is necessary. It can be explained: contrary to what has been developed here, affirming that Brazilian positive law would already allow considering a truly intelligent robot as subject of rights and as a person, if there were no preconceptions and the anthropocentric paradigm, in common law countries, where there is also prejudice and the same paradigm, there is a gradation of the ability to have civil rights of robots.

It is not a question of grading similar to that of European continental law, as in Brazil, with absolutely incapable, relatively capable and capable. The hierarchy is of another order.

The understanding is defended by Inayatullah[419] who, citing

---

[418] Negroponte, N., *op. cit.*, p. 171.
[419] MILNER, Neal apud INAYATULLAH, Sohail. *The rights of robots: technology, culture and law in the 21st century*. Retrieved from: <http://74.125.95.132/search?q=cache:Fv0dYY_djEgJ:www.meta-

Neal Milner, thus considers that there are the following stages:

I) His first stage in this theory is imagery. Here imagery stressing rationality of the potential rights-holder is necessary;

II) The next stage of rights emergence requires a justifying ideology;

III) The next stage is one of changing authority patterns. Here authority patterns of the institutions governing the emerging rights holders begin to change;

IV) Next comes the development of social networks to reinforce the new ideology, thus forming ties with potential clients, lawyers, and intermediaries;

V) The next stage involves access to legal representation. This is followed by routinization, wherein the legal representation is made routinely available. Finally, the government uses its processes to represent the emerging rights-holders.

VI) One of the most complete articles on the subject brings the following considerations:[420]

> While society is abuzz today with the novel and increasingly troublesome problem of human-inspired computer crime, a related yet far more profound issue may be lying ahead — the humanly created machine as a 'criminal' in its own right.

Controversial question covers the capabilities of AI machines, which are proven capable of mimicking the behavior of other machines; learn from their own mistakes; to show curiosity, since

---

future.org/Articles/TheRightsofRobots.htm+MCNALLY,+Phil%3B+INAYATULLAH,+Sohail.+The+rights+of+robots:&cd=1&hl=pt-BR&ct=clnk&gl=br&client=firefox-a>. Last access date: February 25, 2009.
[420] Lehman-Wilzig, S. N, op. cit., p. 424.

they have a high power of investigation around their environment, besides being as creative and determined as the humans in search of their purposes.

In short, "a generation of robots is evolving rapidly. A race that can see, read, speak, learn and even feel emotions."[421]

The evolution achieved by the machines of Artificial Intelligence does not have equivalence because the mechanisms of self-repair assure them an unlimited time of durability, and their reproduction can occur in five different ways. Among these, the fifth mode — "probabilistic of self-reproduction" — resembles biological evolution through mutations, so that the highly efficient, complex and powerful cellular automaton can evolve from an inefficient, simple and weak cellular automaton.

Cyberneticists have realized that automaton/human equivalence is rapidly becoming a reality due to the structural limitations of the human brain compared to the potentiality of machines.

Clarke[422] notes that the cells that make up our brains are slow, bulky and waste a lot of energy — compared to computer elements that theoretically can be the size of an atom, that is, the electronic cell has an efficiency 10 billion times greater than the protoplasmic cells.

Thus, the ground has already been prepared for the arrival in the not-too-distant future of "humanoid" artificial intelligence machines that will display all the important traits and characteristics of a Man. Will (he) it be ready to "serve us" (?). If we are ready for it, that is another matter.

Lehman-Wilzig[423] still delves deeper into robotic crime, noting that the freedom of robots will lead to some harmful behavior, even if well-intentioned. This would be partly because of the literal

---

[421] Rorvik, D. (1971). *As man becomes machine.* (p. 35). New York: Pocket Books. *apud* Lehman-Wilzig, Sam N., *op. cit.*, p. 443.
[422] Clarke, A. C. (1964). *Profiles of the future.* (p. 28). London: Pan Books. *apud* Lehman-Wilzig, S. N., *op. cit.*, p. 444.
[423] Lehman-Wilzig, S. N., *op. cit.*, p.445.

spirit of the robot, which is logical, but it is not sensible or reasonable and therefore can fulfill orders in an absurd way.

It needs to be clarified, however, that such a perception takes into account models of computerized machines such as those currently in existence, not considering the advent of advanced (real?) artificial intelligence that can ponder these orders, because of a table of values or interests of machines or even selfish ones.

As Kemeny[424] notes, "The problem with modern computers is that they actually do exactly what we tell them to do and not what we really want them to do."

Cyberneticists have already begun to discuss the possibility of artificial intelligence psychopathology. Minsky[425] believes that the first self-developed intelligent machines become 'psychotic' in many ways resulting in long-term development to stabilize them. Not to mention that paranoid behavior is already programmed on computers.

Under such circumstances, Lehman-Wilzig[426] ponders, it cannot be expected that machines will always toil for the sake of humans. If his moral criterion for the hierarchy of life is intelligence, then the intelligent robot will relate to us in the same way that we relate to the ants, since, with intelligence that we believe is superior, they probably have purposes and objectives that do not match those of humans.

The author expresses the understanding that from the current juridical point of view, the most advanced computers, robots, and humanoids could be considered nothing more than inanimate objects, subject to the present laws, similarly, kept in due proportion, than represented the slaves to the ancient civilizations. In both cases, the absence of humanity would be based on the conceptions

---

[424] Kemeny, J. G. (1972). *Man and Computer.* (1972). (pp. 10). New York, Charles Scribner's Sons. apud Lehman-Wilzig, S. N. *op. cit.*, p. 445.

[425] Misky, M. (1979). *Computer science and the representation of knowledge. In*: Dertouzos, M. L.; Moses, J. (eds). The computer age: a twenty-year view. (pp. 394). Cambridge: MIT Press. apud Lehman-Wilzig, S. N., *op. cit.*, p. 446.

[426] Lehman-Wilzig, S. N. *op. cit.*, p. 446.

of mind, intelligence, and moral understanding — supposedly ren-
egade to both slaves and machines/robots.

Such characteristics lead to a parallel between the two realities, making us believe, Lehman-Wilzig[427] says, that just as the
slave was progressively given a more humane character, granting
him rights and obligations attributed to the free man, the humanoids of artificial intelligence could also be progressively treated as
quasi-human, relative to the moral, aesthetic, creative, and logical
sphere. In any case, as seen before, some understand that, in Rome,
the slaves were not deprived of rights.

In the legal world, the verisimilitude of the thesis advocated
above would classify robots through a progressive scale from conception as a property to the concept of a legally responsible and
legally responsible entity. It should be emphasized that the legal
relevance of such classification would rest on the need for social
pacification and definition of the roles represented by each character. As stated above, Lehman-Wilzig[428] understands that robots will
traverse an evolutionary legal path to the attainment of the quality
of the person, in the form as summarized below.

Thus, the first stage is that of responsibility for the product,
which provides that the damages resulting from the actions of the
robots would cause civil liability for the product malfunction. This
would be the manufacturer's responsibility. Others that also would
be held liable would be importers, distributors, resellers (and their
employees, if they acted negligently), maintenance staff, installers,
inspectors and certifiers and even the end user, in damages to third
parties but not to himself.

Although legally well-formulated, the idea of product liability encounters problems of various kinds. Initially, in the field
of procedural legitimacy, the identification of the manufacturer
is complex and there are different manufacturers in the elabora-
tion of a robot — one, for the hardware (the physical structure
of the machine) and one for the software (the institutional pro-

---

[427] *Ibidem*, p 447.
[428] *Idem et seq.*

268

gram). It should also be clarified that, in Brazil, the software is protected by copyright, distancing it from the nature of product and service.

Secondly, one can identify the problem arising from the 'inherent risk' principle. If there is an inherent risk in the very nature of the product, then the liability will only be attributed if the manufacturer does not warn the user of the possible risks or if the product has a defect that exceeds the normal limits of the inherent risk of the product. In this way, the inherent risk of a computer with a wide diversity of functions is not as obvious as that of a lawn mower, and the problem will worsen when fourth-generation computers have the power to self-program.

The second stage relates to *dangerous animals* since the independence and evolution of these machines can cause risks and damages to society. In this way, the burden of responsibility can be transferred from the manufacturers/distributors to the final users/owners, following the legal principles that regulate "dangerous animals". Therefore, the doctrinal current to be followed could be related to subjective responsibility (derived from negligence) concerning animals or, as the majority of doctrine argues, relating to objective responsibility.[429]

The third stage would be *Slavery*. The term 'robot', as seen before, comes from the Czech word *robota*, which means servant or forced laborer. From the beginning of the robots, its purpose was to serve as a modern slave of humanity. The real difficulty of the robot-slave legal parallelism is not in the question of the owner's responsibility, but in the sanction to be applied to the robot in cases where no responsibility is attributed to its *dominus* (*v.g.* the criminal conduct of the robot that did not derive from a request of the owner).

---

[429] Castro Júnior, M. A. de. (2001). *Responsabilidade Civil do Hacker* [Hacker's Civil Liability]. Thesis (Master's Degree in Law) – School of Law, Federal University of Bahia, Salvador. In this dissertation I advocate the thesis of a specific treatment of civil responsibility in the digital environment in a gradual way, due to the specific characteristics of each person.

But how could you 'punish' a robot? It could not be as simple as 'pulling the plug'. Conscious actions need not be linked to *intent* to cause injury. Thus, there are two most viable solutions: rehabilitation and compensation. The first would involve reprogramming the guilty robot. The second would be to compel the same to compensate the victim for the damage caused.

The fourth stage takes into account the *reduced capacity*, insofar as the law has developed a differentiated approach for individuals who have a reduced capacity for discernment, including the consequences of the practice of certain acts. In this case, the law is concerned with *mens rea* ("criminal mind") as well as with the *animus* of committing a crime. Within the category, there are two different types of mental incapacity: the permanent and the temporary. To the humanoid, the most common would be temporary mental incapacity due to transient malfunctioning or even programmed humanoids with the Three Laws of Asimov, which could be temporarily disoriented when they see a human getting injured, which can aggravate the injury or injure others.

The fifth stage is related to children and adolescents. The issue addresses legislation concerning minors or incapable or relatively capable, which would apply to humanoids in that it deals with an intelligent entity but with little moral responsibility. The examples stand out in the field of self-learning and self-programming, which would give computers methods of trial and error. In other words: the physical consequences of a specific action could be understood without imputing to them the due legal consequence. Here a problem can be the speed of learning and individual evolution of the robot, which could or could be of such magnitude that prevents a traditional educational process.

However, as noted by Prosser, referred to by Lehman-Wilzig[430] regarding the legal *status* of the child, countries adopting the Common Law do not attribute to parents unrestricted responsibility for the acts of their children, they only recognize the aforemen-

---

[430] Lehman-Wilzig, S. N., *op. cit.*, p. 446.

tioned responsibility under certain conditions (inadequate education or neglect), differently from what happens in countries with a civil tradition. In the future, society would have to establish a balance between the responsibility attributed to the 'parents' of the robot and the need to protect the rights of the victim.

The sixth stage is linked to the robot's vision as a *Representative* since, in almost all circumstances, the robot/humanoid acts in the service of some human mandator. In such cases, the agent is a mere instrument of the mandator. The only essential requirement for the relationship between mandator and agent is that the latter acts on behalf of the mandator and under his order, and there is no need to discuss any liability between the principal and the agent in the event of any damage caused. This relationship differs from the employee/employer relationship, in which the employee occupies a position of subjection to the control and direction of the employer. In this latter case, the employer is jointly and severally liable for any damage done by the employee during the service or for the purpose of favoring the business with which he is engaged.[431]

Finally, it could reach the stage of *Person*. This seventh category represents an emotional-philosophical milestone from a human perspective. Can there be something like 'free will' for artificial intelligence? According to Lehman-Wilzig, Hofstadter comments that, in relation to the origin of the sense of free will, it may be said that it comes from the brain — a piece of hardware that has not been created or chosen. The human being is not a 'self-programmed object', but continues to have a sense of desires, which comes from the physical substrate of his mind. In the same way, machines may one day have desires, although no program will suddenly emerge in their memory (self-programmed). Indeed, in a last level of uniqueness, the machines would have desires by virtue of the organization of the structures in the diverse levels of *hardware* and *software*, as is the case with humans.

---

[431] *Idem.* It should be noted that we are dealing here with *the common law*.

There are no definitive answers, Lehman-Wilzig says. The future may override philosophers, theologians, biologists, psychologists, with a reality difficult to explain.

After all, Lehman-Wilzig[432] concludes: "What does it mean to be a person? As seen before, one can certainly not argue that to be a person means to be human. Could an artifact be human? For me, the answer is clear: yes. A robot can do many things of which we discuss: locomotion and reproduction; predict and choose; learn; understand and interpret; analyze, decide; and it can feel."

Therefore, in this step, it can be affirmed that the technological singularity could result in robots that are legal persons.

5.4 Perspectives

In a speech promoted by the Artificial Intelligence film's producers, Kurzweil said:

> In 2030 there will be no clear distinction between humans and Robots. Around the first quarter of the twenty-first century, we will know everything about the human brain and will be able to reproduce it with perfection in machines. Machines will be able to do all the things we do, including love. [...] In 2029 a computer with the price of a current PC will have the computing capacity of the human brain.[433]

And it will probably pass in the Turing Test, it must be added.

Rather, he said that by 2020, we will connect computers to our brains and build machines as smart as ourselves.

Around 2050, Kurzweil[434] understands that it will be possible to choose to replace parts of our organic body with robotic, cybernetic pieces. Lungs, hearts, kidneys etc., will be able to be replaced.

> In 2060, a $ 1000 machine will be more capable than all human brains added. By 2100, we may see a new species,

---

[432] *Idem.*

[433] Kurzweil, R. (2001, July). Inteligência artificial [Artifical Intelligence]. *Superinteressante.* (Year 15, n. 7, pp. 48-54).

[434] *Idem.*

partially robotic, partly human, appear in proportion to our desire. At that time, "a one-cent chip will have a computing capacity one billion times greater than that of all the human brains of Earth added."

It should be remembered that between the first flight of the first plane and the arrival of Man on the Moon, only 66 years passed, and many people have experienced both events! If Kurzweil's Law of Accelerating Returns is correct — and he makes a good demonstration of its validity — these prognoses may come true[435]. His projections are in line with those of Moravec and other experts in robotics and artificial intelligence, although — let it be clear — many scholar authors disagree.

Regarding predictions, it is also worth recalling some by John Kemeny,[436] dean of Dartmouth University. He predicted,

---

[435] Kurzweil, R. (1999). *The age of intelligent machines.* (3rd reprint). MIT Press, Cambridge.

[436] Kemeny's Crystal Ball. Retrieved from: <http://www.dartmouth.edu/comp/about/history/unplugged/crystalball.html>. Last access date: February 17, 2009. Lee Michaelides: In his 1972 book "Man and The Computer," Dartmouth's former chairman included his predictions for the future of computing. Let's see how much he was right on his predictions:
Prediction: "I fully expect that within the next generation we will see computer memories capable of embracing the content of the largest library in the world."
Result: Correct. Arrival of the online libraries.
Prediction: "The next decade will probably see the development of huge computer networks."
Result: Correct. Networks were taking their first steps in 1972, but within a decade, networking became the wave of the future.
Prediction:
"I'm confident that in 1990, millions of Americans will have the ability to do meaningful searches in their homes. They would buy a computer that costs as little as a black and white television to access one of the nine strategically located computing centers."
Result: Right and wrong. In 1990, the average person could locate all kinds of information online without leaving their home. But Kemeny erred about using terminals to connect to one of nine computing centers.
Prediction: "I want to argue that it is fully feasible for the [New York] Times to provide personalized service to each of their readers."
Result: Correct. Newsletters, newspapers and personalized portal pages are part

among other things, that:

I) There would be enough digital memory to store the world's largest libraries.[437]

II) The appearance of huge information networks and the possibility of millions of people doing searches from their homes, at low-cost terminals.

III) Provision of personalized content for each person.

IV) Companies would keep stock lists on their computers for access by any customer.

---

of the daily routine of millions of people.

Prediction: "Companies could keep the stock list within the computer's memory, and any customer in the region could conduct a simple search on the computer to check what's available in a particular store."

Result: Right and wrong. Kemeny was right about the stock list. But he has not predicted the possibility for companies like Amazon.com to sell to anyone, anytime, to any place on the planet.

Prediction: "A computer system could control all Manhattan traffic lights and base its decision on up-to-date information about traffic flows and traffic jams."

Result: Correct. In major metropolitan areas, computerized traffic control systems have increased the capacity of highways without increasing the amount of runways.

Prediction: "I predict that the widespread use of videotelephones will have a huge impact on employment patterns and office location."

Result: Correct. Although videotelephones are currently dispensable, web-based teleconferencing is already here and growing rapidly.

[437] In fact, there is space in the various types of digital storage media, enough to store all human knowledge already produced.

For further information, check Kelly, K. *Scan this book!* Retrieved from: <http://www.nytimes.com/2006/05/14/magazine/14publishing.html?_r=1&scp=1&sq=Kevin%20Kelly%050%20petabytes&st=cse>. Last access date: January 22, 2009. The article informs that all human knowledge, so far, fits in 50 petabytes. That is, a single small building can store that amount of data that corresponded to 32 million books, 750 million articles, 25 million songs, 500 million images, 500,000 movies, 3 million videos and 100 billion web pages.

V) A computer system could control all traffic lights in Manhattan.

VI) The wide use of videophones.

It turns out, therefore, that the scholars of the themes here related, for some time, have been right to a great extent on the formulated prognoses. Certainly one cannot accept a determinism of the future of man. It is a being of multiple facets and characteristics, impossible to be grasped in its entirety, as well as everything else.

Man always created, dared, innovated, tried everything that was possible and even what seemed impossible. All that was possible to Man he accomplished. Nothing that was impossible became real. This plexus of achievements and impossibilities did not take or fully take into account ethical, moral, religious or legal criteria. Human intelligence is something that overcomes human understanding about it, demonstrating its limitation and its breadth.

What will happen in the future, whether near or remote, is the consequence of something that is done now, done in the past or will be done. Can we face the evidence that points to an increasing and exponential pace of evolution, just as technological evolution, as described by the Law of Accelerating Returns, maintains the lead in shaping the world? Or will we be swallowed up by our own achievements, treading and picking up a neurotic routine, the neurotic enjoyment of repetition that causes us harm? Are there any exits from this situation? Does the Law have the power to direct, control and shape the future? Or the Law must remain attached to its paradigm to regulate only after something occurs?

These issues go beyond this work and sharpen or should sharpen minds attentive to the meaning of having machines as intelligent as Man or more. The work has been limited to demonstrate or at least trying to demonstrate, that the means to create such intelligent machines exist, or are in the process of becoming real, perfecting their virtuality, as well as Brazilian and other countries law is sufficiently elastic to include robots with legal personality.

"I will not sing the future world."[438] The future, which will affect the human species, has already begun to be created in the past and continues to be in the present. At the present stage of things, being inert is the only unacceptable condition. Thus, with this work, in addition to pointing out a doctrinal position, it is possible to facilitate that others advance with the problems posed by robotic law, allowing to find the best possible solutions.

---

[438] Andrade, C. D. de, op. cit., p.78.

CONCLUSIONS

1. The fundamental paradigm of the current Law is anthropocentrism.

2. Anthropocentrism has been losing ground since the discovery that the Sun, not the Earth, is the center of the Solar System, as well as from the development of the Darwinian theory of evolution.

3. Human rationality was called into question by psychoanalysis with its notion of the unconscious.

4. The increasing technological advance opens the door to the creation of machines potentially smarter than humans, which may be decisive for the decay of anthropocentrism.

5. The concept of Person is constantly evolving. In this way, there will be a moment when this concept, faced with such reality, will have to be modified to include robots, cyborgs and alike.

6. There is a certain degree of biological identity registered in DNA among all living beings, such as the genes for sight and organization of the body.

7. The evolution experienced on Earth may have begun in crystalline forms, passed into the present biological stage, and may proceed through cybernetic beings. Thus, the mineral-animal-mineral cycle would be completed.

8. Intelligence is a concept with varied content, whose dimension cannot be accurately measured. Thus, one cannot categorically re-

ject other species as having this attribute. Intelligence is an effect and not something intrinsic.

9. Consciousness, either, cannot be taken as an exclusive attribute of mankind, as can be observed, for example, in the communication process of bees, through dances and body movements, or in primates.

10. What happens inside a computer, when in operation, is often an unfathomable mystery, as it is still the mystery of what occurs in the brain when we think.

11. Brain and computer are not equivalent, which does not matter, therefore, whether its manifestation is an effect or an intelligent act, what causes it will have to be intelligent because what remains in thought cannot be evaluated in any way, only its result.

12. The legal concept of person is changeable and is constantly evolving, as can be observed, for example, from the analysis that Afro-descendants were excluded from it at the time of slavery. Therefore, one cannot relate the legal concept of a person with *Homo sapiens*.

13. Etymologically, the word "robot" means forced labor. The traditional concept of the worker is tied to the Human Being. For this reason, considering that the present concept of person is "the holder of rights and obligations," nothing prevents robots from being included in it.

14. Post-humanity will be the continuity of the human evolutionary process, no longer on totally biological bases, or even, at some point, partly biological, but on a cybernetic, synthetic basis.

15. Once the elements which, together or individually, have resulted in the legal personality of the individual, one can say that if another entity is found endowed with these same elements, the logical conclu-

sion is that the same legal *status* of a person is attributed to this entity.

16. Today the legislation in force in Portugal and Brazil abolished adjectives of their concepts of person. This opened the door for understanding as a person with legal personality not only the Man, but the fashion of the Eastern vision on the equality of the dignity of all beings with Man, giving possibilities to the theory of animal law and, as well the robotic law for a robot to be legally qualified as a person.

17. In common law countries, in principle, according to specialized doctrine, there are no obstacles to gradually recognizing the legal personality of robots.

18. The birth of a robot is its start-up. The unborn is the virtual Man, in potential form, just as the projects are the virtual robot. If born, it will be person and Man, if not born will not be, but already gathers, as well as the seed, all the elements necessary to be so. The same can be said of feasible and achievable robots' projects.

19. One can understand a living system as an autopoietic machine, so it can be concluded that a robot — concept under which are encompassed, computers, cyborgs, androids etc. — can be treated as a living system.

20. A robot, from a classical perspective, is characterized by programmability, mechanical capability, and flexibility.

21. Experience shows that it is common for human beings to have feelings, especially anger, about computers and other machines, treating them as if they were subjects with their own will.

22. Children, when small, recognize that computers are somewhat alive because they have intelligence, but distinguish them from people because only people have feelings. The attribution of human characters to robots is increasing.

23. Nanotechnology and the use of superconducting materials will eliminate the two-dimensional, physically-related thermal barriers of physics from silicon components, making it possible to build a superlative gain on the previous generation of silicon, surpassing the gains, the returns of Moore's Law.

24. This gain will enable the appearance of machines much more intelligent than us and all humanity together, with all our capabilities and more.

25. The Law of Accelerating Returns reports that technologies applied to artificial intelligence grow and develop exponentially. Thus, the development curve now doubling the processing speed with the same cost every 2 years (Moore's Law) will soon be multiplied by n. The curve of the graph concerning the vertical assigned to the time will become parallel to this axis. This will happen when it reaches the singularity that results, among other factors, from the joint application of nanotechnology, neural networks, superconducting materials and quantum computation that will have explosive potential when it can achieve a unifying theory.

26. The Law of Accelerating Returns also applies to biological evolution.

27. Some authors point out that the time when machines will exceed human capabilities will occur around 2030 or 2040, which is why so many humans who are alive today will be able to see this happen.

28. The moment a computer has the same intelligence as a Man, Man will be outdated, because computers are networked and therefore can learn much faster than humans.

29. There has been an increasing need to legally discipline the performance of robots or their interaction with men since they are

becoming more and more present and begin to cause damage and even deaths. International legislation on the subject is incipient, and many national laws are non-existent.

30. Robotics laws are not legal laws.

31. Brazilian positive law, as well as Portuguese law, specifically the Civil Codes, already allow robots to have similar legal treatment endowed with the characteristics that make the human being legally recognized as a person.

32. The law that will regulate the life of robots may be a human, hybrid or robotic law, if any law can intermediate these relations, in the face of projected robotic intelligence superior to the human, which may lead to unwanted changes by the human species.

33. Given that the current legal paradigm is overcome, the end of the Law could be considered, as we know the Law, but we cannot completely predict a new paradigm.

34. Given the technological framework that is presented, there are no definitive answers, hence the future may present a situation that contradicts philosophers, theologians, biologists, psychologists, jurists, etc. with a reality difficult to explain.

35. The anthropocentric paradigm will surely be abandoned in a short time. This is already happening, as animal rights are being recognized, which may be followed by the recognition of forest rights, ocean rights, robot rights, etc., not necessarily in this order.

36. Post-humanity, by taking into account the human frame of reference, at the time when it may result in the end of *Homo sapiens*, perhaps preceded by a period of hybrid beings, will continue as long as the robot shall prevail. The robot is, to some extent, a creature of Man, transforming man from the creature into the creator,

resulting in the perishing of the species as a way of perpetuating it in accordance with the theory of evolution and autopoietic balance.

37. If the most recent exponential human evolution is set up, at the same pace of technological evolution, based on the Law of Accelerated Returns, it is possible that the gap between human and artificial intelligence is maintained and Man will not be surpassed by the machine.

38. Knowledge requires us to be constantly alert against the temptation of certainty, to accept that our certainties do not prove the truth as if the world each individual sees is the world, not a collectively constructed world. Knowledge forces us because we cannot deny the fact that we know we know.

39. Our point of view is the product of a structural coupling in the experiential domain, as valid as that of the opponent, even if the product of the opponent seems to us undesirable. It is up to us to seek the broader perspective of an experiential domain in which the other can equally participate, and together we can erect a world.

40. Regarding the legal nature of personality rights, it is argued that they are formed by certain attributes, physical or moral qualities of the person, individualized by the legal system. They are spiritual and physical representations of the person, a special set of subjective rights, which are revealed through the fundamental characteristics of the person.

REFERENCES

Aras, A. (2006). *Fidelidade partidária: a perda do mandato parlamentar* [Party loyalty: the loss of parliamentary mandate]. Rio de Janeiro: Lumen Juris.

Arendt, H. (2008). *A condição humana* [The Human Condition] 10th ed. 7th reprint. São Paulo: Forense Universitária.

Asimov, I. (2007). *As três leis da robótica.* [The Three Laws of Robotics] (M. Persson, Trans.). Porto Alegre: L&PM.

Asimov, I. (1994). *O homem bicentenário.* [The Bicentennial Man] (R.S. de Biasi, Trans.). Rio de Janeiro: Record.

Asimov, I. (1994). *Visões de robô* [Robot visions] (R. S. de Biasi, Trans). Rio de Janeiro: Record, 1994.

Balkin, J.M. *Deconstructive Practice and Legal Theory.* Retrieved March 30, from <http://www.yale.edu/lawweb/jbalkin/articles/decprac1.htm>.

Banfi, A. (1986). *Galileu* [Galilean] (A. P. Ribeiro, Trans). Lisboa: Edições 70.

Beer, S. (2009). *What is cybernetics?* Retrieved February 12, 2009 from:
<http://www.nickgreen.pwp.blueyonder.co.uk/beerWhatisCybernetics.pdf>.

Brasil. (2004). *Código Civil, Código de Processo Civil e Constituição Federal* [Civil Code, Code of Civil Procedure and Federal Constitution] 6th ed. São Paulo: RT.

Bressane, R. *Morrer datou.* [Dying is outdated]. Retrieved February 14, 2009 from: <http://impostor.wordpress.com/2008/11/01/morrer-datou/>.

Brooks, R. A. (2002). *Flesh and Machines: how robots will change us.* Nova York: Pantheon Books.

Capek, K. *R.U.R. (Rossum's Universal Robots): A play in introductory scene and three act.* (D. Wyllie, Trans). Retrieved February 25, 2009, from <http://ebooks.adelaide.edu.au/c/capek/karel/rur/>.

Castoriadis, C. (2007). *Sujeito e verdade no mundo social-histórico.* São Paulo: Civilização Brasileira, 2007.

Castro Júnior, M. A. de. (2000) *Direito robótico?* [Robotic Law] *Jornal Correio da Bahia,* Salvador, December 29.

Clarke, R. *Asimov's Laws of Robotics: Implications for Information Technology.* Retrieved February 12, 2009, from <www.anu.edu.au/people/Roger.Clarke/SOS/Asimov.html>.

Cordeiro, A. M. (2004). *Tratado de Direito Civil Português: parte geral,* vol. I, tomo III [Treaty of Portuguese Civil Law: general part, vol. I, tome III]. Pessoas: Almedina.

Costa, N. C. A da. (1999). *Lógica paraconsistente aplicada* [Paraconsistent applied logic]. São Paulo: Atlas.

Covre, M. de L. M. (2006). *O que é cidadania* [What is citizenship?]. São Paulo: Brasiliense.

Cristofoleti, R. *As três leis da robótica* [The Three Laws of Robotics] Retrieved February 3, 2009, from <http://74.125.47.132/search?q=cache:B5Ulxx_xRTwJ:cea.eti.br/tecnologia.blog/%3Fp

%3D6+lei+zero+da+rob%C3%B3tica&hl=pt-BR&ct=clnk&cd=2
&gl=br&client=firefox-a>.

Dallari, D. de A. (1998). *Direitos humanos e cidadania* [Human rights and citizenship]. São Paulo: Moderna.

Darwin, C. R. (2008). *A origem das espécies por meio da seleção natural* [Origin of species through natural selection] (A. C. Mesquita, Trans). Tome I. 2nd ed. São Paulo: Escala.

Dawkins, R. (2008). *O gene egoísta* [The selfish gene]. (R. Rubino, Trans). São Paulo: Companhia das Letras.

Dray, G. M. (2006). *Direitos de personalidade: anotações ao Código Civil e ao Código do Trabalho* [Personality rights: annotations to the Civil Code and the Labor Code]. Coimbra: Almedina.

Fernandez, A; Fernandez, M. (2008). *Neuroética, direito e neurociência: conduta humana, liberdade e racionalidade jurídica* [Neuroethics, law and neuroscience: human conduct, freedom and legal rationality]. Curitiba: Juruá.

Fiamenghi, C. M. (2008). Imperativo superegóico e culpa na clínica [Superego imperative and fault in the clinic]. In Gerbase, J. Editor. *Avatares do Supereu*. Salvador: Associação Científica Campo Psicanalítico.

Flynn, J. R. (2007). *What is intelligence?: Beyond the Flynn effect*. Cambridge: Cambridge University Press.

Foucault, M. *A ordem do discurso*. Retrieved March 31, 2009, from <http://www.unb.br/fe/teef/filoesco/foucault/>.

Freud, S. (1969). *Além do princípio do prazer* [Beyond the pleasure principle] (C. Monteiro, Trans). Vol. 18. Rio de Janeiro: Imago.

Freud, S. (1969). *O estranho* [The Uncanny]. (J. Salomão, Trans). Vol. 17. Rio de Janeiro: Imago.

Gagliano, P. S., & Pamplona Filho, R. (2009). *Novo curso de Direito Civil: parte geral* [New course in Civil Law: general section]. 11th ed. São Paulo: Saraiva.

Galvão, E. F. (2007). *O que é computação quântica?* [What is quantum computing?]. Rio de Janeiro: Vieira & Lent Casa Editorial Ltda.

Ganascia, J. G. (1997). *Inteligência artificial* [Artificial Intelligence]. (R. C. C. de Moraes, Trans). São Paulo: Ática.

Garcia, E. C. (2007). *Direito geral da personalidade no sistema jurídico brasileiro* [General personality law in the Brazilian legal system]. São Paulo: Juarez de Oliveira.

Gates, B. (2008). Um robô em cada casa [A robot in every home]. *Scientific American Brasil*, edição especial n. 25, pp. 6-13.

Gelernter, D. *et al. Gelernter, Kurzweil debate machine consciousness*. Retrieved February 13, 2009, from <www.kurzweilai.net/meme/frame.html?main=memelist.html?m=4%23688>.

Gerschenfeld, N. (1999). *When things start to think*. Nova York: Henry Holt and Company.

Goldstein, R. (2008). *Incompletude: a prova e o paradoxo de Kurt Gödel* [Incompleteness: the proof and paradox of Kurt Gödel]. São Paulo: Companhia das Letras.

Gordilho, H. J. de S. (2008). *Abolicionismo animal*. [Animal abolitionism]. Salvador: Evolução.

Grinberg, K. (2008). *Código Civil e cidadania* [Civil Code and citizenship] 3rd ed. Rio de Janeiro: Jorge Zahar.

Guimarães, A. S. O homem de seis milhões de dólares [The man of six million dollars]. *Revista filosofia, ciência & vida*, ano I, n.3, p. 23-26.

Habermas, J. (2006). *O futuro da natureza humana: a caminho de uma eugenia liberal?* [The future of human nature: on the way to a liberal eugenics?] Coimbra: Almedina.

Hayles, N. K. (1999). *How we became posthuman: virtual bodies in cybernetics, literature and informatics*. Chicago: The University of Chicago Press.

Hillis, D. (2000). *O padrão gravado na pedra: a idéias simples que fazem os computadores funcionarem* [The pattern engraved on stone: the simple ideas that make computers work] (L. Neves, Trans). Rio de Janeiro: Rocco.

Houaiss, A. *et al. Dicionário Houaiss de língua portuguesa* [Dictionary Houaiss of Portuguese language]. Retrieved February 9, 2009, from <http://houaiss.uol.com.br/busca.jhtm?verbete=consciencia&stype=k>.

Inayatullah, S. *The Rights of your robots: exclusion and inclusion in history and future*. Retrieved January 29, 2009, from <http://www.kurzweilai.net/meme/frame.html?main=/articles/art0266.html?>.

Karlsson, N., & Jarrhed, J.O. (1993). Um sensor capacitivo para detecção de humanos em uma célula robótica [A capacitive sensor for detecting humans in a robotic cell]. *Conferência sobre tecnologias de Instrumentação e Medidas*. IMTC/93.

Kato, G. *Eu Robô* [Me Robot]. Retrieved January 5, 2009, from http://bravonline.abril.com.br/conteudo/artesplasticas/artesplasticasmateria_292516.shtml.

Keller, A. J. *Dicionário escolar alemão* [German school dictionary]. Retrieved February 25, 2009, from <http://michaelis.uol.com.br/escolar/alemao/index.php?palavra=Dasein>.

Kelly, C. W. *Can a machine Think?* Retrieved January 26, 2009, from <http://www.kurzweilai.net/articles/art0214.html?printable=1>.

Kelly, K. *Scan this book!* Retrieved January 22, 2009, from <http://www.nytimes.com/2006/05/14/magazine/14publishing.html?_r=1&scp=1&sq=Kevin%20Kelly%050%20petabytes&st=cse >.

Kolman, E.; Frolov, I. P. (1958). *La cibernética y el cérebro humano* [Cybernetics and the human brain]. Montevidéu: Pueblos Unidos.

Korzeniewski, B. *Cybernetic Formulation of the Definition of Life.* Retrieved February 13, 2009, from <www.idealibrary.com>.

Kurzweil, R. (2008). A proximidade da união mente e máquina [The proximity of the mind and machine union]. *Scientific American Brasil*, edição especial n. 25.

Kurzweil, R. *After the singularity: a talk with Ray Kurzweil.* Retrieved January 5, 2009, from <www.kurzweilai.net/meme/frame.html?main=/articles/art0451.html?>.

Kurzweil, R. (2001). Inteligência artificial [Artificial Intelligence]. *Superinteressante,* ano 15, n. 7, p.48-54.

Kurzweil, R. *How technology's accelerating power will transform us*. Retrieved February 22, 2009, from <http://www.ted.com/index.php/talks/ray_kurzweil_on_how_technology_will_transform_us.html>.

Kurzweil, R. (1999). *The age of intelligent machines*. 3rd reprint. Cambridge: MIT Press.

Kurzweil, R. (2005). *The Singularity is near:* w*hen humans transcend biology*. Nova York: Penguin Books.

Lacan, J. *A terceira conferência proferida no 7° Congresso da Ecole Freudienne de Paris em 31 de outubro de 1974* [The third conference given at the 7th Congress of the Ecole Freudienne of Paris on October 31, 1974]. Retrieved January 11, 2009, from <http://www.freudlacan.com/articles/article.php?url_article=jlacan031105_2>.

Lacan, J. (2008). *Seminário XVI* [Seminar 16]. São Paulo: Zahar.

Lehman-Wilzig, S. N. *Frankenstein Unbound: towards a legal definition of artificial intelligence*. Retrieved February 22, 2009, from: <profslw.com/wpcontent/uploads/academic/40._Frankenstein_Unbound.Towards_a_legal_definition...pdf>.

Lemos, A. (2008). *Cibercultura: tecnologia e via social na cultura contemporânea* [Cyberculture: technology and sociaty in contemporary culture]. 4th ed. Porto Alegre: Sulina.

Levy, P. (1996). *O que é o virtual?* [What is virtual?] (P. Neves, Trans). São Paulo: Ed. 34.

Lieberman, D. E. (2014). The Story of the Human Body: Evolution, Health, and Disease New York: Vintage Books.

Lima, H. L. A. de. (2004). *Do corpo-máquina ao corpo-informa-*

ção: o pós humano como horizonte biotecnológico [From body-machine to body-information: the posthuman as a biotechnological horizon] Doctoral dissertation (Ph.D. in Sociology) – Faculty of Law, Federal University of Pernambuco, Recife.

Loureiro, J. C. (2006). Nota de apresentação [Presentation note]. In HABERMAS, Jürgen. *O futuro da natureza humana: a caminho de uma eugenia liberal?* (M. B. Bettencourt, Trans). Coimbra: Almedina, p.7-38.

Maturana, H., & Varela, F. (2004). *De máquinas y seres vivos. Autopoiesis: la organización de lo vivo.* [Autopoiesis and Cognition: The Realization of the Living] 6th ed. Buenos Aires: Coedição Editorial Universitaria e Editorial Lumen.

Mazini-Covre, M. de L. (2008). *O que é cidadania.* [What is citizenship?] 3rd ed. 16th reprint. São Paulo: Brasiliense.

Mcauliffe, K. (2009). Are we still evolving? Our history is far from over: humans are actually changing faster than ever. *Discovery Magazine*, March, pp. 51-59.

Microsoft Press. (1998). *Dicionário de informática* [Computing Dictionary] (V. Chamon, Trans.). 3rd ed. São Paulo: Campus.

Minsky, M. (1988). *The society of mind.* New York: Simon & Schuster.

Minsky, M. (2008). A Ascensão dos robôs [The rise of the robots]. Scientific American, ed. especial n.25, pp.14-21.

Moravec, H. *Entrevista concedida a RobotBooks.com.* [Interview given to RobotBooks.com]. Retrieved February 27, 2009, from <http://www.robotbooks.com/Moravec.htm>.

Moravec, H. (1992). *Homens e robots: o futuro da inteligência humana e robótica* [Men and robots: the future of human intelligence and robotics] (J. L. M. F. Lima, Trans.). Lisboa: Gradiva.

Nero, H. S. Del. (1997). *O sitio da mente: pensamento, emoção e vontade no cérebro humano* [The site of the mind: thought, emotion and will in the human brain] São Paulo: Collegium Cognitio.

Negroponte, N. (1997). *A Vida digital* [Being Digital]. (S. Tellaroli, Trans.). 2nd ed. 2nd reprint. São Paulo: Companhia das Letras.

Negroponte, N. (1996). *Being digital.* New York: Vintage books.

Nogueira, S. (2009). Legislação robótica: cientistas querem código de conduta para aqueles que acreditam, estarão cada vez mais entre nós [Robotics legislation: scientists want a code of conduct for those they believe will be more and more between us]. *Revista Galileu*, n. 211, February.

Oliveira, O. M. (2006). *O conceito de homem: mais humanista, mais transpessoal* [The concept of man: more humanistic, more transpersonal]. Ijuí: Unijui.

Patrocínio, J. T. V. *Tornar-se pessoa e cidadão digital: aprender e formar-se dentro e fora da escola na sociedade tecnológica globalizada* [Becoming a digital person and citizen: learning and training in and out of school in the globalized technological society] 2004. Doctoral Dissertation (Ph.D. in Education and Development Sciences) – Faculty of Sciences, Universidade Nova de Lisboa, Lisboa.

Pimentel, A. F. (2000). *O direito cibernético: um enfoque teórico e lógico aplicativo* [Cybernetic right: a theoretical and logical application approach]. Rio de Janeiro: Renovar.

Rosenberg, J. M. (1986). *Dictionary of artificial intelligence and robotics*. Toronto: Wiley & Sons.

Rover, A. J. *Dados e informações na internet: É legítimo o uso de robôs para formação de base de dados de clientes?* [Data and information on the internet: Is it legitimate to use robots to build customer databases?] Retrieved February 13, 2009, from <http://www.infojur.ufsc.br/aires/arquivos/manole2aires.pdf.>.

Rover, A. J. (2000). *Direito, sociedade e informática: limites e perspectivas da vida digital* [Law, society and computing: limits and perspectives of the digital life]. Florianópolis: Boiteux.

Rover, A. J. *O Uso de técnicas computacionais inteligentes no domínio do direito: uma introdução* [The use of intelligent computational techniques in the field of law: an introduction]. Retrieved February 13, 2009, from <http://www.infojur.ufsc.br/aires/arquivos/porto%20IA%20introducao.pdf>.

Rover, A. J. *Para um direito invisível: superando as artificialidades da inteligência* [For an invisible Law: overcoming the artificialities of intelligence] Retrieved February 25, 2009, from <http://www.infojur.ufsc.br/aires/arquivos/direito%20invisivel%202005.pdf>.

Ruiz, E. T. (1998). *La inteligencia artificial: máquinas y personas* [Artificial intelligence: machines and people] Madrid: Editorial Debate, Madrid.

Santos, L. G. dos. (2007). *A inteligência das espécies* [The Intelligence of the species]. *O Estado de São Paulo*, São Paulo, September 23, Caderno 2.

Sterling, B. *Estadão online*. Retrieved February 14, 2009, from <http://www.estadao.com.br/vidae/not_vid317678,0.htm>.

Sterling, B. *Tomorow now*. Retrieved February 14, 2009, from <www.estado.com.br/editoriais/2007/09/23/ cad-1.93.2.20070923.30.1.xml>.

Supiot, A. (2007) *Homo juridicus: ensaio sobre a função antropológica do Direito* [Homo juridicus: essay on the anthropological function of Law] (M. E. de A. P. Galvão, Trans.). São Paulo: Martins Fontes.

Taube, M. (1967). *Os computadores: o mito das máquinas pensantes* [Computers: the myth of thinking machines] (R. S. de Biasi, Trans.). Rio de Janeiro: O Cruzeiro.

Tavares, A. R. (2003). *Curso de Direito Constitucional* [Course of Constitutional Law] 2nd ed. São Paulo: Saraiva.

Teixeira, J. H. M. (1991). *Curso de Direito Constitucional* [Course of Constitutional Law]. Rio de Janeiro: Forense.

Telles Júnior, G. (2003). *Direito quântico: ensaios sobre o fundamento da ordem jurídica* [Quantum law: essays on the foundation of the legal order] 7th ed. São Paulo: Juarez de Oliveira.

Tenório, R. M. (2003). *Cérebros e computadores: a complementaridade analógico-digital na informática e na educação* [Brains and computers: the analogical-digital complementarity in information technology and education]. 4th ed. São Paulo: Escrituras.

Tribe, L. *Ten Lessons our constitutional experience can teach us about the puzzle of animal right: the work of Steven M. Rise*. Retrieved March 29, 2008, from <http://nabrlaw.org/Portals/10/PDF%20Files/ Tribe_10ConstitutionalLessons.pdf>.

Turing, A. M. *Computing machinery and intelligence*. Retrieved

April 20, 2004, from <http://www.loebner.net/Prizef/TuringArticle.html>.

Turkle, S. (1997). *A vida no ecrã: a identidade na era da internet* [Life on the Screen: Identity in the Age of the Internet] (P. Faria, Trans.). Lisboa: Relógio D'Água Editores.

Turkle, S. *Whither psychoanalysis in a computer culture?* Retrieved March 15, 2008, from <http://www.kurzweilai.net/meme/frame.html?main=/articles/art0529.html>.

Vasconcelos, P. P. de. (2006). *Direito de personalidade* [Personality Rights] Coimbra: Almedina.

Vaz, R. de O. Sentimentos fabricados [manufactured feelings]. *Revista filosofia, ciência & vida*, ano I, n.3, p. 42-47.

Vinge, V. *What is The Singularity?* Retrieved February 13, 2009, from <http://74.125.47.132/search?q=cache:2UA--AmSFT0J:mindstalk.net/vinge/vingesing.html+singularity+vernor+vinge&hl=pt-BR&ct=clnk&cd=1&gl=br&client=firefox-a>.

Volkov, G. (1967). *Era of man or robot? The sociological problems of the technical revolution*. Moscou: Progress Publishers.

Ward, P. (2009). Que futuro espera pelo *homo sapiens*? [What May Become of Homo sapiens]. *Scientific American Brasil*, n. 81, ano 7, pp. 56-58.

Welborn, S. *Race to create a "living computer"*. Retrieved February 9, 2009, from <http://74.125.47.132/search?q=cache:GkVsrFC5jvIJ:members.fortunecity.com/y2kprepare/livecomp.htm+%E2%80%9CRace+to+Create+A+%E2%80%98Living+Computer%E2%80%99%E2%80%80%

9D&cd=1&hl=pt-BR&ct=clnk&gl=br&client=firefox-a>.

Wiener, N. (1993). *Cibernética e sociedade: o uso humano de seres humanos* [The human use of human beings: Cybernetics and society] 9th ed. (J. P. Paes, Trans.). São Paulo: Cultrix.

Wiener, N. (1971). *Deus, Golem & Cia: um comentário sobre certos pontos de contato entre cibernética e religião* [God & Golem, Inc.: A Comment on Certain Points Where Cybernetics Impinges on Religion]. (L. Hegenberg, O. S. da Mota, Trans.). São Paulo: Cultrix.

Wildman, P. (1999). Blood sweat and gears: some present implications of cloning and other life futures. *Australian Rationalist*, n.49, p. 35-36.

Wilkinson, R. (editor); Leroi, A. M. (director). (2009). *What Darwin didn't know*. Directed and produced by Tima Lambit. London: BBC. CD-ROM.

Wilks, Y., & Ballim, A. *Liability and consent*. (1991). In Narayanan, A., & Bennun, M. (editors). *Law, computer, science and artificial intelligence*. New Jersey: Ablex Publishing Corporation.

Wilks, Y., & Ballim, A. *A Bola de cristal de Kemeny* [The Crystal Ball of Kemeny]. Retrieved February 17, 2009, from <http://www. dartmouth.edu/comp/about/history/unplugged/crystalball.html>.

Wilks, Y., & Ballim. *Nation death on the job jury awards $10 million to heirs of man killed by robot at auto plant*. Retrieved February 26, 2009, from <http://nl.newsbank.com/nlsearch/we/Archives?p_ product=PI&s_site=philly&p_multi=PI&p_theme=realcities&p_ action=search&p_maxdocs=200&p_topdoc=1&p_text_direct-0=0EB295F7D995F801&p_field_direct-0=document_id&p_perpage=10&p_sort=YMD_date:D&s_

trackval=GooglePM>.

Wilks, Y., & Ballim. (2008). Robô-cientista consegue raciocinar e criar teorias [Robot-scientist can reason and create theories]. *Jornal A Tarde*, Salvador, April 5, Caderno 4, pp. 7.

Wilks, Y., & Ballim. *The automation of science*. Retrieved April 6, 2008, from <http://www.sciencemag.org/cgi/content/abstract/sci;324/5923/85?maxtoshow=&HITS=10&hits=10&RESULTFORMAT=&fulltext=robot++ross+king&searchid=1&FIRSTINDEX=0&resourcetype=HWCIT>.

Wilks, Y., & Ballim. *The first human killed by a robot*. Retrieved February 26, 2009, from <http://74.125.47.132/search?q=cache:YjkxTxTaoMMJ:www.cbc.ca/news/interactives/tlrobotics/+%22death+by+robot%22+Kenji+Urada&hl=pt-BR&ct=clnk&cd=10&gl=br&client=firefox-a>.

www.ingramcontent.com/pod-product-compliance
Lightning Source LLC
Chambersburg PA
CBHW030609220526
45463CB00004B/1234